Digital Education and Learning

Series Editors
Michael Thomas
University of Central Lancashire
Preston, UK

John Palfrey
Phillips Academy
Andover, MA, USA

Mark Warschauer
University of California
Irvine, USA

Much has been written during the first decade of the new millennium about the potential of digital technologies to produce a transformation of education. Digital technologies are portrayed as tools that will enhance learner collaboration and motivation and develop new multimodal literacy skills. Accompanying this has been the move from understanding literacy on the cognitive level to an appreciation of the sociocultural forces shaping learner development. Responding to these claims, the Digital Education and Learning Series explores the pedagogical potential and realities of digital technologies in a wide range of disciplinary contexts across the educational spectrum both in and outside of class. Focusing on local and global perspectives, the series responds to the shifting landscape of education, the way digital technologies are being used in different educational and cultural contexts, and examines the differences that lie behind the generalizations of the digital age. Incorporating cutting edge volumes with theoretical perspectives and case studies (single authored and edited collections), the series provides an accessible and valuable resource for academic researchers, teacher trainers, administrators and students interested in interdisciplinary studies of education and new and emerging technologies.

More information about this series at
http://www.palgrave.com/gp/series/14952

Bill Johnston • Sheila MacNeill
Keith Smyth

Conceptualising the Digital University

The Intersection of Policy, Pedagogy and Practice

Bill Johnston
School of Psychological Science and Health
University of Strathclyde
Glasgow, UK

Sheila MacNeill
Academic Quality and Development
Glasgow Caledonian University
Glasgow, UK

Keith Smyth
Learning and Teaching Academy
University of the Highlands and Islands
Inverness, UK

Digital Education and Learning
ISBN 978-3-319-99159-7   ISBN 978-3-319-99160-3 (eBook)
https://doi.org/10.1007/978-3-319-99160-3

Library of Congress Control Number: 2018957460

© The Editor(s) (if applicable) and The Author(s), under exclusive licence to Springer Nature Switzerland AG 2018
This work is subject to copyright. All rights are solely and exclusively licensed by the Publisher, whether the whole or part of the material is concerned, specifically the rights of translation, reprinting, reuse of illustrations, recitation, broadcasting, reproduction on microfilms or in any other physical way, and transmission or information storage and retrieval, electronic adaptation, computer software, or by similar or dissimilar methodology now known or hereafter developed.
The use of general descriptive names, registered names, trademarks, service marks, etc. in this publication does not imply, even in the absence of a specific statement, that such names are exempt from the relevant protective laws and regulations and therefore free for general use.
The publisher, the authors and the editors are safe to assume that the advice and information in this book are believed to be true and accurate at the date of publication. Neither the publisher nor the authors or the editors give a warranty, express or implied, with respect to the material contained herein or for any errors or omissions that may have been made. The publisher remains neutral with regard to jurisdictional claims in published maps and institutional affiliations.

Front cover image © Rainer Mook / Getty

This Palgrave Macmillan imprint is published by the registered company Springer Nature Switzerland AG
The registered company address is: Gewerbestrasse 11, 6330 Cham, Switzerland

Foreword

Today's permanent and increasingly accelerated revolution of technology, the main bastion of capitalism against socialism, alters socioeconomic reality and requires a new comprehension of the facts upon which new political action must be founded. (Paulo Freire 1997)[1]

Although Paulo Freire penned these words more than twenty year ago, they actually ring truer today than ever. At a breakneck speed, new technological gadgets are introduced to the marketplace, as the great societal panacea of our generation. Technology is touted in even redemptive terms, akin to religious fervour. The consumerist values of capitalism are well-embedded into marketing discourses framed around issues of relentless competition, heightened productivity, innovation, instrumentalism, and marketisation. Nowhere has neoliberal technological discourse become more fierce than in the context of university life. And although the corrupting force of neoliberalism on universities has been well-documented over the last three decades, the discourse of economic globalisation continues to move internationally like hellfire across the reaches of university life.

With the fallacious promise of time-saving efficiency, our labour within the university was systematically increased and accelerated by the

---

[1] Freire, P. (1997). *Pedagogy of the Heart*. New York: Continuum (p. 56).

arbitrary and commonsensical introduction of technological tools that have held faculty and staff captive. In the midst of this phenomenon, few critiques or alternatives have been able to interrupt the burgeoning and disproportionately skewed myths that have deepened managerial and technicist university practices, meant primarily to harness digital technology in the service of the marketplace. In the process, the culturally oppressive epistemology that undergirds values tied to technological practices has resulted in, as the authors of *Conceptualising the Digital University* well confirm, the impoverishment and reductionist account of the digital university today. It is, then, precisely a systematic and eloquent rethinking of these values and practices—offering, as Freire insists, *a new comprehension of the facts*—that is at the very heart of this volume.

Rethinking the Culture of the Digital University

> *Technologized media themselves now constitute Western culture through and through, and they have become the primary vehicle for the distribution and dissemination of culture.* (Richard Kahn and Douglas Kellner)[2]

Within the life of twenty-first-century universities, we would be hard-pressed to find a cultural milieu where a Western positivist epistemology of technology, anchored by extension upon scientific hubris, has not all but supplanted humanist educational values. This represents a central concern, in that neutral or depoliticised views of the digital university ignore or fail to contend with the inseparability that exists between culture and power. Without the tools for critically examining the manner in which the expansion of technology has shaped the neoliberal culture of universities, educators cannot effectively fashion academic spaces where contradictions to emancipatory visions, as well as partial and competing viewpoints, can be critically interrogated and transformed. The unfortu-

---

[2] Kahn, R. & D. Kellner (2007). Paulo Freire and Ivan Illich: Technology, Politics, and the Reconstruction of Education in *Policy Futures in Education*. V. 5, N. 4 (p. 431).

nate consequence here is an inability to politically unsettle through our pedagogical labour those essentialised or carte blanche approaches to digital technology that negatively impact the social agency and decision-making of faculty, students, and the larger community—generally excluding them from genuine participation in decision-making related to technology and other issues that directly impact their lives.

In response to these concerns, Johnston, MacNeill, and Smyth begin by acknowledging that our understanding of technology has generally emerged as a *discursive construction*—where an 'idea is brought into the social world by being talked about or written about without necessarily being subject to analysis or research'[3]—in their quest for finding an effective strategy for exploring the digital university. Through forging a critically profound lens of investigation, they produce a brilliant analysis of the historical, political, economic, and pedagogical agendas that have driven the positivist culture of digital technology in ways that have betrayed emancipatory and pluralistic visions of university life. What results is a complex unveiling of the ways in which the cultural underdevelopment of pedagogical theory and organisation development practice within the digital university has functioned to reproduce and perpetuate structures of inequalities that betray our emancipatory efforts.

However, beyond their critique, their sound understanding of discursive construction has also provided them the dialectical basis upon which to offer a more substantive and nuanced reading of technology, as well as a set of innovative cultural values that privilege liberatory notions of pluralism, through a perspective of the current context as *both a challenge and an opportunity* to transform the digital university. In this way, Johnston, MacNeill, and Smyth's perspective revolutionises how we conceptualise the dynamics of academic and organisational development in the digital university, illuminating key aspects of a matrix for practical uses in the integration of technology as a liberatory tool for individual and community empowerment.

---

[3] Jones, C. & R. Goodfellow (2014) The "Digital University": Discourse, Theory and Evidence in *International Journal of Learning and Media*. V. 4; N. 3–4 (p. 60).

Deconstructing the Political Economy of Digital Hegemony

Highly capitalized tools require highly capitalized men. (Ivan Illich)[4]

In centring the political economy of learning in their treatise, Johnston, MacNeill, and Smyth signal the importance of material conditions to any critical examination of the digital university and, moreover, any attempts to transform the digital hegemony that permeates university contexts. Ivan Illich's concern, for example, for the tyrannical manner in which economic policy options unfold under capitalism seems especially pertinent to the discussions of digital technology within the neoliberal university. It is evident, moreover, that the oppressive and alienating forces of advanced capitalism have largely shaped the manner in which digital technology as a tool has been capitalised within the university and society. This has required, as Illich rightly argues, *highly capitalized* men and women who commonsensically embrace the underlying myths of technology as neutral and non-obstructive to our labour and, thus, acquiesce to the changing forms of university work—even when such changes strip us of *conviviality*[5] or the freedom of choice.

For example, in the early 1990s, university professors were suddenly mandated to establish email accounts. For the most part, there was little pushback to the rhetoric of innovation and time-saving promises made to faculty across universities. In the excitement of the novelty, there was little argument against the fact that technology would overnight add two to three hours of labour daily to our already full workloads and that we would become enslaved to our email 24/7. As a consequence, our productivity did increase without necessarily an increase in our salary, as was the case across many industries. The result was not only heightened labour expectations, in which we did not have a voice, but also a loss of autonomy for our labour that until this day is seldom discussed. It is this loss of autonomy and infringement into our creative production that

---

[4] Illich, I. (1973). *Tools for Conviviality*. New York: Harper & Row (p. 66).
[5] Ibid.

well-illustrates a mechanism by which academic workers became further capitalised. Similarly, technology in the neoliberal university has also led to the standardisation and instrumentalisation of curriculum development and pedagogical activities within the classroom that have grossly interfered with the autonomy, fluidity, and creative processes of educators. In the name of progress, this has led to increasing conditions of surveillance and control of our labour, often shrouded, once again, by the distorted rhetoric of efficiency and heightened productivity—a sort of radical positivist proclamation.

With this in mind, Johnston, MacNeill, and Smyth work meticulously to reveal the underlying myths behind deceptive transformative claims and descriptions of the digital university, which function to intensify the political economic grip of neoliberalism. From this standpoint, the authors expose the unevenness of digital development over the last three decades and across multiple levels of university life, unveiling gross disparities related to technological practices and the adoption of technology. In this way, the reader is moved towards critically exploring the emancipatory potential and benefits of digital technologies for teaching and learning, as well as the possibilities for genuine transformative change to the digital culture of higher education. Through an eloquent engagement with notions of porosity, open education practice, and the concept of the commons, Johnston, MacNeill, and Smyth demonstrate the mounting need for widening participation from both within and without the university. By so doing, the authors counter the oppressive exclusionary culture of neoliberalism, asserting the power of open, democratic relationships and participation in building a new political economic ethos for the digital university.

Critical Literacy and the Digital University

Critical literacy is also necessary to hold to critical scrutiny many of the claims made by those heralding this brave new world of the 4IR. (Peter Mayo)[6]

---

[6] Mayo, P. (2018). Personal email correspondence of August 14, discussing the "Fourth Industrial Revolution" (4IR) phenomenon.

Given the great hoopla that is currently underway among global university discussions of the Fourth Industrial Revolution—the nascent intensification of old neoliberal values now more aggressively twisted by an economic determinist rhetoric linked to the imminent takeover of drones, Artificial Intelligence, and other technological forces—never has there been a timelier moment for this outstanding volume. Countering the economic opportunism associated with the political priorities and interests of the few (at the expense of the many) points to the necessary pedagogical scrutiny of critical literacy for disrupting hegemonic myths and shattering deceptive arguments. In the overwhelming neoliberal milieu of the digital university today, Johnston, MacNeill, and Smyth rightly argue that critical literacy is essential to countering the material and social conditions of inequality and exclusion within and outside the digital academy—conditions unequivocally preserved by technologically driven structures, policies, practices, and relationships that conserve the status quo.

Towards this end, *Conceptualising the Digital University* holistically critically examines a variety of pressing concerns tied to information literacy and the curriculum, considering themes of digital capability, social agency, and personhood, as key dimensions of the digital university committed to social justice. Moreover, by making critical literacy a central feature of their emancipatory design, Johnston, MacNeill, and Smyth consistently provide a much-needed critique of marginality at all levels of university academic development. In this way, a critical view of digital literacy is presented as a substantive focus in the evolution of curriculum development, particularly with respect to critiques of neoliberalism, the globalisation of technology, and struggles for democratic life in higher education. As would be anticipated, critical pedagogy underpins their discussions of redesigning technological learning spaces and environments. Here, a radical understanding of space is effectively deployed to engage salient questions of digital, pedagogical, and social relations—whether these exist in or out of the university—in order to expand possibilities for the democratisation of learning and an understanding of the digital university as public good.

Foreword   xi

Reinventing the University as Public Good

In this possibly terminal phase of human existence, democracy and freedom are more than just ideals to be valued—they may be essential to survival. (Noam Chomsky)[7]

Just as Noam Chomsky has often reminded us of the essential need for freedom and democracy, Johnston, MacNeill, and Smyth also build their germane arguments for the reinvention of the digital university on a similar premise. Grounded in a clear recognition of how political economy, education, and democracy always comingle, the authors insist that critical pedagogical alternatives of the university as public good must be founded upon values that unquestionably support the exercise of democracy and freedom, within universities and the larger society. This reinvention encompasses the digital university as a significant site of struggle and contestation, as well as a potentially democratic space for both educational and societal transformation.

Here, the values of critical pedagogy, open education, and academic praxis are significant features connected to knowledge production, intellectual formation, and community participation in the interest of the common good. Furthermore, an innovative conceptual matrix and digitally distributed curriculum paradigm are presented as critical democratic tools to guide collective reflection, dialogue, decision-making, and action. This dynamic design of the university as public good fittingly privileges digitally enriched learning spaces that reinforce democratic learning and co-creation, by way of porous boundaries between knowledge, spaces, and formal organisation. More importantly, these spaces comprise a pedagogical and political essential for reinventing how we comprehend the place and purpose of technology in education and the world today.

In this difficult historical moment, where our very humanity seems at risk to destructive technological forces linked to political irresponsibility, social exclusions, and economic greed, *Conceptualising the Digital University* constitutes a powerful clarion call for educators of conscience

---

[7] Chomsky, N. (2010). Noam Chomsky in *Speaking on Democracy: A Factual Alternative to the Corporate Media.* See: https://speakingofdemocracy.com/quotes/noam_chomsky/

committed to critical education, democratic political ideals, and economic justice. The book issues a critical call to action engendered by what Paulo Freire called radical hope[8] and an emancipatory vision of the digital university—one that is founded on political and pedagogical actions that engage the liberatory possibilities of academic leadership, embrace the democratising value of pluralism, and enact democratic organisational policies and practices unapologetically committed to the building of a more just and loving world.

Loyola Marymount University, USA Professor Antonia Darder
International Scholar,
Public Intellectual, Educator,
Writer, Activist and Artist

---

[8] Darder, A. (2015). *Freire and Education*. New York: Routledge.

Acknowledgements

The writing of this book has very much been a discursive process and the culmination of many discussions and dialogues around the vague concept, questionable assumptions, and actual realities of realising any sort of vision and plan for the 'digital university'.

Collaboration has been at the heart of this book, and the thinking and ideas we present within it. A series of blog posts by Bill and Sheila in 2011 prompted Keith to get in contact in 2012 about a project he was leading, which led in turn to our collective endeavours in further exploring the concept of the digital university, and the place of 'the digital' in Higher Education. Our efforts in doing so have encompassed our own joint dialogue, reflections, and writing, our further reading and research, and crucially also the dialogue we have had with colleagues across the sector, through workshops at a range of universities, and through presenting our thinking, as it developed, at a number of conferences, symposia, and events.

Now, six years later, we have this book.

Finding and developing our shared critical understanding of the concept of the digital university has been a challenging and humbling experience, and one which saw our own thinking move away from questioning the concept of the 'digital university' to also questioning the purpose of universities, and Higher Education, in relation to the constraints, purpose, and possibilities of digital technologies, spaces, and practices, and in relation to the ideas and ideals of critical and public pedagogy, openness, and democracy. As we have contextualised our understandings, we have given each other hope in a shared critique which we in turn hope our readers will share and use as a starting point for many more critically informed discussions, based on a shared recognition of the need for critical love and hope to challenge the neo-liberal dominance of our age.

There are a number of people we need to thank. Firstly, the team at Palgrave Macmillan for recognising the potential for a book in our work, and their continued support throughout the writing process. Our work draws from many sources and we are continually inspired by all of our professional networks and the encouragement we have received from our peers at conferences where we have presented our work, and the opportunities that we have been given to publish. This has given us the faith to carry on and develop our thoughts from conversations and debates into this most tangible of outputs, a book.

We'd like to give special thanks to some key colleagues and friends. We warmly thank Antonia Darder for her immediate and continued engagement, support, and critical love for our work. We were fortunate to meet Antonia at a pivotal point in the preparation of our book, and the time we spent with Antonia, both learning from and being inspired by her, left an indelible mark on our thinking and across the final version of this text. We also thank Helen Beetham, Catherine Cronin, Alex Dunedin, and Martin Weller for taking the time to read the book and for their generous endorsements of our work. Their own respective work has had a significant impact on our thinking and the structure of this book, as has the work of Mark Johnson, who introduced us to the concept of Value Pluralism which we explore at several points.

There are almost too many other people to thank, and we realise frustratingly that we cannot put a name to everyone we have had the benefit of speaking with as we have developed our work. However, we would like to give a special mention and thanks to a number of colleagues and friends who have supported and encouraged us as we started to clarify and structure our ideas into the form in which they are now presented, or with whom we were fortunate to have important discussions at important points of our journey. In addition to those already mentioned above, we thank Gordon Asher, Linda Creanor, Jim Emery, Julia Fotheringham,

Peter Hartley, Jennifer Jones, Ronnie MacIntyre, David McGillivray, Neil McPherson, Beck Pitt, Frank Rennie, Peter Shukie, John Alexander Smith, Panos Vlachopoulos, David Walker, Gina Wall, and Nicola Whitton.

In the above context, we extend a particular thanks to Richard Hall. Chapter 8 of our book, as indicated in the chapter, incorporates and extends material published in the paper by Hall, R. and Smyth, K. 'Dismantling the Curriculum in Higher Education' (2016), published in the Open Library of Humanities. We are grateful to Richard and the Open Library of the Humanities for allowing us to repurpose this material in our narrative. Richard also draws upon aspects of the aforementioned paper in his recent book *The Alienated Academic: The Struggle for Autonomy Inside the University* (2018, also published by Palgrave Macmillan).

To our respective families, thank you for your patience and understanding and tolerance of lost weekends over the past year. Thanks also to colleagues at Glasgow Caledonian University and the University of the Highlands and Islands for your support and understanding at points where our work on this book had an impact on other activities. Finally, we'd like to give a special mention to the Black Isle Bar in Inverness for providing a welcoming space for warmth, laughter, pizza, and the occasional glass of red wine.

In solidarity, love, and hope.

Praise for *Conceptualising the Digital University*

"I read this book with a sense of both recognition and urgency. This is not a manifesto about utopian digital futures, but rather a provocative invitation to re-think higher education and its role in increasingly open, networked, and participatory culture. Written in a language of "hope and critique" (Giroux, 2011), the authors use the lenses of critical pedagogy and praxis to offer a compelling case for troubling the existing boundaries of universities – and thus for greater openness and democratic engagement within and beyond higher education. The questions and analytical frameworks proposed by the authors should stimulate much dialogue and debate by educators, academic developers, policy makers, and all interested in the future of higher education. A vital and timely book."

—Dr Catherine Cronin, Strategic Education Developer, *National Forum for the Enhancement of Teaching and Learning in Higher Education, Dublin, Eire*

"This is a timely and necessary book. All universities are in some form negotiating their relationship with the digital context they now operate within – what does it mean for students, staff, ways of learning, methods of research and the role of the university in society. What and how should we teach in order to give students the appropriate skills to operate as effective citizens in a digital world? These are all questions which the higher education sector seeks answers for. The issue is that often the answers to such questions are provided by those with a vested interest – technology vendors or ed tech consultants. What this book does is place these types of questions within a meaningful and well reasoned framework. The book addresses this in three sections, looking first at the broadly

neo-liberal context within which the digital university operates, and what this means. In the second part, how the digital university might be conceptualised and practically implemented is considered. Lastly, the authors address how such a digital university is situated within a social context. By addressing these elements, a comprehensive, critical and nuanced picture of the digital university can be established, rather than one determined by a technological perspective alone. It is therefore essential reading for anyone with an interest in the digital evolution of the university."
—Professor Martin Weller, *The Open University, UK*

"This timely work examines the power of the digital in context with what is happening to education today, and in particular to Higher Education. Understanding education in terms of human development, it is comforting that narratives of education as a public good are being related through the digital. We live with the golden promises of technology to emancipate and extend social and intellectual benefits to the many, however this thinking needs to be matched with the practical details whilst not shying away from critique of expanding a successful monoculture. Just as with the industrial revolution before, our technology industries are proposing revolutions which lead us round the same circle, down the same paths of behaviour. Scrutiny of formal education reveals how learning has been commodified and narrowed; just as we have come to consume the natural world we have come to consume education. This book provides robust analyses and alternative envisioning to the consumption of education exploring how technology can be used as a tool to open up vital opportunities to everyone, as well as essential vistas to those in the academy if it is not to atrophy as an intelligent organ of human society."
—Alex Dunedin, *Ragged University*

"We've been waiting for this: a book-length critique of the 'digital university' that gives full attention to the political context. Johnston, MacNeill and Smyth explore the role that digital technologies have played in corporatising the academy, from the curriculum to learning environments, and from business models to terms of academic employment. They're hopeful enough and engaged enough in the wider world to also show how alternative digital pedagogies and strategies might be pursued, reframing higher education as an open, critical and democratic project."
—Helen Beetham, Education Consultant, writer, researcher, commentator (https://helenbeetham.com/about/)

Contents

Section I Visioning the Digital University   1

1 Neoliberalism and the Digital University: The Political
   Economy of Learning in the Twenty-First Century   3

2 The Digital University: An Impoverished Concept   19

3 Exploring the Digital University: Developing and
   Applying Holistic Thinking   39

Section II Deconstructing the Digital University   61

4 The Myth of Digital Transformation   63

5 Digital Participation and Open Communities: From
   Widening Access to Porous Boundaries   85

6 Information Literacy, Digital Capability, and Individual Agency 105

7 Digitally Enriched Learning Spaces 127

8 The Digitally Distributed Curriculum 149

Section III   Reimagining the Digital University 177

9 An Extended Conceptual Matrix for the Digital University 179

10 Institutional Practice and Praxis 203

11 Academic Development for the Digital University 217

12 Conclusion: Advancing the Digital and Open Education Agenda 235

Index 245

List of Figures

Fig. 3.1	Work phases to date (MacNeill 2014)	40
Fig. 3.2	Key constructs of the Digital University	41
Fig. 3.3	The Conceptual Matrix for the Digital University (MacNeill and Johnston 2012)	42
Fig. 3.4	Towards a Digitally Distributed Curriculum (DFWG 2014)	53
Fig. 5.1	Macro, meso, and micro participation. (Adapted from Buckingham-Shum 2011)	99
Fig. 8.1	The Digitally Distributed Curriculum	164
Fig. 9.1	The Revised Conceptual Matrix for the Digital University	184
Fig. 9.2	The Revised Conceptual Matrix as the intersection of open educational practice, critical pedagogy, organisational development, and praxis	188

xxi

Section I

Visioning the Digital University

1

Neoliberalism and the Digital University: The Political Economy of Learning in the Twenty-First Century

Introduction: Locating 'The Digital' in a Contested Environment

Our aim in this book is to conceptualise 'The Digital' as a feature of the change forces influencing higher education in the twenty-first century. These forces include (i) neoliberal policies to reposition higher education as a market of providers and consumers; (ii) the expansion of the number of institutions and increase in the numbers of students; (iii) overemphasis on the contribution made by universities to economic growth and competitiveness; (iv) introduction of external mechanisms to measure the quality of teaching, research, and the performance of staff; (v) digital technology itself, primarily positioned as a practical means of enhancing learning and teaching; and (vi) critical responses to negative changes. It is within this complex nexus of forces that we locate 'The Digital' in relation to the university. However, we also contend that 'The Digital' is best understood as contestable territory in relation to the overall strategic policy directions universities choose to define their place in society. So it is in the space of critical approaches to strategic direction that our efforts

© The Author(s) 2018
B. Johnston et al., *Conceptualising the Digital University*, Digital Education and Learning, https://doi.org/10.1007/978-3-319-99160-3_1

will converge and focus, particularly on academic and organisational development in universities.

We will show in Chap. 2 that these change forces elicit contradictory responses to the idea of the digital university. Some commentators are extremely positive, whilst others are highly sceptical, voicing concern that the intrinsic motivations of students and scholars are under threat from a repositioning of higher education as a market in knowledge and qualifications. From our perspective the contradictory nature of response is of most interest, and our approach to the argument and narrative development in the book embraces contradiction as the focal point for conceptualisation of the digital university. We will seek to answer the question 'what is the digital university' by a dialogic process, and it is only through creating opportunities for critical dialogue that affords opportunities to all stakeholders that radical digitally enabled transformation can actually occur. We look to critical pedagogy as a key theoretical focus to create the appropriate supportive spaces for these dialogues to be instantiated and evolve. We look to highlight the positive elements of radicalisation, as something that is based on human values that allows everyone to find their voice, to be valued, and to question the many illusions of consumer choice that our neoliberal society and in turn education systems currently operate. We see this as the way to create a meaningful alternative narrative to that of the increasingly managerialist, education as a service with customer's approach that senior managers within universities are embracing.

Our aim in this introductory chapter is to expose and challenge the power of neoliberalism to shape higher education and universities. We contend that neoliberalism impoverishes higher education and in response introduce an alternative framing of change and educational transformation. Our values are drawn from notions of critical pedagogy, public pedagogy, and openness as defining characteristics of university institutions.

We interpret critical pedagogy as a theory and practice of learning and teaching derived from radical educators such as Paulo Freire, Henry Giroux, and Antonia Darder, which engenders critical consciousness of the oppressive social and economic conditions influencing learners and teachers. Critical pedagogy in action is often described in relation to the term praxis, which denotes collective understandings derived from cycles of dialogic and experiential learning, and a commitment to challenging and changing that which needs challenged and changed.

We recognise and explore the challenges of value pluralism, that is "the view that different values may be fundamentally and defensibly correct in different contexts, but may also be incommensurable" (Johnson and Smyth 2011, pp. 211–212) in relation to the place of the digital in our universities. This expresses our view of organisational tensions between differing concepts of the digital, pedagogy, curriculum, and the university, and we recognise that such tensions will be manifest in the behaviour of institutional actors on the organisational stage and in the substance of their decisions about strategy, funding, structures, and daily practice.

We interpret openness as entailing notions of open educational practice, open pedagogy, open educational resources, and critical and public pedagogy. We see openness as a way to provide increased opportunities for participation and knowledge creation, and the sharing of knowledge created through pedagogic engagements within and through the university. As we come on to argue and explore at several points, openness is not the sole preserve of online or digital environments. There are many ways in our physical environments where an open ethos can provide alternative ways to extend our notions of physical learning spaces, and where a co-location and intersection of the physical and digital can enrich and extend educational opportunities.

These principles are at the centre of our conceptualisation of the digital university and interconnect with each other as we consider the politics, practices, and pedagogies of modern universities and the potential for radical change.

Our main intellectual strategy is to treat the 'digital university' not so much as a discrete type or kind of university; rather we adopt the notion of 'discursive construction' (Jones and Goodfellow 2012) in relation to the term 'digital university' to express our sense that what is required is holistic investigation of the concept rather than the establishment of hard and fast categories of description. We will take the process of discursive construction further by employing Freire's sense of praxis as involving not simply discussion but also challenge and action to change oppressive elements in our environment. Allied to this is the related notion of public pedagogy within which we contend that academic work undertaken in a university should matter in relation to social needs and the wider good (Giroux 2000). In line with this critical strategy, we will explore both 'The Digital' and 'The University' as problematic and contestable constructs, which are subject to definition and redefinition by powerful sociocultural forces and political and economic interests. However, we contend that the agency of staff and student can be interposed to counter such forces, generate alternative visions of the nature and purpose of universities, and redraw the boundaries of participation to engage a much wider and more varied university population.

On the Nature of 'The Digital'

'The Digital' has become a talismanic phrase in general use suggesting a powerful socio-economic force. In everyday parlance, 'The Digital' is mainly associated with computer technology applications such as data recording, storage, and transmission, and specific examples including digital TV. However, a much wider horizon of meaning is evident and includes terms such as 'digital age', 'digital generation', and 'digital revolution'. When espoused by the management consultancy McKinsey (Dörner and Edelman, 2018) in relation to universities, we find the following assertion:

> … we believe that digital should be seen less as a thing and more a way of doing things. To help make this definition more concrete, we've broken it down into three attributes: creating value at the new frontiers of the business world, creating value in the processes that execute a vision of customer experiences, and building foundational capabilities that support the entire structure.

Whether the McKinsey copywriter has actually made the definition 'more concrete' by invoking high-level management speak, or has simply appropriated the term to serve corporate interests, is a matter for debate.

It is unsurprising, therefore, that universities are contributing to the debate by using the phrase 'digital university' to attempt a redefinition of the university in the twenty-first century. However, when it comes to the practicalities of what a university 'being digital' might look like, different perspectives are being embedded in the policy, provision, and futures planning of higher education institutions. We suggest that development is hampered by the term being used in narrow contexts, mainly relating to digital technology and infrastructure, or to developing student digital skills and/or digital literacies. Equally we are concerned that a corporate style of top-down management is determining the nature of digital developments in universities and constraining staff and student capacity to shape their learning and teaching experiences.

These different, often competing, understandings are informed by the responsibilities that different individuals or departments have for specific aspects of digital practice within the institution. This variety represents a form of what we described above as value pluralism (Johnson and Smyth 2011), in university organisation, and we will elaborate this important concept in later chapters in concert with our advocacy of critical pedagogy. Hereafter we will use the form—the digital—and express the various connotations in the particular context of our discussion at given points in our narrative. Also we will expand our consideration of the nature of the digital in Chap. 2 in the context of a number of key commentators on the digital university.

Neoliberalism and the Neoliberalisation of the University: The Architecture of the Digital University

We see neoliberalism as the primary shaping influence on contemporary universities, exemplified by notions of higher education as a market comprising universities as providers and students as consumers. Consequently, it is essential to preface any discussion of what a digital university might be, with a discussion of what a neoliberal university is and what alternatives can be adduced.

Headline features of neoliberal political economy include (i) valuing private property over public ownership; (ii) appropriation of public resources through government policy of privatisation; and (iii) introduction of corporate management styles to public sector organisation. As an intellectual construct, neoliberalism has been carefully analysed (Mirowski and Plehwe 2009; Birch 2017) and critiqued (Harvey 2005; Streek 2014; Maclean 2017). As both economic doctrine and political practice, neoliberalism has dominated state policy in the UK, the EU, North America, and many other nations, since at least the 1970s, and has come to dominate contemporary cultural frameworks. At the time of writing, it is strongly associated with the austerity policies enacted in response to the 2008–2009 financial crash.

We describe neoliberalism from three perspectives:

- Philosophy of economic and social dominance by the rich and powerful at the expense of socialist and social democratic values; a long-term economic project to prize market values and ensure corporate power.
- Practice: shrink the state, suppress organised labour, accept wage stagnation, deregulate enterprise, use zero-hour contracts and other employment mechanisms to increase precariousness of work, minimise welfare systems, sanction welfare claimants, install austerity.
- Presentation: there is no alternative; negative attitudes to workers, welfare claimants, immigrants and 'experts'; control of media messages to grab attention, shape public opinion and voting behaviour; stifle critical thinking.

Neoliberalism is claimed by some to be an economic and political structure in crisis (Mason 2015; Srnicek and Williams 2016) exemplified by the economic shocks post the 2008 financial crash including stagnant wages, low interest rates, low productivity, precarious employment, and a weakening of public services. Both sets of authors make out cases for radical alternatives involving digital technology and new ways of collaborative working. Nevertheless, neoliberalism remains the primary influence of the strategic direction on higher education and management of universities.

In essence the neoliberal approach to higher education is as an industry 'producing' degrees, to be 'purchased' by student customers with the intention of career benefit to the consumer and the economy as a whole. The strong tendency, therefore, is to curtail ideas of an education with wider personal, social, and democratic purposes. In addition, neoliberal thinking influences staff and student consciousness, arguably in the direction of purely economic goals and away from notions of holistic development and critical citizenship. Commenting from a North American perspective, the radical educator Antonia Darder is unequivocal:

> As the liberal democratic purpose of higher education became more and more obfuscated, universities across the country become more deeply aligned with the narrow rationality of neoliberal objectives. (Darder 2011, p. 420)

In universities established perspectives and practices are threatened by neoliberal managerialism, and new more radical propositions such as the Entrepreneurial University (Gibbs et al. 2012) are being promoted in the spirit of neoliberal thinking. This approach has driven change in UK higher education since the late twentieth century and has been enshrined in national policy over several decades to constitute a project of neoliberalisation of the idea, nature, and practice of universities.

Within a neoliberal ideological architecture, education and pedagogy are constrained by the policy imperative of student employability as the primary learning outcome and control of pedagogical practice as a key underpinning strategy in achieving that outcome. These outcomes are directly linked to the economic success of the nation as well as individual graduates, and in both cases there is a powerful narrative favouring STEM (Science Technology Engineering and Maths) subjects and work-related skills. In this formulation value for money is presented as a key determinant of student experience, and institutions are required to provide tangible evidence of the value for money they represent to students. The review of higher education in England and Wales announced by the Prime Minister, Theresa May, in February 2018 underlines the point that the UK Government is still determined to treat higher education as a market. In effect there is no alternative to continued neoliberalisation of UK higher education in the eyes of the present UK Government.

Institutional management in turn is predicated on norms and practices derived from the corporate sector. In terms of institutional practice, this approach is exemplified by control mechanisms such as the Teaching Excellence Framework (TEF), described by the Office for Students website (2018) as "a national exercise, introduced by the government in England. It assesses excellence in teaching at universities and colleges, and how well they ensure excellent outcomes for their students in terms of graduate-level employment or further study", with its attendant league tables of universities, which can be viewed as an attempt at measuring learning and teaching in market-specific terms. The newly formed UK Office for Students (OfS) whose aim is to ensure that "every student has a fulfilling experience of higher education which enriches their lives" (OfS 2018) will have significant power over the higher education sector. This centralising and controlling approach can be interpreted as a direct response by government annoyed that universities have not operated the fee cap as a competitive pricing mechanism. Thus organisational development has been firmly shaped by the prescriptions of a neoliberal mission to introduce a market for higher education in universities, with academic development subordinated to that purpose. We will challenge this approach to academic development in Chap. 11.

We view the present neoliberal hegemony as an impoverishing and inequitable influence, and argue for an alternative conceptualisation aimed at reforming the experience of higher education as an inclusive public good as opposed to a neoliberalised market. We will discuss the nature of the concept of public good in subsequent chapters. However at this point, several characteristics of our thinking on the public good can be identified: (i) advocacy of access to more inclusive and progressive forms of higher education; (ii) critique of the limitations of a view of wider access as simply increased access to the current experience of higher education; (iii) co-location of the university with non-traditional constituencies in its community; (iv) commitment to more democratic dissemination of knowledge and knowledge artefacts created within the university.

The process of impoverishment is also challenged by scholars such as Stefan Collini (2012, 2017) who critiques the loss of academic autonomy, intellectual freedom, and collegiality instigated by the neoliberal project. The dynamics of the debate on the purposes and future of higher education are therefore contradictory and contested, yet individual universities are creating strategic visions to align with the dominant political economy rather than engaging in more fundamental appraisals of their situation. Within this difficult environment, it seems that the institutional approach to the digital is predominantly technist, with the overriding aim of growing the technological infrastructure and harnessing it to market and consumer-based educational objectives. Our aim in this book is to outline an alternative approach based on critical pedagogy, openness, and reconciling value pluralism, in relation to our conceptualisation of the Digital University.

Technology in the Neoliberal University

The neoliberal university treats digital technology as a servant of market strategising, and it is introduced to achieve objectives such as (i) increasing student numbers, (ii) distributing degree matter online, (iii) enhancing learning and teaching, (iv) enhancing the analytic capabilities of administration, (v) meeting student expectations, and (vi) improving student satisfaction scores such as the NSS (National Student Survey) in the UK. A number of these objectives align to notions of markets and students as customers, particularly these based on the assumption that students will be attracted to and satisfied by the digital experiences provided by their university. In addition, digital technology is usually positioned as in some way aligning with what 'young people' do with technology in their private lives and as part of the contemporary digital society overall. The assumption being that the digital university must in some way become part of the Silicon Valley and big tech worldview and economy if it is to advance further along the neoliberal lines ordained by the state.

Several thought-lines can be discerned emerging from neoliberalism in relation to visions of digital universities:

(i) An apocalyptic vision of complete disruption of existing campus-based models of provision and its replacement with a new tool such as Massive Open Online Courses (MOOCs), the 'coming avalanche' vision (Barber et al. 2013). We will challenge this vision throughout the book.

(ii) A managerialist, technist approach taken by institutions and staff seeking to augment and enhance existing aims and practices. The biannual UK UCISA (Universities and Colleges Information Systems Association) Surveys provide an informative vision of this more moderate approach in action. We will explore the limitations of this approach and develop a critique drawing on critical pedagogy, open education, and a revitalised collegiality amongst staff.

Faced with these contradictory lines of thought, our task is to discover how best we can problematise what academics do under conditions of neoliberal management. Whilst a major focus will be on the digital aspects of contemporary higher education, we are determined to produce a pedagogical response to the neoliberalisation of higher education. Hence our interest in the work of the radical educator, Paulo Freire.

Critical Pedagogy: Paulo Freire and Higher Education

The very title of Freire's book *Education for Critical Consciousness* (1974) expresses an alternative view of what education might be for. Rather than simply reproducing the values and desired technical skills of a neoliberal political economy, critical pedagogy would engage learners and teachers in a mutual project aimed at extending critical thought from narrow disciplinary issues to a wider critique of self, community, society, and democracy. A 'university education for critical consciousness' would undoubtedly be anathema to the neoliberal consensus on what a university is for! That conflict would be a challenge to our perspective, and we anticipate a sharp response from politicians, senior managers, and their partisans.

We will explore the potential to introduce a critical pedagogy for universities through the practices of course redesign, educational development, and innovative approaches to how digital technology is used (Chaps. 7 and 8). Given that this is likely to be contested territory, we will provide persuasive arguments and examples of how criticality can be introduced in practice. This will include a dialogue with current theory-based approaches and will involve close description of digital pedagogy in practice.

Freire's approach to contextualising education within the wider sociopolitical context is presented a radical transformation around the power relationships with education and the wider state. Learning is positioned as being based on mutual respect between the educator and the educatee which empowers authentic learning through the development of education as a collective, critical dialogic activity and not a top-down one-directional transmission (Rugut and Osman 2013). Freire's approach countered the banking metaphor approach to education, where knowledge is deposited by those in power (the elite), and so the status quo is maintained as students become passive recipients (Freire 1974).

Freire sought to transform this situation through the development of culture circles where learners were encouraged to share their understandings of their world and how they interacted within it (Rugut and Osam, ibid.). These collective experiences created generative themes, that is, something that is of material significance to a particular group of students. Working in primarily adult literacy, Freire then encouraged students to produce (a mix of visual images and words) codifications of these generative themes, which can then be used as a basis for critical discussion. This should be distinguished from simply 'teaching' literacy, to a much more critical process of raising consciousness and exploring contradictions in the cultural context. This process of codification allows for the development of a shared contextualisation of a real situation based on authentic experiences. The subsequent dialogue engendered by the codification process should allow for the development of individual freedom from oppressive systems through critical reflection on personal experience and practice—what he termed praxis, which he describes as:

reflection and action directed at the structures to be transformed. (Freire 1974, p. 126)

Several value propositions arise from this account of Freire's work which characterise how it might be developed and experienced in contemporary higher education:

- Reinstatement of active, critical and creative qualities in design of learning experiences and the notions of learning experiences and the recognition that education is part of a political process and plays a pivotal role in democracy.
- Development of human capacities distinct from the current neoliberal social order, particularly the distinction between the details and power structures of the digital world (devices, media etc.) and the world of social relationships (critique, community, humility, love).

Given our emphasis on higher education as an inclusive public good, the question of participation and the wider public realm needs to be discussed also, and issues of political uncertainty and economic dislocation taken into account as influences of the nature and motivations of a participating public.

Thematic Overview

We will concentrate on three major approaches in our consideration of the change forces influencing the strategic direction of change in universities:

(i) Neoliberal political economy
(ii) Academic/pedagogical development
(iii) Organisational/institutional development

As the book unfolds, we will show how these themes intersect in both theory and practice to shape options for institutional strategy; curriculum design and implementation; pedagogical practice; learning spaces; and the options for transforming institutional identity, management, and organisation.

To these ends we will:

- Approach our themes analytically from macro, meso, and micro perspectives (detailed in Chap. 5).
- Advocate a range of approaches to pedagogic practice, academic development, and organisational development underpinned by critical ped-

agogy perspectives, as a means to revive the value of higher education as an inclusive public good and to shape educational practice through harnessing digital technology, space, and place creatively, effectively, and for more democratic educational purposes.
* Argue the need to advance the current discourse on openness and open practice in education and with respect to the location and co-location of the university, the curriculum, and engagement in higher education learning opportunities, and in relation to notions of porosity, community, and public pedagogy.

The basis of our educational thinking is developed from Freire's ideas of critical consciousness (Freire 1974), and we will engage with our themes in the dialectical spirit of Freire's work. Consequently, our writing will display that dialectical character of praxis as will our conceptualisation of the implications of our thinking for strategic direction, academic structures, and academic development. Our approach to writing is a blend of experience, ongoing reflection, analysis, dialogue, and advocacy to promote long-term and comprehensive innovation, leading to significant transformation of what a university education can mean.

The ideas and arguments in this book have taken some years of discussion, presentation, and local initiatives to develop. To some extent the narrative of the book reprises that process. In our own practice, we worked as 'thought collective' rather than three separate authors, and this approach is described more fully in Chap. 3. Throughout we were careful to avoid closing down discussion or adopting overly prescriptive positions. Our aim was to stimulate and engage rather than provide easy solutions and blueprints.

Conclusion and Forecast of the Book

We argue that the entry point for discussion of the digital university is through the portal of the neoliberalisation of the university. Neoliberalism impoverishes the university, and we counterpoise the ideas of critical pedagogy and openness as an enrichment of the university. Neoliberalised curriculum denies students' opportunities and experiences, such as development of critical consciousness, by channelling their efforts in the direction of a narrow definition of value, that is, value for money calculated as graduate earning power.

Surely students should have the opportunity to follow their own paths and have the tools to do so? For example, if we can impose a 'portfolio' tool on students to 'record' career development, why not give them the chance to co-create an alternative form of portfolio? This later could be viewed as a portable aspect of their personhood and could be a record of their 'journey' to complex epistemological development in the sense of achieving an evaluativist epistemology. This opportunity should be a right and a mark of intellectual and social value.

In Chap. 1 we established our main positions on neoliberalism, technology, and pedagogy. In Chap. 2 we scope the territory of the digital university using selected exemplars. In Chap. 3 we describe our process of praxis, which has shaped our thinking, and then in Chaps. 4, 5, 6, 7, 8, and 9, we deal with our major themes in more detail. In Chaps. 10 and 11, we focus on academic and organisational development of universities, and we present our conclusions and proposals for future activity in Chap. 12.

References

Barber, M., Donnely, K., & Rizvi, S. (2013). *An Avalanche Is Coming: Higher Education and the Revolution Ahead*. IPPR. https://www.ippr.org/publications/an-avalanche-is-coming-higher-education-and-the-revolution-ahead. Accessed 28 Apr 2018.

Birch, K. (2017). *A Research Agenda for Neoliberalism*. Cheltenham: Edward Elgar Publishing.

Collini, S. (2012). *What Are Universities For?* London: Penguin.

Collini, S. (2017). *Speaking of Universities*. London/New York: Verso.

Darder, A. (2011). Teaching as an Act of Love: Reflections on Paulo Freire and His Contributions to Our Lives and Our Work. *Counterpoints, 418*, 179–194.

Dörner, K., & Edelman, D. (2018). *What 'Digital' Really Means*. McKinsey & Company. http://www.mckinsey.com/industries/high-tech/our-insights/what-digital-really-means. Accessed 28 Apr 2018.

Freire, P. (1974). *Education for Critical Consciousness*. London: Bloomsbury Academic.
Giroux, H. A. (2000). Public Pedagogy and the Responsibility of Intellectuals: Youth, Littleton, and the Loss of Innocence. *JAC: A Journal of Composition Theory, 20*(1), 9–42.
Harvey, D. (2005). *A Brief History of Neoliberalism*. Oxford: Oxford University Press.
Johnson, M., & Smyth, K. (2011). Diversity, Value and Technology: Exposing Value Pluralism in Institutional Strategy. *Campus-Wide Information Systems, 28*(4), 211–220.
Jones, C., & Goodfellow, R. (2012). The "Digital University": Discourse, Theory, and Evidence. *International Journal of Learning and Media, 4*(3–4), 59–63.
Maclean, N. (2017). *Democracy in Chains: The Deep History of the Radical Right's Stealth Plan for America*. New York: Viking.
Mason, P. (2015). *PostCapitalism: A Guide to Our Future*. London: Alan Lane.
Mirowski, P., & Plehwe, D. (2009). *The Road from Mont Pelerin: The Making of the Neoliberal Thought Collective*. Cambridge, MA: Harvard University Press.
Office for Students. (2018). *Office for Students Strategy 2018 to 2021*. Office for Students. https://www.officeforstudents.org.uk/publications/office-for-students-strategy-2018-to-2021/. Accessed 28 Apr 2018.
Rugut, E. J., & Osman, A. A. (2013). Reflection on Paulo Freire and Classroom Relevance. *American Journal of Social Science, 2*(2), 23–28.
Srnicek, N., & Williams, A. (2016). *Inventing the Future: Postcapitalism and a World Without Work*. London/New York: Verso.
Streek, W. (2014). How Will Capitalism End? *New Left Review, 87*, 35–64.

2

The Digital University: An Impoverished Concept

Introduction

Change in universities in response to the Internet and digital technologies should be uniformly progressive and enriching given the communicative power of the technologies and their obvious links to educational practice. Yet our survey of key representative contributors to the literature shows the responses to be more complex and indeed sharply contradictory. For example, some commentators on the digital university have been characterised as "Boosters", whilst others are characterised as "Doomsters" (Selwyn 2014). There is also a strong sense that predictions of radical educational change (Barber et al. 2013) have been exposed as overblown hype by a more mundane, and perhaps disappointing, reality:

> There is no doubt that digital technologies have had a profound impact upon the management of learning. Institutions can now recruit, register, monitor, and report on students with a new economy, efficiency, and (sometimes) creativity. Yet, evidence of digital technologies producing real transformation in learning and teaching remains elusive. (Luckin et al. 2012, p. 8)

Our critique of the neoliberal university in Chap. 1 suggests why this might be the case. Firstly, neoliberal thinking defines higher education as a market where the value of education is increasingly expressed as graduate earning power and contribution to national economic competitiveness to the detriment of other potential choices. Alternative perspectives and objectives for learning are thereby marginalised or simply ignored. Secondly, Silicon Valley-style radical visions of the Internet and the digital influence strategic thinking about the nature and future functioning of higher education in society. Hence the more apocalyptic presentations of the digital as a fundamental upending of traditional values, structures, and practices in universities. Thirdly, the rise of managerialism in university organisational practice serves to constrain the options for educational development and pedagogical innovation in practice. The net result is a university system dominated by a logic of self-interested consumerism, supposedly driving up teaching standards, with the digital technologies harnessed to the service of that logic.

From our critical perspective, this suggests that neoliberalisation entails a conceptual impoverishment of the notion of what a university is for, and undermines any conceptualisation of the digital university, which accepts a neoliberal approach without critiquing its dangers. Neoliberalism operates in practice across the macro, meso, and micro levels of the higher education system, and in universities, to channel thinking and practice into its own narrow perspective. Within the organisational and developmental structures of universities, this conceptual impoverishment limits the awareness of possibilities for critical pedagogy, including the possibilities for digital innovation. The practical context for these limiting tendencies is an ongoing redefinition of the nature of academic work, including (i) precarious employment, (ii) excessive workloads, (iii) overemphasis on research productivity, (iv) contested approaches to academic publishing, (v) declining pay and pension rights, and (vi) a general sense of loss of worth and academic freedom. In combination, these features represent an impoverishment of the academic role and employment experience.

The combination of conceptual and practical impoverishment also tends to circumscribe the range of possibilities for more open participation and engagement with universities in the public arena. However, such impoverished circumstances also stimulate critical responses and generate alternatives to neoliberal principles and ways of working, which we will explore in this book.

On the Nature of the Digital: A Basis for Critical Discussion

To continue our contribution to the current debate on the digital within the higher education sector from Chap. 1, it may be helpful to propose a working description of what the digital is taken to be in general terms and as it can be discerned in universities. We see the digital typically portrayed in plain language and in broad terms as:

> The convergence of the Internet, WWW, computers and mobile devices to produce and share information for a diverse range of economic, social, political and educational purposes in modern society.

A digital university might therefore simply be a centre of such convergences. This rather neutral and technical sounding formulation is offered as a starting point for a more nuanced and critical discussion of what the digital is and how it might be reframed. Our discussion embraces notions of the digital in the internal environment of the university and in terms of interactions between universities and their wider social context.

We can identify broad aspects of society where this general description of the digital is relevant. Often subsumed within notions of the 'digital age', these include (i) professional and academic practice; (ii) economic organisation, production, and consumption; (iii) political and public policy; (iv) media and communication sectors; (v) health and wellbeing; and (vi) the everyday lives of people. This later aspect is diverse, including leisure, personal development, and many life situations observed in a wide variety of formal and informal contexts. It is particularly relevant to our aim of highlighting the importance of participation in higher education as an inclusive public good, and also in emphasising the importance of information as the life-blood flowing through the Internet and connected digital systems. We develop our account of these two concepts in Chaps. 5 and 6, respectively.

Specific configurations of the digital can be identified in universities: "… most notably computers, the internet and mobile telephony—are now integral features of higher education" (Selwyn 2014, p. 3). A more systematic and longitudinal account is provided through the Universities and Colleges Information Systems Association (UCISA) biannual Surveys of Technologically Enhanced Learning (TEL). At the time of writing, the most recent survey available was published in 2016. UCISA offers a working definition of TEL as follows:

> Any online facility or system that directly supports learning and teaching. This may include a formal VLE, e-assessment or e-portfolio software, or lecture capture system, mobile app or collaborative tool that supports student learning. This includes any system that has been developed in-house, as well as commercial or open source tools.

The 2016 Survey (Walker et al. 2016) findings report a palate of technologies in use and identify trends, institutional priorities, and potential new directions, thereby offering a comprehensive picture of the main headline features of the current state of the digital art in UK universities and colleges. The UCISA approach is concerned primarily with institutional engagement with TEL and aligns with the organisational aspect of our interest in conceptualising what a digital university might be. We will return to the UCISA Survey contents in more detail in later chapters.

The UCISA Surveys describe the trajectory of technology uptake in UK universities over time and raise crucial issues of organisation and management. For example, how has the composition of the workforce changed? What practices are being modified and how? How are organisational structures changing? What are the barriers to innovation? The overall impression given is not one of revolutionary change, rather change seems incremental and limited to particular zones of practice embodied in the technological infrastructure of universities, which contextualise learning and teaching. All these features of technology uptake are subject to Government funding constraints and policy changes, which in the UK are determinedly neoliberal. We will return to these issues in subsequent chapters.

In short digital technologies institute changes in a range of social and cultural activities, which alter daily life and appear irreversible. A similar process of adjustments and modifications to practice can be observed in universities, particularly in respect of teaching. Let us look more closely at how these change processes are being interpreted in respect of higher education and university development.

Patterns of Critical Consciousness: An Engagement with the Literature

Our aim in this section is to highlight and critique several major facets and trends in the emerging accounts of the digital university. We will mount this discussion through a selective outline of the thinking displayed in some key texts. Our selection includes academic commentators alongside contributions from management consultants, think thanks, and university internal policy statements. We interpret this literature as being to an extent ideologically grounded, so our review highlights the ideological nature of the contributions. In some cases, the ideological framing is clearly neoliberal, whilst other contributions are oppositional and framed by alternative philosophies of education and society.

The UCISA approach described above is pragmatic and suggestive of a view of technology as an institutional overhead incurred in supporting core activity such as teaching. Although there is reference to 'pedagogies', there does not seem to be a focus on educational thinking about the nature of learning. So, UCISA provides a 'manager's guide' to the contours of TEL rather than an educationalist's perspective on the use of technology in specific learning contexts, for example, PBL (Problem Based Learning). This is not to marginalise observable good practices in any sense. However, we suggest that gradual, incremental initiatives, focused on short-term and sectional projects, for example, will not really evolve the university into a new organism. This is an area we will revisit in subsequent chapters when we discuss pedagogical thinking and practice in more detail.

So, where can we locate the digital in the university beyond the domain of technology specialists and professional managers? For example, it is visible in:

- Government policy
- Scholarly perspectives
- Consultants and think tanks
- University mission statements

We will consider each type of source in turn as facets of the pattern of thinking about the digital university. We will also outline our critique of the digital, which we will develop in subsequent chapters.

Government Policy: Value for Money

The UK Government has proceeded along clear neoliberal lines and fostered the idea of a market in higher education. The current UK Government Review of higher education (2018) is a further example of the dominance of neoliberal ideology over higher education and the universities. The Review is predicated on the assumption that there is no alternative to the market and that a mix of student fees and competition between institutions for student enrolments will somehow drive up teaching standards and deliver student satisfaction. Hence the point of the Review is to make the articulation of relations between the university providers and the student consumers more transparent and 'market efficient'. There is no suggestion (at time of writing) that alternatives to student fees and competition between institutions would get serious consideration if they somehow emerged from the Review. The announcement of the Review was attended by the notion of creating an information base using data sets of pupil, student, and employability (graduate earnings) to create league tables of universities in terms of differences in . graduate income outcomes aligned to subject departments.

How such an approach would work in relation to historically low-paid graduate careers like nursing is an open question. For example, would departments of nurse education in universities be run down based on the salaries of their graduates? Or would the departments simply be shifted into other kinds of non-university tertiary education? Equally is it credible that Oxford, Cambridge, and the Russell Group institutions will lose their appeal to students if they slip down a given 'league table' for a period of time? Indeed, will the league table be separated out into divisions? One for the elite and perhaps several lower divisions along the lines of the USA? In any case it is difficult to see how any moves towards critical pedagogy would survive in such a system.

As to the place of the digital in this ideological approach, it appears that the 'search engine' to drive this turbocharged market system is to be an App, designed to enable prospective students to access information about 'employability' and 'graduate income' to assist their choice of university/ subject of study. Evidently universities would have to respond by aligning their educational strategy and practice to these sorts of metrics, allied to digitised consumer behaviour, and revise their recruitment/selection methods accordingly. This seems to be the digitised epitome of consumerised higher education and contradicts established notions of academic excellence, learning as critical inquiry or higher education as a public good. It also builds on the appropriation of the digital to narrow, neoliberal ends, which we have noted.

The Scholars: Collini, Selwyn, McCluskey, and Winter

The following scholars have been chosen to illustrate different perspectives in relation to our developing thesis on the failings of the neoliberal approach, and the need for a critical alternative, as they may cast a light on the concept of the Digital University. Collini and Selwyn take different approaches—one is a renowned humanist scholar and public commentator, the other is a distinguished educationalist—but both are broadly critical of the neoliberal position. To an extent therefore, they align with that aspect of our thinking, and we believe they also support our 'impoverished conception' theme in this chapter.

McCluskey and Winter are American educationalists, who seem less sceptical of the digital and more interested in the practical 'how to' aspect of digital practice. To that extent they seem to us to offer a more nuanced account than the UCISA Survey's, with the added value of offering insights into aspects of improved practice. We can align to that approach in terms of the demands of practical educational development in universities, but remain true to our view that a critical alternative is required.

Collini

Stefan Collini is Professor Emeritus of Intellectual History and English Literature at the University of Cambridge and therefore a high status commentator. As an opening contribution to our review of scholarly thinking, we cite his 2017 text:

> We need to be able to articulate an understanding of what universities are for that is adequate to our time if we are to be able to decide what to do. (Collini 2017, p. 4)

Collini's challenge is well made and illuminates our ambitions for this book since he goes on to signal that the fundamental values, traditions, and contradictions of our times should be included in debating his question of purpose, rather than simple acceptance of the conventional wisdom of the day. This view accords with our notions of praxis as critical dialogue. His perspective includes critical opposition to state interference in academic discretion over research, marketisation of knowledge and educational opportunity, and the dominance of narrow instrumentalist/human capital agendas in university organisation and staffing. By contrast he expresses support for education as a humanist project to explore and develop knowledge, individual curiosity as a fundamental motivation, and the importance of arts and humanities. Collini's views therefore stand in stark contradiction to neoliberal thinking about the purpose of a university and its contemporary embrace of neoliberal perspectives expressed through Government policy and enacted through managerialist control of institutions.

We should also note from the perspective of our interests that Collini says little about the digital. For example: "New technologies promise to alter the most basic mechanics of the teaching process" (Collini 2017, p. 2). This is hardly a detailed response to technological influences on pedagogical change, although it implies acceptance of the notion that technology will in some manner radically change practice. Collini's main contribution to our perspective is his powerful critique of universities and their leaders for becoming too much like corporate businesses driven by business aims, metrics, and management speak. He is not alone, for example, *The Assault on Universities: A Manifesto for Resistance* (Bailey and Freedman 2011) and *A Manifesto for the Public University* (Holmwood 2011). Both have similarities with Collini's critique but have perhaps more politically radical perspectives. It should be said that neither of these books indexes the terms 'digital' or 'technology', which may give some measure of the emphasis in their perspective.

Collini is a distinctive and much cited voice in the debate given his direct challenge to Government policy and robust advocacy for an ideal of university education at odds with the neoliberal emphasis on providers and consumers in a higher education marketplace. To an extent his work has shaped the public mind given his high-profile and sharp wit. The following commentators are perhaps more specialist in their provenance but nonetheless bring distinctive and important ways of thinking to the emerging conceptual map of the digital university.

Selwyn

Neil Selwyn is Professor of Education at Monash University in Australia. In our reading of his work, we focus on his book *Digital Technology and the Contemporary University* (2014). Three chapters (1, 7, and 8) are chosen for attention.

We chose Chap. 1, 'Universities and digital technology: Hype, hope and fear', as evidence of a thread of critical analysis of the digital in relation to universities and higher education, which identified contradictory tendencies in the presentation of the digital. Specifically, the perception that much is promised—the hype and the hope—however there are negative and potentially damaging implications, is the fear. In this chapter Selwyn's 'forty years on' review of the various strands of discussion over the decades, which he neatly categorises into 'booster' accounts and 'doomster' accounts, suggests a mixed utopian/dystopian landscape.

His argument for seeking a more subtle analysis and focussing on what really happens in practice (Chaps. 3, 4, 5, and 6) again supports our approach and underlines a similar view that although great changes have not happened, there is a discernible 'digital footprint' across various parts of institutional function, policy, and organisational management. If not altogether benign, this hasn't developed into a complete overthrow of the traditional university values, structures, practices, and patterns of participation. Selwyn is clearly dissatisfied with the way the digital has developed in practice and particularly in terms of changed organisational culture.

The title of Chap. 7, 'Looking back: making sense of universities in the digital age', expresses Selwyn's commitment to looking at the wider social, political, and economic factors constituting 'the digital age' as influences on universities and university engagement with the digital. He is also clear that this is not mere 'background' to digital university life, but a powerful, direct influence on framing the digital, understanding managerialism, and illuminating the question of what university is for in the twenty-first century. The arguments and themes Selwyn advances form the basis of a critical discussion of the issues he cites: power, commodification, values, and so on. One could see this chapter being a 'reading' for a PG Cert group for example. How the ideas in this chapter could be introduced to institutional strategic thinking and organisational change would need some thought as he presents a critique, which tends to undermine the legitimacy of contemporary governance and management authority. That said, Selwyn's perceptions align with our own.

The macro is much to the fore in this chapter and is strongly linked to our theme of 'organisational development', and very much in a mode of critical analysis of contemporary managerialist orthodoxy and practice. He presents a perspective that suggests the digital is not only an impoverished concept, but also potentially detrimental to academic practice. His account of the dark side of the digital is well done and implies a Borg-like state of organisational being, with people assimilated to the institution's digital systems on the grounds that "resistance is futile". Clearly, Selwyn does not agree and neither do we.

Our final selection from Selwyn is Chap. 8: 'Looking forward: Reimagining digital technology and the contemporary university'. The central theme seems to be Selwyn's "…critical, pessimistic approach…", which characterises his analysis of the failings of the digital as both innovative technology and transformative ideology, and provides a platform for his thinking on what to do about the situation. His posture seems to be grounded in the identification of alternative uses of digital technologies and speculation on the prospects for engaging various communities to take action for change. The dialectic seems to be between the negative position of a digital technology for universities shaped by neoliberal corporatism and institutional managerialism, and a potential for 'grassroots' opposition to those shaping powers. In effect Selwyn seems to present the way forward as residing in a 'counter cultural' challenge to the dominant forces of digital development in universities.

His proposals include:

(i) Emphasis on the (macro) social nature of digital technology situated in particular (meso/micro) settings;
(ii) Call to 'problematise' digital technology and subject it to critical analysis;
(iii) Adoption of some version of 'nudge' tactics to change perceptions and behaviour;
(iv) Re-phrasing the language used to describe technologies;
(v) Reconfiguration of physical space to expose the digital component;
(vi) Collective action to produce alternative statements, for example, Bill of Rights/Manifesto;
(vii) Individuals asserting their rights and perspectives against corporate/institutional dominance of technology;
(viii) Widening the range of 'publics' engaging in 'problematising' technology and proposing alternatives;
(ix) Engaging more organisations and groups in the debate, for example, trade unions, charities.

Selwyn's proposals warrant a critical response. For example, we think (i) and (ii) are correct, (iii) is dubious, (iv) and (v) are attractive and plausible, (vi) is attractive, (vii) is essential, (viii) is an essential challenge, but (ix) looks doubtful—would a trade union really be able to take up these issues as negotiating objectives? Would government and management forces committed to a neoliberal/corporate position really listen to a union policy statement, which is critical of their stance? In essence the conclusion is a call to arms couched in terms, which we characterise as 'left activist'.

McCluskey and Winter

Our choice from their book *The Idea of the Digital University* (2012) is Chap. 18—'The major elements and essence of the digital university'.

Their approach is quite different in tone from Selwyn and Collini, and much more of a 'how to' chapter, in that it seems to largely accept digital technology as a given and proceeds by describing how to get the best out of it rather than mounting any form of critique. The argument is quite proscriptive—lots of 'musts' and 'shoulds'—aimed at getting things done rather than encouraging reflection.

There is a strong emphasis on data, measurement, analytics, tracing, and so on allied to a belief in rational, purposive action as the basis of positive change. Much of what they write about data analytics sounds like an updated form of information management. This is a useful perspective if applied from the perspective of the politics of metrics—who decides, uses, and owns the metrics? Are there alternatives? How can they be used without encouraging more reification of the university experience? These questions would repay further discussion.

Some key points from McCluskey and Winter include:

(i) The 'market smart, mission driven' mantra of business management as applied to universities;
(ii) Need for student 'digital literacy' for employability;
(iii) Strong support for academics in traditional roles but enhanced by digital technology;

(iv) Differentiation between categories and kinds of universities based on mission and performance;
(v) Promotion of local data analytics to shape the experience of student cohorts, identify achievement of learning outcomes, and exemplify mission success;
(vi) Promotion of large-scale external data collection for quality regulation and sector direction—TEF and LEO (longitudinal educational outcomes) spring to mind;
(vii) Advocacy for 'critical thinking' across the curriculum;
(viii) Promotion of some level of STEM subject knowledge and methods across the curriculum;
(ix) Proposals to distinguish academic and administrator roles in relation to technology and business processes;
(x) Strong support for the use of 'dashboards and data warehouses' along with 'digital report cards'.

The chapter concludes with a rather vague set of paeans to the virtual, the empowerments of 'digital natives' and an uncritical cheer for the 'digital revolution', which will, inevitably, force a refocusing of higher education. In effect they offer a 'how to' advocacy of digital technology as a guide to enhance practice. In the short to medium terms, this approach may be unavoidable, pragmatic, and to an extent beneficial. However, it is arguable that this approach could become part of the problem of neoliberalisation and managerialist approaches to university organisation if not critiqued.

The Management Consultancy: Price Waterhouse Cooper (PWC)

PWC in its 'The 2018 digital university: staying relevant in the digital age' briefing paper (2018) offers university leaders an off-the-shelf primer for a comprehensive digital strategy. The advice founds on certain assumptions about the digital including (i) it is here to stay; (ii) it is transformational; (iii) it is essential to keeping up the university place in modern society; and (iv) it is a skillset for all areas of academic practice. The tone is not as apocalyptic as The Coming Avalanche (Barber et al. 2013); indeed they acknowledge that MOOCs "… have yet to gain traction …".

However, the audience are left in no doubt that digitally driven change is inevitable, that "…digital disruption in teaching methods" is the order of the day, and that failure to act now would be the gravest folly. The following quote should suffice to illustrate PWC's uncritical promotion of neoliberal thinking:

> … as competition from credible substitutes to Higher Education, such as Higher Apprenticeships, continues to grow, as does the fierce competition to attract the best students in both the UK and internationally, universities need to demonstrate that they are able to provide the digital experience that students now take for granted. In today's digital age where the voice of the customer is more prevalent than ever, turning your customers into advocates for your university is one of the most powerful marketing tools available.

The brief comes complete with prescriptions for 'How to successfully harness digital' and a comprehensive bullet pointed 'digital blueprint' for a university to incorporate in its strategic thinking. In effect PWC advocates harnessing the university to the supposedly defining features of our neoliberal time: globalisation, competitive knowledge economy, digitally networked society; and their blueprint is a simple statement of managerialist principle and practice. We are not convinced by the overly positivist spin on the digital promise.

The Think Tank: Leading the Entrepreneurial University: Meeting the Entrepreneurial Development Needs of Higher Education (Gibbs et al. 2012)

The origin of this perspective is in the Said Business School at the University of Oxford and arguably makes it a suitable counterpoint to Collini's Cambridge Don status. It is also arguably much more detailed and sustained an argument than PWC's broad-brush portrait of the university in the digital age. The report is a powerful statement of the case for universities becoming entrepreneurial as their defining mission and mode of organisation. Entrepreneurship in this formulation denotes the philosophy and practices of capitalist notions of value and modes of accumulation and may be regarded as a particularly robust expression of the general neoliberal approach to transforming universities.

As applied to universities, this philosophy includes objectives for student learning as well as paradigm for a university's own ways of working. So it is a view which not only sets about shaping the nature of institutional culture and operations but also the nature and experience of the curriculum. The report highlights the impact of an external environment largely described by capitalist political economy and cutting-edge business thinking. Both are assumed to be positive and are clearly aligned to a prospectus for university organisational development and individual academic responses.

The leadership challenge posed by this paradigm shift is clearly described as a drive to generate a university as an entrepreneurial business, wherein management and leadership development are designed to achieve an entrepreneurial mission. The argument is couched very much in a language and mind-set, which Collini might characterise as 'management speak'. That said, it is a well-researched and clearly argued contribution. However, where Collini is sceptical of contemporary changes in universities, Gibbs et al. are uncritically positive in pursuit of new forms of higher education.

The digital is mentioned in this account in quite instrumental terms, for example, as part of the external environment to be accepted and adopted as a process activity contributing to the overall mission. In terms of given technologies, there is mention of MOOCs and Big Data, both depicted as challenging but necessary and uniformly positive. The technological dimension is closely linked to university knowledge transfer initiatives and is therefore aligned to the business function account of a university. In this respect, the authors deploy the Mode 1/2 account of knowledge creation to describe the 'public' knowledge function of the university.

The authors acknowledge the debate over the 'idea' of a university and cite Collini. Indeed, they recognise the concerns over knowledge capitalism as an unwelcome threat to traditional academic values, nonetheless they hold to the view that the entrepreneurial direction is the right one. The digital is also posited as a challenge to older academics, but treated as a matter of managers finding practical accommodations for such staff rather than exploring the possibility that 'older academics', with their hard-won experiences, might have points worth considering.

Gibbs et al. distinguish between the entrepreneurial model and other models such as a presumed mainstream corporate business model. Key overlaps include strong elements of business professionalism applied to organisational management and development and a philosophy and practice of the marketisation of knowledge as a commodity. The paper serves to identify a polar opposite to Collini's position, but also to illuminate the spectrum of emphasis and the potential for radical organisational answers to Collini's questioning of what universities are for.

In Collini's terms, universities are primarily for knowledge, education, scholarship, and personal growth as social goods in their own right. In the entrepreneurial/business dispensations, the view of what a university is for tips decisively in favour of the integration of academic activity in a competitive global knowledge economy and a digitally networked society. Consequently, knowledge is produced primarily for economic gain, and student learning is presumed to induce the relevant skills for recruitment to the knowledge workforce. The implication is that staff research, teaching, and administrative responsibilities will be subordinate to such aims.

The Institutional Mission Statement: Monash University

(Office of the Vice Provost, Learning and Teaching (2013). "Better Teaching, Better Learning Agenda".)

In this institutional macro level statement, Monash presents itself to the world as a major academic institution operating in line with modern socioeconomic values for higher education and, we believe, as a serious competitor to its longer established neighbour, the University of Melbourne. In effect a modern business/technology institution set alongside one of the Australian Sandstones.

This illustrative specimen of a university strategic learning and teaching statement is clear and emphatic on themes of progressive change, innovative pedagogy, and the priority of global ambitions for students. Drawing on local experience, 'blended learning' is presented as a confusing term for academics, which needs to be refocused in order to avoid a simplistic assumption that basic importation of technology into existing course designs is sufficient. Interestingly, the digital is described as not only an infrastructure but also as integrated in pedagogy and subject to ongoing improvement. In essence the development strategy uses 'bottom-up' feedback to modify the direction of change. Senior academic leadership is invested with responsibility for change. Thus we see a system of macro, micro, and meso level engagements with the digital—described in this case by reference to blended learning—to refine pedagogical practice allied to a modernising institutional mission.

A cyclical model of organisational change/engagement is proposed, focused on the systematic alignment of course units and modules with the macro perspectives of the institutional learning and teaching strategy. A faculty working party approach is the preferred mode of organisational development, and there is reference to specific generic digital tools, for example, Turnitin and content and resource repositories. There is a section on 'learning spaces', which briefly discusses technology as a function of space utilisation and a key aspect of design and chimes with our thinking in Chap. 7.

In essence this is a fairly recognisable University policy statement of the period. By contrast to Gibbs et al., we would argue that it is more indicative of a pragmatic, incremental change driven as much by agreed curriculum themes as a full-on embrace of technology and entrepreneurialism. So it looks closer to our impression of the situation in the UK as described in the UCISA Surveys. Equally there is little to suggest that Collini's more critical appraisal is having an influence, although it may be that Collini's views are implicit and embedded in academic practice at Monash.

Conclusion: Reflections on the Literature

It seems the territory is divided between those commentators like PWC and Gibbs et al. embracing a neoliberalism technist account of the university and those like Collini and Selwyn who are critical and tend to reject the new dispensations in favour of alternative positions. How an actual university might behave in this contradictory and contested territory may be gleaned from the Monash example above and our own experiences described in Chap. 3.

The argument, which we can adduce from the sources above, is along the lines that there are powerful, competing positions available to describe and locate the digital in university experience. However current reality, certainly in the UK, is not so much affected by the academic and professional commentaries save that the thrust of the EULP model is probably more dominant on university practice than Collini's critique of managerialist culture or Selwyn's detailed analysis of digital developments. By contrast McCluskey and Winter are accepting of the neoliberal slant and offer pragmatic responses for pedagogical and organisational adjustment. The Monash mission statement is possibly a reasonable guide to what strategic leaders would like to see in their institutions. It can be argued, then, that the universities' response to digital change has been transactional rather than transformational. The transactions can be observed in terms of the steady adjustments and modifications of practice reported by UCISA and given strategic expression in documents like the Monash strategy statement.

The actual transformation of the university resides more in the domain of the neoliberal project and can be observed in the positions detailed in the PWC briefing paper and the much more substantial account given by Gibbs et al. Our task in the following chapters is to develop a new and critical vision, which challenges the powerful myth of digital transformation (Chap. 4). In addition, we can provide a more 'professional' account of the digital and pedagogical practice than Collini has attempted and a less uncritical analysis than offered by McCluskey and Winter. Selwyn's views are closer to ours and we will draw down on them in Chaps. 10 and 11.

A key outcome of our literature review and our own thinking relates to the theme of 'impoverishment' consequent on neoliberalisation. As educationalists we are faced with an impoverished concept of the digital university largely because we are faced with an impoverished concept of the university. This stems from the adoption of neoliberal ideology by the state and various actors on the university stage. There is a discernible process of 'normalisation' of the neoliberal idea in progress, and this process is part of the challenge we face. It is a major challenge as strands like the entrepreneurial univeristy paper are clearly well argued and persuasive.

Our perception from experience and literature is that the concept of the digital university is impoverished because it is both:

* Disproportionally skewed in the direction of a neoliberal, technist, and managerialist account of the university.
* Underdeveloped in the realms of pedagogical theory and organisational development practice.

The contradictory and partial accounts of the digital university discussed above have influenced our thinking and spurred us to seek an alternative, holistic orientation. In the following chapters, we will detail the evolution of our thinking and present our current views on the concept of the digital university. Our intention throughout will be to advance an enriched rather than an impoverished concept of the digital university.

References

Bailey, M., & Freedman, D. (Eds.). (2011). *The Assault on Universities, A Manifesto for Resistance*. London: Pluto Press.

Barber, M., Donnely, K., & Rizvi, S. (2013). *An Avalanche Is Coming: Higher Education and the Revolution Ahead*. IPPR. https://www.ippr.org/publications/an-avalanche-is-coming-higher-education-and-the-revolution-ahead. Accessed 28 Apr 2018.

Collini, S. (2017). *Speaking of Universities*. London/New York: Verso.

Gibbs, A., Haskins, G., Hannon, P., & Robertson, I. (2012). *Leading the Entrepreneurial University: Meeting the Entrepreneurial Development Needs of Higher Education* (2009, Updated 2012). NCEE. http://eureka.sbs.ox.ac.uk/4861/.

Holmwood, J. (2011). *A Manifesto for the Public University*. London: Bloomsbury Academic.

Luckin, R., Bligh, B., Manches, A., Ainsworth, S., Crook, C., & Noss, R. (2012). *Decoding Learning: The Proof, Promise and Potential of Digital Education*. NESTA. https://www.nesta.org.uk/report/decoding-learning/. Accessed 15 Feb 2017.

McCluskey, F. B., & Winter, M. L. (2012). *The Idea of the Digital University: Ancient Traditions, Disruptive Technologies and the Battle for the Soul of Higher Education*. Policy Studies Organisation. Washington: Westphalia Press.

Office of the Vice Provost Learning and Teaching. (2013). *Better Teaching, Better Learning Agenda*. Monash University.

PWC. (2018). *The 2018 Digital University Staying Relevant in the Digital Age*. PWC. https://www.pwc.co.uk/assets/pdf/the-2018-digital-university-staying-relevant-in-the-digital-age.pdf. Accessed 21 Nov 2017.

Selwyn, N. (2014). *Digital Technology and the Contemporary University: Degrees of Digitization*. Abingdon/New York: Routledge.

Walker, R., Voce, J., Swift, E., Ahmed, J., Jenkins, M., & Vincent, P. (2016). *2016 Survey of Technology Enhanced Learning for Higher Education in the UK*. Oxford: UCISA. https://www.ucisa.ac.uk/tel/. Accessed 6 Oct 2017.

3

Exploring the Digital University: Developing and Applying Holistic Thinking

Introduction: Praxis, Process, and Products

In the preceding chapters, we highlighted the contradictory nature of responses to the notion of the digital university within the current context of increasing political pressures to redefine the purpose, redirect funding, and corporatise management structure of universities. With the consequence that universities are expected to be run as businesses, with students cast as customers and technology engaged under a rubric of enhancing learning and teaching. The digital university emerges not so much as a jubilant technological transformation of the academy, but rather as an educational business operation cloaked in some digital finery.

The alternative educational narratives and practices surrounding higher education as a public good, and a cornerstone of democratic development, are marginalised in the neoliberal script. In the context of the neoliberalisation of university strategic management and practice, our arguments for openness and critical pedagogy are therefore aimed in part at overcoming the contradictory nature of current formulations of the construct of the digital university and partly offered as a preferable alternative.

In this chapter we reflect on our initial pragmatic response to addressing the challenges of lack of consistency and definition of 'the digital university' and the tension between system- and surface-level digital 'transformation' through a variety of technology-driven solutions. This reflection is consistent with our commitment to the idea of praxis as a way of working systematically on pedagogical issues and our intellectual strategy of treating the digital university as a discursive construction, a work in progress, developing by dialogue, activity, and critical reflection.

It has never been our intention to simply present more packaged 'solutions' to the digital university conundrum, or presume to define what a digital university is. Rather we are intent on expressing our experience of praxis through the text of this book to engage readers in adapting that mode of working to their own needs, and to develop our ideas on academic and organisational development in universities.

In effect we are reflecting on the evolution of our analysis over time of the ways in which the digital university can be conceived beyond the

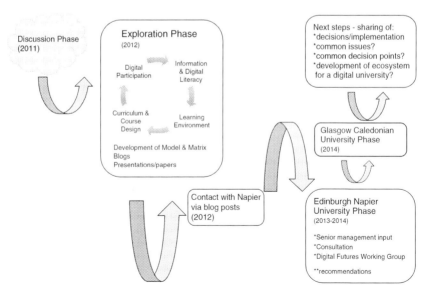

Fig. 3.1 Work phases to date (MacNeill 2014)

Exploring the Digital University: Developing and Applying...

contradictory positions we observed in the literature and our experiences of institutional practice. Figure 3.1 sets out the key phases in our discursive journey and introduces two key yields:

- Our model of a new way of conceiving of the dynamics of academic and organisational development in universities. (Fig. 3.2)
- Our Matrix illuminating key aspects of each element in the model. (Fig. 3.3)

Both the model and the Matrix have been (i) openly shared with other educationalists through blog posts, (ii) presented and debated in academic conferences, (iii) disseminated to the sector though publications, and (iv) tested against the realities of supporting change in specific universities. We will detail those experiences below, and in so doing elaborate both the discursive processes involved and the nature and relationships between the elements of model and the detail on the Matrix. This discussion will provide the necessary conceptual backdrop to Chaps. 4, 5, 6, 7, and 8, and we will revisit the Matrix in an extended form in Chap. 9.

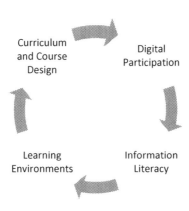

Fig. 3.2 Key constructs of the Digital University

Digital Participation	Information Literacy
*Glocalization *Widening access *Civic role and responsibilities *Networks (human and digital) *Technological Affordances	*High level concepts and perceptions influencing practice *Staff & student engagement development *Effective development and use of infrastructure
Curriculum and Course Design	**Learning Environment**
*Constructive alignment *Curriculum representations, course management, pedagogical innovation *Recruitment and marketing *Reporting, data, analytics	*Physical and Digital *Pedagogical and social *Research and enquiry *Staff and Resources

Fig. 3.3 The Conceptual Matrix for the Digital University (MacNeill and Johnston 2012)

Early Directions in Understanding the Digital University: What Is a University for?

The initial framing of our work took a very open, conversational, and increasingly dialogic approach. In trying to articulate our own understanding of what a digital university was, or perhaps more pertinently what it could be, we quickly realised that the addition of the word 'digital' to university did not make answering the fundamental question of 'what is a university?' or 'what is university for?' (Collini 2017) any easier. A review of the literature at that time was both unsatisfactory and contradictory as elaborated in Chap. 2. For example, whilst McCluskey and Winter (2012) explored the idea of the digital university, they did so from an almost exclusively North American perspective coupled with an almost unwavering faith in the positive impacts of digital technology.

> While it is true that the digital revolution has disrupted the university, if we embrace that same technology, it can see us through this crisis to the other side. (McLuskey and Winter, p. 226)

They also seemed to have embraced the 'education is broken meme' that was particularly prevalent during the early 2010s. We suggest this meme was used deliberately by politicians to pressurise universities to adopt neoliberalisation as the remedy for their apparently 'lamentable teaching' as described by the then UK Cabinet Minister responsible for universities, Jo Johnston in an article in The Times (2016). These views contrast with the more critical approaches of both Selwyn (2014) and Collini (2017).

At this time, there was also an emerging literature around digital literacies and capabilities (Beetham et al. 2009; Littlejohn et al. 2012; Sharpe and Beetham 2007). However this appeared to be more focused on the development of individual capabilities and literacies, which did not really satisfy our desire to understand the notion of a digital university holistically at an institutional level. That said, it represents an important strand of the discussion which we take up in Chap. 6.

Finally, there were and continue to be a growing number of white papers from the commercial sector that did address the digital at an institutional level, and in particular about developing strategies for the implementation of technology platforms. For example, the recent (2018) PWC paper, discussed in Chap. 2, 'The Digital University: Staying Relevant in the Digital Age', provided a strongly corporate account of how the digital might be incorporated into institutional strategy and practice. In this corporate rhetoric, digital developments can be seen to be adding to the increasingly politicised nature of recent and current debates over the role and place of higher education in society. One where the 'solution' to a broken education systems' 'problems' and 'challenges' is provided by new technologies to manage systems, staff, and students in the service of an image of the university as a *business*.

As the preceding chapters have illustrated, our early critical work was influenced by a number of commentators, in particular, the work of Stefan Collini (2017, p. 204) with his ongoing critique of the purpose of universities and Holmwood (2011) in their manifesto of a university for the public good. Taken together these commentators enlarged our horizons and encouraged our ambition to mount a challenge to the conceptual impoverished of the contemporary university.

Contextual Influence and Response: Were Universities Being 'Transformed'?

At this point it is useful to reflect on some of the major influences for change impacting the educational sector when we started our work in late 2011.

2012 has been badged by many in the edtech (educational technology) industry as "the year of the MOOC". American Ivy Leagues academics Andrew Ng and Daphne Koller led the charge. Both secured multi-million-dollar angel investment for Udacity and Coursera MOOC platforms. This much-hyped revolution of education through digital transformation led to many claims about the future of universities. Including one from Ng that in 10 years there would be only 50 universities left in the world.

The UK was not immune to this hype, with former Government advisor, Sir Michael Barber, co-authoring a much-hyped paper 'An Avalanche is coming: higher education and the revolution ahead' (2013), again heralding the demise of the traditional university system and the rise of a digital revolution in the delivery of (higher) education that would be driven largely by MOOCs. In essence higher education was apparently to be modernised by a mixture of corporate finance and digital technology—the fourth industrial revolution had arrived on campus!

The conceptualisation of the digital university was not immune to this influence. Siemens, Gasevic, and Dawson published their 'Preparing for the digital university' paper in 2015. It was a timely attempt to redress the apparent lack of awareness of the existing educational research into distance and online learning that some of the new 'MOOC kids on the block' had apparently not been aware of. The authors state:

> it is our somewhat axiomatic assessment that in order to understand how we should design and develop learning for the future, we need to first take a look at what we already know. Any scientific enterprise that runs forward on only new technology, ignoring the landscape of existing knowledge, will be sub-optimal and likely fail. To build a strong future of digital learning in the academy, we must first take stock of what we know and what has been well researched.

This paper was important in redressing some of the imbalance around the history and development of distance and online education within the HE sector. However, it differed from our work as it was a review of distance, blended, and online learning as opposed to an investigation of how universities were being changed by neoliberalisation and what role technology would play in that project.

Developing a Discursive Construction: A Dynamic Model and Conceptual Matrix for the Digital University

From our own experience and early literature reviews, we identified four key constructs—digital participation, Information Literacy, learning environment, and curriculum and course design—and set them in dynamic relationship with each other (Fig. 3.2).

Whilst none of these constructs were novel in and of themselves, we felt that they, and crucially the interrelationships between them, provided a novel yet pragmatic way to prompt meaningful dialogue and reflection on current and future practice, policy, and infrastructure within a university. One that could allow a route for some deconstruction of the institutional power relationships that digital technologies can be seen to maintain (Selwyn 2014) and one that provided hooks for all members of a university community—not just those with responsibilities for managing the technological infrastructure.

This schematisation of the dynamics of a digitally empowered university challenged both the apocalyptic and more mundane conceptualisations of the time, which we elaborated in Chaps. 1 and 2. It also offered a sounder basis to develop and explore emerging critical themes in our thought, including *openness and community* (Chap. 5), *digital capability and agency* (Chap. 6), *enriched learning spaces* (Chap. 7), and the *nature of curriculum* (Chap. 8).

Our model assumes that a university is a complex system comprising certain elements, which are widely acknowledged as defining the educational nature and purpose of the institution. In our case the presence of learning environments and the practice of curriculum and course design are two such defining features, without which an institution would struggle to function as a university (MacNeill and Johnston 2012). Nonetheless, within a complex system there are other elements, which appear to be in the background, but are of major, if initially unrecognised, significance for change management. When digital developments begin to take place in universities, the foreground features are subject to palpable change, but so too are the less familiar features. Recognising and illuminating the dynamic relations between foreground and background elements offers the ability to direct change in new and exciting directions.

At its most basic, the introduction of digital technology to the university system offers opportunities to change existing practices, but there is also an opportunity to explore new educational horizons and re-evaluate the university's purpose and potential for new forms of social engagement. Inevitably there will be a certain degree of misperception if the change is assumed to be a radical transformation, but is in effect really a modification of the form of a learning environment. For example, a simple exchange of analogue for digital practice can be presented to give the impression that course design has been fundamentally altered, or indeed transformed, when in fact only particular facets of the technological infrastructure of the learning environment have been modified. Thus the aims and objectives of learning may remain relatively constant, whilst the interface with learning materials and academic administration by staff and students simply moves into a VLE/MLE format, without necessarily leading to innovative or theoretically informed pedagogical development.

From our perspective the large-scale adoption of critical pedagogy and greater participation would represent a radical change in direction of the university, whereas simply acquiring a VLE would not. Clarifying such misperceptions is one benefit of our model, but we will show in this book that it can offer deeper insights and help to change the conceptualisation of a digital university.

An Overview of the Conceptual Matrix

During 2012, two of the co-authors (MacNeill and Johnston) set out to further develop the model in the form of a Matrix, which would provide a multidimensional, holistic lens through which to view the concept of the digital university. We felt that this format could offer a flexible tool for engaging staff in identifying and formulating systematic programmes for change through harnessing, or developing, digital spaces, practices, and provision. The Conceptual Matrix set out to develop the four key constructs of our model more explicitly and to provide prompts that identify some of key dimensions of the digital university. These prompts were chosen as 'hooks' or prompts to stimulate discussion around the people, processes, space, and technologies used to fulfil each of the quadrants. We were open to, and indeed encouraged, these prompts to be developed or replaced within a particular institutional context.

With respect to the meanings and interrelationships between the four categories, the Matrix positions *digital participation* as involving public engagement by the university with government digital inclusion policy, and also the growing potential of social and 'consumerist' interactions offered by digital technology and the Internet to engage new forms of wider participation in a potentially more democratic venture, thereby restoring the balance between the current neoliberal domination over universities and the ideal of higher education as a public good. *Information Literacy* enables Participation through developing information awareness and skills, and identifies those both of academic relevance and relating to personal development as an informed citizen. Both *digital participation* and *Information Literacy* are channelled through the university's *learning environment*, which is conceived in both technological and, critically, in academic and pedagogical terms. All three then influence and condition *Curriculum and Course Design*.

The process we adopted in the development of the Matrix was one of discursive construction (Jones and Goodfellow 2012), where discussion was invited from our peers of our perception that much of the dominant discourse was based on a very techno-centric or techno-dominant point of view. By contrast our developing point of view was that a meaningful idea of a digital university can only occur where there is an equal balance between technology and staff/student developments driving innovation and creativity. This perspective underpinned our next move, which was to take the dynamic relations of our model, presented in Fig. 3.2, and represent them as a Matrix (Fig. 3.3) to offer educational and organisational focus on the micro, meso, and macro aspects of the digital university as they might apply to particular institutions whilst also retaining a strong sense of sociocultural context.

In terms of developing our discursive approach, we took an open, conversational stance through a series of blog posts entitled "A Conversation around what it means to be a digital university" (MacNeill and Johnston 2012). These posts were our initial articulation and description of what would become the conceptual Matrix for the digital university. In each post we deconstructed each of our four constructs and invited questions and reflection. We were pleasantly surprised with the level of engaged response that the post received. This encouraged us to take the framework and our work to a number of national, UK, and international conferences (including ASCILITE 2013, SEDA 2013, ALT-C 2014, EDEN 2015) to gain more feedback from an informed community within the academic/educational technology development disciplines. The response to our framework was positive, and the level of debate it engendered at each outing strengthened our belief that we were developing a useful dialogic tool.

Digital Participation and Information Literacy: Addressing the Essential and the Unfamiliar Through the Matrix

Of the four constructs within the Matrix, we felt that typically digital participation and Information Literacy receive less attention in organisational discourse than notions of learning environment and curriculum. It was as if these two dynamics were not part of the core business of universities, and this did not seem to reflect the actual technological and sociocultural circumstances of the early twenty-first century. The Matrix sets out to redress this imbalance by giving more attention to Participation and Information Literacy and placing them on a par with the more familiar aspects of *learning environment* and *curriculum development*. With this balancing focus, the Matrix brings with it a different perspective on the digital, going beyond the familiar categories of technological infrastructure and applications to enhance teaching, learning, and the public good.

Based on our own practice and research interests, we used Information Literacy as a lens to explore a number of internal and external drivers for institutional change and to explore notions of the term 'digital university'. As we will show in Chap. 6, Information Literacy offers a disciplinary field of scholarship and research influencing practice, which can be extended to enhance approaches to understanding and changing areas such as digital capability, student learning, and educational development in the curriculum.

Initially we were working from a shared understanding that the popular term digital *literacy* is an extension of Information Literacy and that one cannot exist without the other. From this perspective we positioned the 'literacy' of the digital university as the literacy of information. This in turn raises wider social issues of digital inclusion in a society rich in information, much of it sourced from the Internet, channelled via digital devices, and presented in the forms and texts of social media. A key part of our discussion involved questioning the positioning of universities in this landscape, and the role universities can play within their communities in terms of the widening participation agenda, but also in terms of becoming more recognised and more fully utilised as technology-rich spaces for community engagement and participation (MacNeill and Johnston 2012).

It was our belief that Information Literacy could act as a gateway to creating dialogue at the institutional level as it provides the means, knowledge, and skills needed to allow meaningful interactions between people, digital content, and technological systems. Using an Information Literacy lens also provided us with a means to produce a coherent outline of a digital university and suggest strategic developments of the digital infrastructure, learning environment, and management culture required to fully achieve the potential of the digital technologies. Chapter 6 provides a more in-depth account of Information Literacy in the context of the digital university.

We surmised that this modelling could support better strategic thinking and change management in universities. Typically, however, the relationships identified in our model and the attendant Matrix are not evident in the strategic thinking and operational practices of universities. Each dimension is more likely to be treated as a separate area, with its own dynamics and priority weightings reflecting the particular development, character, and espoused mission of a specific institution. This situation seemed to us to hamper the development of new and more holistic educational and organisational thinking in universities, particularly so if the culture and value system is being distorted by a neoliberal ideology of market relations, consumerism, and managerialist direction of staff effort, as the imperatives driving universities.

Our design of the Matrix centred on creating an artefact that prompted questioning and contextualisation of each of the four quadrants, and we used the Matrix to present generative themes and focal questions in our engagements with development workshops in universities. For example: how is digital participation managed in the (your) university—is this within widening access initiatives or lifelong learning provision? Where is Information Literacy visible in the university—is this in library programmes, or perhaps staff and student development provision? How is the learning environment currently conceived in the university—as a unified concept or divided between technical infrastructure and estate, or learning and teaching? And who has the locus in Curriculum and Course Design at the levels of development and management—where do decisions reside, and how influential are overall institutional objectives on outcomes common to all courses (e.g. employability, citizenship) in shaping practice at ground level?

These questions are illustrative of how the Conceptual Matrix can be, and has been, applied in practice. The key point being that the Matrix and the dimensions within it can be used to provide a focus on activities such as (i) synthesising relevant pedagogical literature and evidence; (ii) analysing particular institutional contexts, settings, and strategic statements; and (iii) identifying plausible lines of action for change. The Conceptual Matrix was intended to support the exploration of the overarching term and concept of the 'digital university' and offer the potential to act as a catalyst for fundamental change throughout an institution from administration to learning and teaching, and from policy formation to practice.

Since being developed the Conceptual Matrix has been successfully applied in aiding strategic discussions and scoping possible future developments at a number of universities in the UK (including the University of Dundee, University of Greenwich, and Glasgow Caledonian University) and also at Macquarie University in Sydney. However perhaps the most significant application of the Conceptual Matrix to date has been in the Digital Futures consultation undertaken at Edinburgh Napier University between 2013 and 2014 (Smyth et al. 2015).

The Edinburgh Napier University Exemplar: Using the Matrix and Developing the Digitally Distributed Curriculum Construct

The broad notion of the Digitally Distributed Curriculum first emerged as an outcome of the work undertaken in applying the original Conceptual Matrix, and associated tools, in the context of an institutional 'Digital Futures' consultation at Edinburgh Napier University (Smyth et al. 2015).

This consultation, led by one of the authors of this text (Smyth) with the other authors acting in 'critical friend' capacities (MacNeill and Johnston), involved an institution-wide exploration of current, emerging, and possible future digital practice across six thematic areas: developing digital literacies, digital student support provision, digitally enhanced education, digital communication and outreach, digital research and leadership, and digital infrastructure and integration. These themes were seen to encompass key areas of importance at the university in question and were explored through a series of dialogues and events that included a Digital Futures Symposium, and which involved every faculty of the university, the students' association, and staff from across the various professional service departments.

The consultation itself was an extensive one, comprising the following stages:

* The formation of a Digital Futures Working Group to undertake the consultation
* Identifying and refining the themes to be explored within the consultation

- Development of 'Position Statements' capturing current institutional practice and key issues within the six themes being explored
- Development of Faculty Position Statements on 'Digitally enhanced education'
- Internal consultations including a series of Digital Futures Open Events
- Research into national policy and initiatives of interest underway at other universities

In terms of key outputs from the Digital Futures consultation, these comprised:

- An 'external benchmarking' document summarising national policy, key reports, and examples of practice within the sector that were of relevance
- A 'rich picture' report that summarised current digital practice, provision, and issues
- Final report setting out recommendations for priorities up to 2016–2017, and a set of future recommendations for the period up until the Academic Year 2019–2020

With respect to the recommendations (explored more fully in Smyth et al. 2015), many of the short-term recommendations were focused on the consolidation and enhancement of the then current digital practice and provision at the university. Longer-term recommendations were of a more aspirational nature and included:

- Providing opportunities within every programme for learners to engage digitally with the professional and discipline-related communities they will become part of
- Locating 'the digital' in a programme-focused approach to curricula including cross-cohort learning and learners contributing to digital bodies of knowledge
- Harnessing open educational practices and approaches in ways that make sense for a post-1992 teaching-focused institution with a strong widening access agenda

Exploring the Digital University: Developing and Applying...

As for how the longer-term aspirations in particular might be instantiated within a 'vision' of the university as a digital university, the final recommendation of the Digital Futures consultation was to explore the potential of the 'Digitally Distributed Curriculum' (Fig. 3.4) as an organising concept for future developments in digital practice at the university.

The idea of a Digitally Distributed Curriculum was defined in the final report of the Digital Futures Working Group as "one that provides an innovate learning and teaching experience, extends learning and teaching across cohorts and communities, can meet diverse needs around work-based learning and continued professional development, and that is digitally sustainable as well as pedagogically progressive" (DFWG 2014, p. 17).

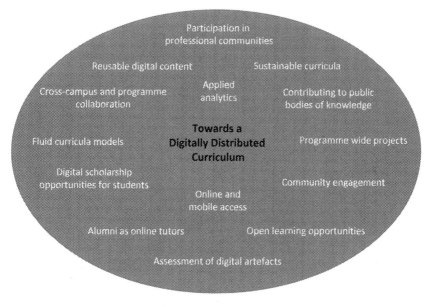

Fig. 3.4 Towards a Digitally Distributed Curriculum (DFWG 2014)

The Digitally Distributed Curriculum: An Initial Holistic Clustering

Through our work in applying the original Conceptual Matrix, and subsequent dialogues concerning the further development of our thinking about the digital university, our initial representation of the Digitally Distributed Curriculum proved a useful focal point for exploring a wider role for 'the digital' in relation to how the curriculum is organised, who is able to engage with and benefit from the activities of the curriculum, and for a 'reframing' of open education practice in the context of the Digital university (MacNeill 2016; Smyth 2016).

However, as we identified at the time, our thinking about what would characterise the Digitally Distributed Curriculum, and how it would be instantiated, was very nascent and 'imperfect' when we first outlined it (Smyth 2016). Our initial thinking, captured in the representation below, was also 'bounded' within, and to a large extent defined by, issues that were being explored within a specific institutional context for a specific institutional purpose.

As our thinking on the digital university has continued to evolve, principally in relation to our increased focus on 'praxis' and in parallel with related activities concerning the nature of higher education curricula, our position in relation to the Digitally Distributed Curriculum has moved from one of a nascent 'organising concept' to a more fully conceptualised idea. We will return to the development of this extended conceptualisation in Chap. 8.

Key Lessons Learned: Developing Critical Consciousness of Curriculum Development

It was perhaps unsurprising, given our backgrounds in academic and educational technology development, that we began to see our approach as one that could constructively align the emerging and existing strategic systems design approach to organisational development with emerging educational/academic development in terms of digital learning and teaching practice and research. As our own discourse and research around the Matrix has extended, primarily through the process of writing this book, we are now questioning our attitudes towards constructive alignment in this context.

The work of Biggs (2003) around constructive alignment has gained significant traction in educational development in the UK and beyond. It can be seen to be an almost de facto agreed process for educational development. In the light of our more critical approach towards the current university socio-political environment, we now question if the very success of constructive alignment is in fact due to it being a very managerial, process-driven approach to curriculum development (Roxå and Mårtensoon 2017)—a process that can lack criticality and may not engage a plurality of viewpoints. From a critical pedagogy perspective, we became convinced that there needed to be more questioning around who sets and perhaps more importantly 'owns' and controls learning outcomes.

From the outset our work has been influenced by contemporary theoretical developments in higher education pedagogy and academic development. For example, the work of Vermunt (2007) was central in our original thinking around learning environments. In relation to constructive alignment, Biggs (2003) again was a key touchpoint. As our discursive reflections evolved, we looked to a number of theoretical approaches such as Threshold Concepts and Troublesome concepts (Meyer and Land 2003) and value pluralism (Johnson and Smyth 2011). Whilst these theories have influenced our thinking, particularly value pluralism which we discuss in more detail in Chaps. 9 and 10, it was critical pedagogy that provided us with a holistic theoretical basis to ground, contextualise, and develop our thinking and to frame the increasing number of questions we were grappling with and to provide a way to evolve the Matrix.

In terms of constructive alignment, we now feel the need to question if the constructive alignment process itself is a tool of educational oppression for both students and teachers (Roxå and Mårtensoon's, ibid.)—one which ultimately is being used to manage curriculum and not extend the potential for creativity and choice. Where is the learner negotiation in the alignment process? Similarly, is the drive for personalised learning delivered through digital systems just a thinly veiled disguise for conformity, and highly structured behaviourist approaches to delivering learning? Is the learner negotiation in this process potentially going to be driven or be replaced by lowest common denominator AI algorithms? We return to these questions in Chap. 11 in our discussion around the development of critical academic development.

Conclusion

Our work in conceptualising and visioning the nature of the Digital university has taken us on a journey from the development of the Conceptual Matrix (MacNeill and Johnston 2012) through the application of the Matrix in the genesis and development of the Digital Futures consultation at Edinburgh Napier University, which has engaged us in furthering our collective thinking and ideas about the nature of the digital university. The Edinburgh Napier consultation process and outcomes have in turn informed a similar process of consultation at Glasgow Caledonian University. Glasgow Caledonian University has used an adapted version of the Matrix as an underlying concept for their internal digital strategy developments. To an extent this consultative work is analogous to the kind of developmental processes described in Chap. 2 in relation to the Monash strategic policy statement.

Both in academic conferences and within institutional contexts, such as Napier and Glasgow Caledonian University, the Matrix itself has proved to be a robust and flexible tool that can be used to identify short- and longer-term priorities. It provides meaningful hooks for all staff and students within a university to begin to have contextualised discussions about the nature of current and potential digital engagement and digital technologies. From that point of view, it has had some success in being a tool for discursive construction.

Our initial work was an attempt to address the apparent gap between the overly positive and strictly corporate depictions, and our interest in critical pedagogy and collegiate communities. Our emerging aim was to create a framework for a more discursive, inclusive, practitioner-focused exploration of the notion of the digital in the context of the digital university. As our work has evolved, we have continued to share our experiences and developing ideas through conference presentations, workshops, and papers. The writing of this book has provided a means to develop a more informed shared perspective on the realities, challenges, and possibilities of the digital university.

As highlighted through the Edinburgh Napier case study, the existing Matrix has been used as a strategic tool to analyse and map policies, channel discussions at various levels across an institution, focus on specific areas, and co-ordinate discussion and actions. We now propose that a far richer dialogic process could be created through an extended three-dimensional version of the Matrix—one that takes a more explicitly critical stance that would allow for more critically informed alignment and actions to be developed.

The framing of our extended critical pedagogy approach draws heavily on the work of Freire. We look to his early work Education for Critical Consciousness (1974). We seek not only to empower the individuals who work in, around, and outwith universities but also to allow a more empowered holistic view of a university as an entity, to allow it to understand, articulate, and engage in a more critical way around the oppression of digital technologies, neoliberal techno-centric 'solutions', and simplistic definitions of the concept of the digital and the notion of the digital university.

Within this context, the Matrix itself becomes a symbol allowing an enhanced critical radicalisation and ownership of the discussions around the digital university concept at micro and meso levels. One which allows the fundamental questions around whether or not the digital is an agent for transforming the university or is the digital age actually causing universities to retreat, to become more closed to transformation which may in turn help explain some of the ambivalence towards open education from senior management.

This chapter has provided an overview of our open, discursive, and participatory approach to the development of our digital university Matrix. Through our own praxis, we have identified critical pedagogy and open education as powerful allies in addressing the dominant, techno-centric narrative around the concept of the digital university. We will return to how we are now positioning the revised Matrix in Section III and in particular Chap. 9.

Before we do that however, it is necessary to explore in more detail our key themes and contextualisation of our discursive praxis around the digital university. In Section II (Chaps. 4, 5, 6, 7, and 8), we deconstruct the neoliberal myth of digital transformation. We then explore notions of digital participation and open education as a viable alternative to current market-driven approaches to extending participation in higher education. This leads to an overview of Information Literacy, digital capabilities, and notions of developing learner agency. We then extend these themes to an exploration of the potential for digitally enriched learning spaces and our new conceptualisation of the Digitally Distributed Curriculum.

References

Barber, M., Donnely, K., & Rizvi, S. (2013). *An Avalanche Is Coming: Higher Education and the Revolution Ahead*. IPPR. https://www.ippr.org/publications/an-avalanche-is-coming-higher-education-and-the-revolution-ahead. Accessed 28 Apr 2018.

Beetham, H., McGill, L., & Littlejohn, A. (2009). *Thriving in the 21st Century: Learning Literacies for the Digital Age (LLiDA Project) Executive Summary, Conclusions and Recommendations*. UK Joint Information Systems Committee (JISC). http://oro.open.ac.uk/52237/. Accessed 23 May 2018.

Biggs, J. B. (2003). *Teaching for Quality Learning at University* (2nd ed.). Buckingham: Open University Press/Society for Research into Higher Education.

Collini, S. (2017). *Speaking of Universities*. London: Verso.

DFWG (Digital Futures Working Group). (2014). Digital Futures Working Group: Recommendations: April 2014 (Final Revision). Edinburgh Napier University.

Freire, P. (2005). *Pedagogy of the Oppressed: 30th Anniversary Edition*. New York: Continuum.

Holmwood, J. (2011). *A Manifesto for the Public University*. London: Bloomsbury Academic.

Johnson, M., & Smyth, K. (2011). Diversity, Value and Technology: Exposing Value Pluralism in Institutional Strategy, Special Issue of *Campus-Wide Information Systems* on Learning Technology and Institutional Strategy, 28(4), 211–220.

Jones, C., & Goodfellow, R. (2012). The "digital university": Discourse, Theory, and Evidence. *International Journal of Learning and Media, 4*(3–4), 59–63.

Littlejohn, A., Beetham, H., & McGill, L. (2012). Learning at the Digital Frontier: A Review of Digital Literacies in Theory and Practice. *Journal of Computer Assisted Learning, 28*(6), 547–556.

MacNeill, S. (2014). Exploring the digital university – Next Steps digital university Ecosystems. https://howsheilaseesit.net/analytics/exploring-the-digital-university-next-steps-digtial-university-ecosystems/. Accessed 6 May 2018.

MacNeill, S. (2016). *Reframing Open in the Context of the Digital University – Part 1*. https://howsheilaseesit.blog/2016/04/14/reframing-open-in-the-context-of-the-digital-university-part-1-oer16/ Accessed 5 May 2018.

MacNeill, S., & Johnston, B. (2012). A Conversation Around What It Means to be a digital university. http://blogs.cetis.org.uk/sheilamacneill/2012/01/26/a-converstaion-around-what-it-means-to-be-a-digital-university/. Accessed 5 June 2018.

McCluskey, F. B., & Winter, M. L. (2012). *The Idea of the digital university: Ancient Traditions, Disruptive Technologies and the Battle for the Soul of Higher Education*. Policy Studies Organisation. Washington: Westphalia Press.

Meyer, J. H. F., & Land, R. (2003). Threshold Concepts and Troublesome Knowledge: Linkages to Ways of Thinking and Practising. In C. Rust (Ed.), *Improving Student Learning – Theory and Practice Ten Years On* (pp. 412–424). Oxford: Oxford Centre for Staff and Learning Development (OCSLD).

PWC. (2018). *The 2018 Digital University Staying Relevant in the Digital Age*. PWC. https://www.pwc.co.uk/assets/pdf/the-2018-digital-university-staying-relevant-in-the-digital-age.pdf. Accessed 11 May 2018.

Roxå, T., & Mårtensoon, K. (2017). Agency and Structure in Academic Development Practices: Are We Liberating Academic Teachers or Are We Part of a Machinery Supressing Them? *International Journal for Academic Development, 22*(2), 95–105.

Selwyn, N. (2014). *Digital Technology and the Contemporary University: Degrees of Digitization*. London: Routledge.

Sharpe, R., & Beetham, H. (Eds.). (2007). *Rethinking Pedagogy for a Digital Age*. Hoboken: Taylor and Francis.

Siemens, G., Gasevic, D., & Dawson, S. (Eds.). (2015). *Preparing for the Digital University: A Review of the History and Current State of Distance, Blended, and Online Learning*. MOOC Research Initiative.

Smyth, K. (2016). *Reframing Open in the Context of the Digital University – Part 2*. https://3eeducation.org/2016/04/20/reframing-open-in-the-context-of-the-digital-university-part-2/. Accessed 5 May 2018.

Smyth, K., MacNeill, S., & Johnston, B. (2015). Visioning the Digital University – From Institutional Strategy to Academic Practice. *Educational Developments, 16*(2), 13–17.

The Times. (2016). Jo Johnson Under Fire for Calling Some University Teaching 'Lamentable'. *Times Higher Education (THE)*. https://www.timeshighereducation.com/news/jo-johnson-under-fire-calling-some-university-teaching-lamentable. Accessed 1 June 2018.

Vermunt, J. D. (2007). The Power of Teaching-Learning Environments to Influence Student Learning. *British Journal of Educational Psychology*, Monograph Series II, *4*, 73–90.

Section II

Deconstructing the Digital University

4

The Myth of Digital Transformation

Introduction

In Chap. 2, we characterised the actual relationship between universities and the digital as more transactional than transformational. However, the myth of digital transformation is a powerful force driving change, and in this chapter we critique this transformation narrative in detail. We will (i) explore the cultural and social context which supports the notion of revolutionary transformation in higher education, (ii) challenge the concept of transformation in relation to the introduction of the digital to university practice, (iii) examine the evidence for transformation, and (iv) consider the emerging possibilities for genuinely transformative change in relation to digitally enabled education and more democratic educational practices.

The early twenty-first century has been arguably one of the most challenging times for the established culture of the higher education sector. The traditional Ivory Tower is no longer safe from changing political and funding structures. Universities are increasingly being seen as businesses and are having to adapt their policies and environments to reflect changing expectations and 'market' pressures, which are themselves reflections of the state of the political economy (Molesworth et al. 2011; Mason 2015). In the UK the introduction of student fees in England and Wales has brought about a different perception of students to that of consumers, even customers. The student journey is no longer centred on personal academic knowledge exploration and development, rather it is increasingly perceived and positioned as a series of administrative steps and business interactions. Within individual universities, and across the sector as a whole, the marketisation of higher education has been further compounded by (and is indeed increasingly a product of) public metrics, frameworks, and league tables that purport to reflect the quality and status of higher education institutions and the educational experience that they offer.

These developments sit in stark contrast to, but alongside, educational narratives and practices concerning higher education as a public good, within which democratising access to higher education and harnessing higher education as a means to develop and improve society and the human condition are pivotal values (Collini 2012, 2017; Giroux 2014).

The tension between these two positions extends to how the digital is positioned in relation to higher education, our educational institutions, and the learning and teaching that occurs within them. On the one hand, there exists the arguably dominant, business- and techno-centric narrative that concerns the range of ways in which digital technology can position universities as global providers of education, and how it can bring greater efficiencies in managing the student experience (both on campus and online) in key operational areas of marketing and recruitment, accessing services and resources, the delivery of teaching and assessment, and alumni relations. If there is a digital 'transformation' to be found here, it is bound in the terms and practices of the neoliberal education project, which yokes the digital to its purposes. On the other hand, from an educational and societal perspective, we can look towards what digital technology can offer us by way of enhancing learning and teaching, enriching knowledge including through connecting learners across rich and varied cultural and geographic boundaries, enabling our learners to develop their digital skills and capabilities, widening participation in formal higher education, and improving access to informal, non-credit bearing learning opportunities for those who could benefit from them.

Regardless of whichever perspective dominates or informs the respective outlooks we may hold, in recent years there has been a rapid rise in claims, and in the number of proposed solutions, that will seemingly transform higher education with and through digital technology and digital educational practices, and which will solve the Silicon Valley "education is broken" narrative (Weller 2014). Most recently the main focus has been on open education, including the potential of large-scale open online courses to widen access to higher education. This is a promise which remains largely unfulfilled, and is perhaps symptomatic of a key challenge of seeking to change or advance education through the use of digital technology, and which lies in the technology itself rarely being the key to sustainable long-term transformation in what we do or how we do it. This and other key challenges that limit the potential to improve higher education with and through digital technologies, and digitally supported practices, are what we will now turn our attention to in this chapter.

Alternative Views of Transformation: The Social Context for Change in Higher Education and What a University Is for

There is a wider societal context and rationale for change in higher education, and within which the potential place of digital technology as a change force in education can be framed. In the very broadest sense, and central to this context, is the relationship between higher education and the wider communities within which our universities sit and should arguably exist to support.

Dewey (1916) was perhaps the first to discuss the complex nature of this relationship and the dual need for educational systems to support the development of the individual while also sustaining the dominant practices, beliefs, industries, and expectations of the 'nation state'. In our post-industrial knowledge economy, within an increasingly networked and globalised society, we might recognise a pragmatic need for higher education to develop in relation to a different and rapidly evolving set of economic and employment demands and opportunities, an increasing number of which are digital in focus and also transnational in nature. For today's learner, living within an increasingly networked and global society, there are challenges related to being able to contend with rapidly developing bodies of knowledge, proliferation of information and data, and being able to harness digital tools and spaces to communicate and collaborate and to curate, create, and share knowledge. There are more fundamental human needs and challenges too, within the wider context outlined above, which are to do with education and educational systems that value and respect difference, engender individual and collective resilience, and support participation in democratic processes, and which are committed to digital participation and inclusion for those who would otherwise be disadvantaged, disenfranchised, or marginalised within education and broader society.

There have been examples of systemic change in higher education in order to respond to societal needs and to widen access to higher education itself. In the UK, this included the initial expansion of higher education resulting from the publication of the Robbins Report in 1963 and which has, in the last three decades in particular, been followed by a further period of growth that has seen the number of UK higher education institutions rise from around 60 in the mid-1980s to approaching 170 today. The government policy that has driven the expansion of UK higher education, including the widening access agenda and the principle of fair access, has to date resulted in a more educated workforce and increased equality in the opportunity to benefit from higher education (while also leading to the heightened competition between higher education institutions and increased adoption of market mechanisms alluded to earlier). Governmental policies and initiatives continue to support the widening of access to higher education globally while also increasingly recognising the need for digital technology and digital engagement to be more effectively embedded in education in order to meet the needs of our learners, economy, and society. In Scotland, relevant policy in this area includes "Realising Scotland's full potential in a digital world: a digital strategy for Scotland" (Scottish Government 2017), while in the USA, the 'National Educational Technology Plan' outlines a commitment for "all involved in American education to ensure equity of access to transformational learning experiences enabled by technology" (US Department of Education 2017).

The obvious question to ask, in the context of such policy and the claims that might be made for how the digital can be harnessed in educational change, is 'what do we mean by transformation?', and by extension 'what is it that is to be transformed, why, and for whom?'

Central to this book is the contention that digital technologies and practices have the potential not only to enhance learning and teaching, but to democratise engagement in education, extend outreach, and reposition and extend higher education and higher education institutions for the public good. However we argue that transformation as a concept, and the boundaries and barriers to change that are to be found within the higher education sector and the university, severely limits and inhibits what is possible.

Transformation as a Troublesome Concept

The ideal or aspiration of transformation has been an increasingly prevalent one in higher education, central to sectoral and institutional policy, and programmes and initiatives for change at national, cross-institutional, and institutional level. Within the USA, notable national-level initiatives focused on technology and change have included the Program in Course Redesign funded by The Pew Charitable Trusts and supported 30 universities and colleges "in their efforts to redesign instruction using technology to achieve quality enhancements as well as cost savings" (Twigg 2003, p. 30). Within the UK, the Transforming Curriculum Design and Curriculum Delivery through Technology programme managed by Jisc between 2008 and 2010 engaged 15 institutions in exploring how technology could support more flexible and creative curriculum models, with a focus on areas of practice including assessment, personalisation, accessibility of learning experiences, retention, and employment. Similarly, the Higher Education Academy's e-Learning Benchmarking and Pathfinder Programme (Mayes et al. 2009) supported over 70 institutions in establishing where they were in regard to embedding e-learning, before working with selected institutions to devise, implement, and evaluate "different approaches to the embedding of technology-enhanced learning in ways that result in positive institutional change" (Jisc/HEA 2008, p. 2).

As the former examples suggest, the decade of 2000–2010 saw significant investment in sector-wide digital 'transformation' initiatives within UK and US further and higher education, and within the middle of this same time period, the Scottish Funding Council (SFC) for further and higher education ran their e-Learning Transformation Programme. This programme saw six cross-institutional projects funded to the combined total of £6M to undertake projects that would promote transformational change in learning and teaching supported by, and through, current and emerging technologies. The SFC defined "transformational change" as requiring "a conscious and deliberate decision made by one or more institutions to do something differently in a systematic way across the whole institution, on a defined timescale of two or more years" (in Nicol and Draper 2009). The projects undertaken included the Re-engineering Assessment Practices (REAP) project (Nicol and Draper 2009), which sought to bring about strategic change in technology-enabled assessment practices across three universities, and the Transforming and Enhancing the Student Experience through Pedagogy (TESEP) project (Comrie et al. 2009). TESEP focused on redesigning current courses across the lead university and two further education partner colleges to place an increasing emphasis on online-supported collaborative learning, and an increase in student autonomy to create and co-create key aspects of their learning experience including harnessing read/write technologies to create digital resources to support and evidence their learning.

Within each of the aforementioned initiatives, and other comparable projects and programmes, there is generally good evidence of change having occurred at the micro level of learning and teaching practice, and with respect to improving curriculum design and delivery, and often there is also evidence of an enrichment or expansion of practice at the meso level of the institution (at least with respect to an increase in the number of courses or programmes that can exemplify or role model different ways of harnessing digital technology to enhance some aspect, or aspects, of the educational experience).

However in returning to the question of what we mean by transformation, and transformation of what and for whom, it becomes apparent that what we see in the majority of change initiatives in the higher education sector that have sought to harness digital technology and digitally enhanced practice in 'transformational', including the initiatives above, have been focused primarily on improvement (in engagement, in efficiency, in perceived quality, in the outcomes of learning) within and to current practice and provision. They are focused in the main on the enhancement of existing processes and pedagogies, or the enhancement and expansion of curricula, rather than challenging and disrupting those processes, or identifying and developing additional or alternative practices that can enrich and evolve higher education, and extend higher education as a wider public good. While we do not challenge the value of or need for enhancement-focused initiatives that will improve learning and teaching, and the learner experience, we would argue that most change initiatives to date are in fact examples of a transactional relationship to the digital rather than one of substantial transformation, even where ethereal notions of transformation are an aspiration.

Where there are disruptive dimensions to institutional transformation initiatives, they tend to be at the micro level of learning and teaching practice, through offering increased choice or empowerment to learners in relation to how they engage, what they produce and how they are assessed, and where conventional tutor and student roles make way for tutor-as-learner and student-as-tutor approaches. Illustrative examples of these approaches include the aforementioned TESEP project (Comrie et al. 2009), several of the projects taken forward through Jisc's Transforming Curriculum Design and Curriculum Delivery through Technology programme, and more recently the work of Gros and Lopez (2016). We can also extend the general point about learning choice and empowerment to curriculum design initiatives in which students are engaged as co-designers of the curriculum, are engaged as partners or leaders in activity design within the curriculum, and are engaged in decision-making about how the digital is to be harnessed within learning and teaching. We further explore such approaches in Chaps. 7 and 8. For now, two questions we feel must be asked across these contexts (i.e. learners co-creating the curriculum, designing learning activities, and determining where the digital is located within the curriculum) are firstly how widespread these practices are, beyond the known examples in the sector, and secondly whether they have the potential to be mainstreamed into areas where there is either a reluctance or inhibition to explore and embed them into learning and teaching and the curriculum?

To reiterate, the location of the digital within established educational structures and practices inside our institutions, for the aim of enhancing learning and teaching, is of and by itself an important priority. However, to return to the central narrative of this book, this particular situating of the digital and digital practice in higher education is limited in supporting us to question: the extent to which digital technologies and practices can allow us to rethink where the university, our curricula, and the educational opportunities the university provides are located and co-located; the extent to which we are supporting our learners (and the wider populace) to develop the digital skills and capabilities they need; and how our harnessing of digital spaces and practices can help us further extend higher education as a public good. It is in this territory that our thinking on critical pedagogy and open education come into the foreground and help us move towards conceptualising alternative approaches and frameworks for practice including the Digitally Distributed Curriculum construct and the Revised Conceptual Matrix for the Digital University we present in Chaps. 8 and 9.

In recent years the emergence of the open education movement has certainly brought with it the potential for disrupting how and for whom higher education is organised and made available. As explored in Chap. 5, there have been considerable advances in policy and practice within the field of open education, and there is considerable promise in currently emerging discourses and practices including in the area of open textbooks (e.g. the UK Open Textbook Project) and associated debate around open textbooks as a social justice.

Occupying a central position within the open education landscape has been the development of the MOOC. However, MOOCs have not served to widen access to higher education in the ways that were originally envisaged. Indeed, there is much evidence to suggest that MOOCs in the varying forms which are being offered by our universities are generally only amplifying access to open online higher education to those who have already experienced a formal higher education (e.g. Zhenghao et al. 2015). This is not to say that many MOOCs are not offering relevant and engaging educational experiences to the learners who enrol upon them, or a sizeable proportion of those learners, but in demographic terms, MOOCs are arguably falling short in providing opportunities to access and benefit from a meaningful higher education learning experience for those who are aspiring to transition into higher education for the first time. In addition, universities that are less resource-rich have found themselves unable to harness the MOOC model on the same scale as the leading (and mainly US based) universities that may be considered amongst the 'global elite' universities of the academy (Haggard 2013).

Where does this all leave us, with respect to the concept of transformation in relation to digital technology and education? Perhaps that transformation is an ill-structured and variously understood idea, open to interpretation but also easy to conflate with enhancement of practice rather than a reimagining of practice. At the same time, within the collective rhetoric concerning digital technology and the transformation of education, we see aspirations towards equity of access to education, systematic change across the institution, and within these contexts co-ordinated efforts to improve pedagogic practice and the learner experience. So where have previous digital transformation developments and initiatives left us, and what wider evidence base is there to draw upon in relation to actual change at sectoral or institutional level, or for the impact of the digital on the learning experience?

The Evidence for Digital Transformation: Macro, Meso, and Micro Engagements

In considering the effectiveness and reach of digital transformation opportunities and interventions within higher education, we can draw upon illustrative examples of policy and sectoral developments, institutional and cross-institutional programmes, and learning and teaching interventions at the macro, meso, and macro levels of digital education practice.

At the macro level, one important consideration is the extent to which national policy and strategy can be observed to be having a direct impact on how digital technologies and practices are being harnessed to address national educational agendas and priorities, for example, in relation to widening access and participation, collaboration within the sector, providing globalised learning opportunities, and contributing to the development of a digitally skilled society and workforce that is equitable with respect to digital participation.

The picture at the macro level is a varied one, in which it is difficult to see the direct influence of national policy and strategy on practice in a number of key areas. This includes the potential for universities to work together to harness digital technologies and approaches to provide a richer, more flexible, and more expansive HE learning experience. The potential opportunities in this area, including specifically for the collaborative development and delivery of online programmes that would be offered nationally and internationally, within which there would be clear opportunities for learners to access a contextually and culturally enriched educational experience through programmes of study that combine curricula strengths and disciplinary expertise from two or more institutions, would seem clear. How to effectively harness such opportunities for collaboratively developed and delivered online education was the focus of the recommendations of the UK Online Learning Task Force 'Collaborate to Compete' report to the Higher Education Funding Council England in 2011 (OLTF 2011), which was informed through an extensive UK-wide national consultation. Yet the obvious opportunities in this area remain largely unexplored, and amongst the proliferation of fully online, mainly postgraduate programmes that are now available from UK institutions, many of which offer the same or similar qualifications, very few are offered in conjunction with other national or international partner institutions.

Perhaps ironically, the above situation is one no doubt reflective of, and compounded by, the increasingly marketised and competitive higher education sector we find ourselves operating within. However, interestingly, there are an increasing number of examples within the sector of individual academics, or course teams, collaborating with colleagues from other institutions to offer students on similar courses or programmes joint online learning opportunities through activities including webinars, social networking events, and in some cases joint coursework activities. Similar grassroots developments are to be seen in the contexts of online open education and professional development for educators (e.g. Nerantzi and Beckingham 2014; Nerantzi and Gossman 2015; and further examples as explored in Smyth et al. 2016). Are these perhaps some of the real changes in how we might harness the digital more creatively and democratically to develop higher education, as opposed to the mythical sector-wide transformations that the dominant rhetoric will have us assume can be realised simply through becoming 'more digital'?

With respect to the emergence of MOOCs within the sector, evidence of impact is also varied. As highlighted above, those learners enrolling on MOOCs tend to possess a higher education already (with the report by Zhenghao et al. 2015, putting this as high as 80%), and in addition the majority are from developed countries and also in full-time employment (ibid.). This currently reflects poorly on the potential for MOOCs to widen participation in higher education, for those seeking to access higher education for the first time, while amongst those who do take part completion rates tend to be poor. At the same time, there is evidence to suggest that MOOCs are effective for those seeking to keep their knowledge of a particular subject area up to date, to flexibly learn about a new area of interest and, as noted above albeit in relation to smaller scale open education opportunities, in meeting the Continuing Professional Development (CPD) needs of educators themselves (as a number of MOOCs have had a focus on educational theory and practice) (Haggard 2013).

We wonder whether the failed promise of MOOCs, purely in relation to widening access to higher education, has in part been a failure to fully consider the diversity of needs of those who may be aspiring to access a higher education experience online, especially those seeking to access such an experience for the first time, in relation to focus and level of the curriculum, cross-cultural relevance of the courses being offered, and the guidance and support offered to enable and foster meaningful engagement both individually and in learning alongside peers. At the macro level, other large-scale online learning initiatives with similar kinds of aspirations to widen access to higher education have faltered or failed due to not fully considering the cultural relevance, transferability, and accessibility of what was being offered to potential learners. This was a major factor in the failure of the US Open University to translate the UK Open University's ethos, model, and curricula to the US context (Krenelka 2009). In the UK itself, the closure of the UKeU (UK eUniversities Worldwide Limited) in 2004, after four short years of operating as a broker, marketer, and technology platform for accessing online degrees from various universities, was at least in part due to an emphasis on technology and delivery mechanisms over an understanding of who the potential students were going to be.

At the meso level, the potential to fully harness digital technology for effective and creative engagement in learning and teaching arguably remains constrained by the limited use that is made of the institutional VLE (Virtual Learning Environment), and other associated technologies, in most campus-based universities. In these contexts, the VLE predominantly remains a repository for basic course materials, with little opportunity for the student to actively engage online with resources, their peers, or their tutors. Furthermore, some of the evidence that supports this also indicates that several of the potentially more progressive and democratising digital education practices are not highly prioritised within universities. In their 2016 Survey of Technology Enhanced Learning for higher education in the UK, to which 110 of a potential 167 universities responded, UCISA reported that "Improving access to learning through the provision of open education resources" and "Improving access to learning through the provision of open education courses" were respectively ranked 28th and 29th (out of a 29) on a prioritised list of driving factors for TEL development across the UK universities that participated in the study (Walker et al. 2016).

Despite the observations above, at the meso and micro levels, there is ample evidence of good practice across the sector within which active and creative use of the VLE and other digital technologies and approaches to enhance learning and teaching, and to do so in pedagogically rich ways, is apparent. The question we previously raised is just how prevalent and widespread these examples are, beyond those that are shared within the literature and/or through transformation projects and initiatives like the exemplars discussed above? The various programmes highlighted have, like many others, generated a rich range of models, resources, and tools to support the development and implementation of digital technologies and practices in learning and teaching. Within the HEA and SFC programmes in particular, there is a legacy of case studies, tools, and rubrics which continue to inform pedagogic practice and curriculum design. This includes the assessment and feedback principles of the REAP project (Nicol and Draper 2009), the 3E Framework originally developed within the TESEP project (Comrie et al. 2009; Smyth 2013; Smyth et al. 2016), and a wealth of curriculum design, assessment and feedback, and digital literacies development resources from Jisc and HEA projects found online in Jisc's The Design Studio.

However, we also arguably need to accept that time-limited change projects and initiatives can only be expected to impact upon practice in selected areas, and that without sustained support and a change in institutional culture and processes, it is extremely difficult to cascade and further embed new or enhanced practices in a sustainable way over time.

This was a central message coming out of both the HEA e-Learning and Benchmarking Pathfinder Programme, and the SFC programme of which it was observed that "it was never likely that transformational change could be demonstrated directly during the short lifetime of the funded project, but it was hoped that the project would serve to establish within the partner institutions a coherent and widely accepted set of principles that would underpin a policy framework for sustainable change" (Comrie et al. 2009, p. 209).

To this end, it becomes important to distinguish between legacy and longitudinal change with respect to digital transformation projects and initiatives, and to perhaps underline again the important distinction between enhancement within the practices, processes, and systems of the university and genuine transformation of those practices, processes, and systems.

At the micro level of learning and teaching practice, we can also consider evidence in relation to quality of learning and 'learning gains' through digitally supported learning and teaching. The picture here is somewhat confusing, with several comparative studies and meta-analysis suggesting that there is no significant difference in the quality of learning between 'traditional' face-to-face learning and blended approaches, or that the blended learning is at least as effective (e.g. Swan 2003; US Department of Education 2010).

This may be misleading, as a comparison of like-for-like on assessed learning outcomes does not account for factors including the increased flexibility of learning; increased opportunities for reflection, discussion, and collaboration; and the development of digital skills and capabilities that digitally enabled learning, in blended and online contexts, can offer. Neither do comparative studies account for the culturally enriched learning experiences that can occur in open online learning, where cohorts of learners from a diverse range of cultural backgrounds and experiences may come together around shared areas of interest.

Beyond this, there is already a well-established body of cognitively focused education research that relates to the increased educational benefits of interacting with various online and other digital educational technologies. We know, for example, that learner-to-learner and learner-to-tutor dialogue and debate through asynchronous discussion can provide increased opportunity for the learner to reflect on their own views, and those of others, before articulating their own thoughts, and that this can be associated with deeper levels of engagement and understanding, increased participation on the part of those who are less forthcoming face-to-face, and also more equitable participation in discussion as it is harder for a smaller number of more vocal students to dominate as they might in the classroom. We also know that engagement with visual and interactive educational multimedia can, under certain conditions, improve comprehension and recall particularly when visual media complement verbal (written or audio) material or when interactive visual media aid 3D visualisation and manipulation of objects that are harder to comprehend when presented in 2D. Furthermore we know there are benefits for learners in developing a richer, more transferable knowledge when digital resources are used to establish more 'authentic' learning environments that realistically represent real-world settings and phenomena, and that increased choice over when and what to learn, through accessing online educational resources, can allow students to engage at a time that is most conducive to their own learning and to focus their efforts in areas of most relevance or challenge. Overview of the research undertaken in the above areas, and evidence of the various ways in which learning has been enabled and enhanced through engagement with different educational technologies, is summarised in several studies and reviews (e.g. Smyth and Buckner 2004; Price and Rogers 2004; Schellens and Valke 2006; Moreno and Mayer 2007).

What we think the above suggests is that many comparative studies at the micro level of digitally supported learning and teaching, between traditional and blended or online 'modes of delivery', are not nuanced enough to capture the rich range of enhanced learning opportunities that digitally supported education offers, and that individual 'learning gains' on formally assessed learning outcomes is a very narrow indicator of the learning that is potentially occurring with and through digital tools and spaces in formal education contexts.

We do, however, argue for the need to be critical and even sceptical of what digital technologies are seen to offer in relation to supporting and enhancing learning, and what is actually offered in practice. We are cognisant in particular of ongoing debates concerning the 'affordances' of educational technology. As originally conceptualised by the ecological psychologist James Gibson (1977, 1979) in his work on visual perception, the term 'affordance' was used to describe the relationship between the individual and the opportunities for action they perceived within objects in their environment. Crucially, it described an emergent relationship. For example, a pen affording the opportunity to write, but predicated firstly on the individual recognising that the object is indeed a pen and could be used for written communication and secondly on the individual having a need to write. Over the last three decades, the term affordance has come into common use to refer uncritically and unassumingly to what different technologies offer in terms of their educational benefits, such as asynchronous discussion boards offering more time to reflect and debate, leading to deeper exchanges and understanding. Concurrently, in the last two decades to the present time, there has been a more critical discourse concerning affordances as it relates to Gibson's original theory (e.g. Conole and Dyke 2004; Parchoma 2014; Evans et al. 2017).

Our perspective shares the more critical view concerning the affordances of digital educational technologies as being emergent properties through which the potential educational benefits of any specific technology are only fully realised when the individual learner recognises what the technology offers and uses the technology in a corresponding and constructive way. For example, an asynchronous discussion board may well offer more time to reflect and debate leading to deeper learning, and may offer less forthcoming learners further time and space to engage with peers. However, this is only so if the learner recognises that and does not engage with a discussion board for the first time immediately before it closes and when they can at best only quickly communicate their own views.

A key implication here concerns the way in which learners can be supported to engage effectively with digital tools and spaces, in ways which make expectations, potential challenges, and the affordances that can emerge from their engagement with digital educational technologies, and their engagement with each other through such technologies, as transparent as possible. As we return to Chap. 7, the need for such transparency becomes even more critical within contexts, pedagogical interventions, and approaches that place more autonomy with students as co-creators of their own learning.

Emerging Possibilities for Transformative Change

We have attempted to challenge what it is we mean by transformation in relation to digital education practice, including the evidence of impact at the macro, meso, and micro levels, and where we may be conflating the 'transformation' of practice with what is actually the enhancement of existing practices in selected areas or contexts. This is not to challenge the value or worth of enhancing learning and teaching practices through harnessing digital tools and approaches; however we do challenge the extent to which we are harnessing digital tools and approaches to extend our practices, and develop new practices, that can better position, enrich, and widen access to higher education as more a democratic, public good.

We have however identified some of the emerging possibilities, for example, the open textbook movement and growing grassroots practices relating to open collaborative learning, professional development, and networking amongst educators. There are other emergent practices, in the open education domain, that are now beginning to offer more democratic and educationally inclusive alternatives to MOOCs and other similar large-scale open online courses. Of particular interest in this respect is the work that has been undertaken by Peter Shukie and colleagues at University Centre Blackburn College to develop and implement Community Open Online Courses (COOCs) (Shukie 2015), which is underpinned by a widening access ethos in which the COOCs online digital learning platform is presented as "a place where anyone can teach and learn anything for free". We might also take encouragement from the ways in which MOOCs themselves might diversify, supported by a growing evidence base which should help enable more representative, democratic forms of engagement in MOOCs going forward and more refined approaches to supporting those who do choose to participate (Wintrup et al. 2015). A current trend in the increased outreach of MOOCs, and similar online open education initiatives, looks to be emerging around supporting large-scale learning in developing areas of the world (e.g. Laurillard and Kennedy 2017). This is promising, but brings with it an even greater need to ensure cultural inclusivity and relevance in curriculum content and a mindfulness concerning the digital means, and digitally rich spaces, that will support engagement for those who might otherwise be disadvantaged, disenfranchised, or unable to participate.

We further explore these issues in Chap. 8, while across Chaps. 7 and 8, we consider other emerging possibilities for what we might cautiously refer to as 'transformative change', including participative and co-creative pedagogic approaches, student engagement in digital public scholarship, the co-location of the curriculum as a digitally enabled space, and the sharing of knowledge created through the curriculum.

Conclusions

Within the sector, there is a 'rhetoric' of digital transformation in relation to higher education, the outreach of our universities, and the learning and teaching experience that is nebulous and therefore open to being interpreted and enacted in various ways. At the very broadest level, as we have explored here and in earlier chapters, the dominant perspective is a neoliberal one that is non-critical and accepting of the digital as a means to deliver higher education more effectively, more efficiently, and on an ever larger scale.

The reality would appear to be somewhat different and offers a more varied picture of what is happening. This includes evidence of faltering practice at sectoral level, evidence of enhancement and enhanced practice at the meso and micro levels, and the existence of a growing base of tools and resources, as legacy of various sector and cross-institutional initiatives, that have a current and continued role to play in shaping effective practice. In terms of developing more pedagogically progressive and democratic approaches to harnessing digital tools, spaces, and approaches in extending higher education as a public good, and in moving towards a further understanding of the Digital University as we conceptualise it, there is encouragement to be taken from the emerging practices above which we will return to.

References

Collini, S. (2012). *What Are Universities For?* London: Penguin.
Collini, S. (2017). *Speaking of Universities*. London: Verso.
Comrie, A., Smyth, K., & Mayes, T. (2009). Learners in Control: The TESEP Approach. In T. Mayes, D. Morrison, H. Mellar, P. Bullen, & M. Oliver (Eds.), *Transforming Higher Education Through Technology-Enhanced Learning* (pp. 208–234). York: Higher Education Academy.
Conole, G., & Dyke, M. (2004). What Are the Affordances of Information and Communication Technologies? *ALT-J: Research in Learning Technology, 12*(2), 113–124. https://doi.org/10.1080/0968776042000216183. Last Accessed 25 Jun 2018.

Dewey, J. (1916, Republished 1966). *Democracy and Education: An Introduction to the Democracy of Education*. New York: Free Press/Macmillan.

Evans, S. K., Pearce, K. E., Vitak, J., & Treem, J. W. (2017). Explicating Affordances: A Conceptual Framework for Understanding Affordances in Communication Research. *Journal of Computer-Mediated Communication, 22*, 35–52.

Gibson, J. J. (1977). The Theory of Affordances. In R. Shaw & J. Bransford (Eds.), *Perceiving, Acting and Knowing* (pp. 67–82). Hillsdale: Lawrence Erlbaum.

Gibson, J. J. (1979). *The Ecological Approach to Visual Perception*. Boston: Houghton Mifflin.

Giroux, H. (2014). *Neoliberalism's War on Higher Education*. Chicago: Haymarket Books.

Gros, B., & Lopez, C. (2016). Students as Co-creators of Technology-Rich Learning Activities in Higher Education. *International Journal of Educational Technology in Higher Education, 13*, 28. https://doi.org/10.1186/s41239-016-0026-x. Last Accessed 30 Oct 2017.

Haggard, S. (2013). *The Maturing of the MOOC: Literature Review of Massive Open Online Courses and Other Forms of Online Distance Learning, BIS Research Paper Number 130*. London: Department of Business, Innovation and Skills. https://www.gov.uk/government/uploads/system/uploads/attachment_data/file/240193/13-1173-maturing-of-the-mooc.pdf. Last Accessed 30 Oct 2017.

Jisc/HEA. (2008). *E-Learning Benchmarking and Pathfinder Programme 2005–2008: An Overview*. York: Higher Education Academy. https://www.heacademy.ac.uk/knowledge-hub/e-learning-benchmarking-and-pathfinder-programme. Last Accessed 30 Oct 2017.

Krenelka, L. M. (2009). A Review of the Short Life of the US Open University. In K. A. Meyer (Ed.), *Lessons Learned from Virtual Universities, New Directions for Higher Education, No. 146* (pp. 65–72). San Francisco: Jossey-Bass.

Laurillard, D., & Kennedy, E. (2017, December). *The Potential of MOOCs for Learning at Scale in the Global South*. Centre for Global Higher Education Working Paper Series, No. 31. London: Centre for Global Higher Education, UCL Institute of Education. http://www.researchcghe.org/perch/resources/publications/wp31.pdf. Last Accessed 24 Jan 2018.

Mason, P. (2015). *Postcapitalism: A Guide to Our Future*. London: Alan Lane.

Mayes, T., Morrison, D., Mellar, H., Bullen, P., & Oliver, M. (Eds.). (2009). *Transforming Higher Education Through Technology-Enhanced Learning*. York: Higher Education Academy.

Molesworth, M., Scullion, R., & Nixon, E. (Eds.). (2011). *The Marketisation of Higher Education and Student as Consumer*. Abingdon/New York: Routledge.

Moreno, R., & Mayer, R. (2007). Interactive Multimodal Learning Environments. *Educational Psychology Review, 19*(3), 309–326.

Nerantzi, C., & Beckingham, S. (2014). BYOD4L – Our Magical Open Box to Enhance Individuals' Learning Ecologies. In N. Jackson, & J. Willis (Eds.), *Lifewide Learning and Education in Universities and Colleges*. Lifewide Education. http://www.learninglives.co.uk/e-book.html. Last Accessed 25 Jun 2018.

Nerantzi, C., & Gossman, P. (2015). Towards Collaboration as Learning. An Evaluation of an Open CPD Opportunity for HE Teachers. *Research in Learning Technology Journal, 23*. https://doi.org/10.3402/rlt.v23.26967. Last Accessed 25 Jun 2018.

Nicol, D., & Draper, S. (2009). A Blueprint for Organisational Change in Higher Education: REAP as a Case Study. In T. Mayes, D. Morrison, H. Mellar, P. Bullen, & M. Oliver (Eds.), *Transforming Higher Education Through Technology-Enhanced Learning* (pp. 191–207). York: Higher Education Academy.

OLTF (Online Learning Task Force). (2011). *Collaborate to Compete: Seizing the Opportunity of Online Learning for UK Higher Education*. Report to HEFCE by the Online Learning Task Force. Higher Education Funding Council for England. http://www.hefce.ac.uk/media/hefce1/pubs/hefce/2011/1101/11_01.pdf. Last Accessed 25 Jun 2018.

Parchoma, G. (2014). The Contested Ontology of Affordances: Implications for Researching Technological Affordances for Collaborative Knowledge Production. *Computers in Human Behaviour, 37*, 360–368.

Price, S., & Rogers, Y. (2004). Let's Get Physical: The Learning Benefit of Interacting in Digitally Augmented Physical Spaces. *Computers and Education, 43*, 137–151.

Schellens, T., & Valke, M. (2006). Fostering Knowledge Construction in University Students Through Asynchronous Discussion Groups. *Computers and Education, 46*(4), 349–370.

Scottish Government. (2017). *Realising Scotland's Full Potential in a Digital World: A Digital Strategy for Scotland*. http://www.gov.scot/Publications/2017/03/7843. Last Accessed 25 Jun 2018.

Shukie, P. (2015). The Big Idea: Community Open Online Courses. https://www.thersa.org/discover/publications-and-articles/rsa-blogs/2015/02/the-big-ideacoocs. Last Accessed 25 Jun 2018.

Smyth, K. (2013). Sharing and Shaping Effective Institutional Practice in TEL Through the 3E Framework. In S. Greener (Ed.), *Case Studies in E-Learning* (pp. 141–159). Reading: Academic Publishing International.

Smyth, K., & Buckner, K. (2004, November 25–26). Towards a Theoretical Framework for Understanding the Nature of Networked Learning. In D. Remenyi (Ed.), *Proceedings of the 2004 European Conference on eLearning*, Universite Paris Dauphine (pp. 375–386). Paris: Academic Conferences International.

Smyth, K., MacNeill, S., & Hartley, P. (2016). Technologies and Academic Development. In D. Baume & C. Popovic (Eds.), *Advancing Practice in Academic Development* (pp. 121–141). New York: Routledge.

Swan, K. (2003). Learning Effectiveness: What the Research Tells Us. In J. Bourne & C. J. Moore (Eds.), *Elements of Quality Online Education, Practice and Direction, Sloan Center for Online Education* (pp. 13–45). Needham: Sloan Consortium.

Twigg, C. (2003). Improving Learning and Reducing Costs: New Models for Online Learning. *Educause Review, 38*(5), 28–38.

US Department of Education. (2010). *Evaluation of Evidence-Based Practices in Online Learning: A Meta-Analysis and Review of Online Learning Studies*. https://www2.ed.gov/rschstat/eval/tech/evidence-based-practices/finalreport.pdf. Last Accessed 30 Oct 2017.

US Department of Education. (2017). *Reimagining the Role of Technology in Education: 2017 National Education Technology Plan Update*. https://tech.ed.gov/netp/. Last Accessed 25 Jun 2018.

Walker, R., Voce, J., Swift, E., Ahmed, J., Jenkins, M., & Vincent, P. (2016). *2016 Survey of Technology Enhanced Learning for Higher Education in the UK*. Oxford: UCISA. https://www.ucisa.ac.uk/tel/. Last Accessed 06 Oct 2017.

Weller, M. (2014). *The Battle for Open: How Openness Won and Why It Doesn't Feel Like Victory*. London: Ubiquity Press.

Wintrup, J., Wakefield, K., & Davis, H. (2015). *Engaged Learning in MOOCs: A Study Using the UK Engagement Survey*. York: Higher Education Academy.

https://www.heacademy.ac.uk/system/files/resources/engaged-learning-in-moocs.pdf. Last Accessed 30 Oct 2017.

Zhenghao, C., Alcorn, B., Christensen, G., Eriksson, N., Koller, D., & Emanuel, E.J. (2015, September 22). Who's Benefiting from MOOCs, and Why. *Harvard Business Review.* https://hbr.org/2015/09/whos-benefiting-from-moocs-and-why. Last Accessed 30 Oct 2017.

5

Digital Participation and Open Communities: From Widening Access to Porous Boundaries

Introduction

As we created our conceptual framework, we were conscious of the need to make explicit the relationship between digital participation and wider social inclusion issues relating to access and cost of access to online services. The digital divide works across multiple levels including geography, finance, and literacy. Universities sit at the intersection of all of these levels. In this chapter we will explore the Digital Participation Quadrant of our Matrix, viewed as a broad social construct with a range of specific implications for educators and educational institutions.

The Matrix highlights a number of different but related areas of digital participation, namely, glocalisation, in terms of the blend of global aspiration within a range of local contexts; widening access, both in terms of extending traditional socio-economic access to higher education and in terms of more flexible approaches and access to tertiary education through digital systems; civic role and responsibilities, in terms of the wider civic role universities play within the communities in which they are physically located and potentially beyond; networks (human and digital), in terms of the potential for enhanced networked participation digital technologies can provide access to; and technological affordances, in terms of the potential role and costs to access to the relevant technologies and digital services to underpin all of the above.

Acknowledging digital participation as a fundamental part of any knowledge economy or information-based democracy is one such implication. We will develop this line of thought by discussing participation in relation to (i) digital access, (ii) open education, (iii) research and academic publishing, and (iv) social inclusion. We will place this discussion in the context of our analysis of digital issues at micro, meso, and macro levels.

We contend that digital participation needs to be optimised to ensure continued economic growth in parallel with the development of an informed, literate citizenship. From our critical perspective, we suggest that a more equal development of the educational aspects of society's economic and democratic dimensions is a necessary corrective to the present unevenness in the university curriculum, which has resulted from the dominance of neoliberalism over higher education policy and practice. We argue that universities are uniquely placed to lead and evolve digital participation for and with their wider communities. In exploring this territory, we tackle the following questions: How can we facilitate more and better engagement between communities? What human and digital networks do we need to foster? What are the underlying infrastructures and connections underpinning access to all of the above? The notion of zones/zones of practice is one which has emerged from our own praxis as one potential area for development.

We will address participation in terms of the current wider participation agenda, and then seek to extend the pedagogical dimension of that frame of reference by exploring the history and current state of play of the open education movement. To that end we will discuss the present mainstream approach to widening access, whilst offering our own views based on critical pedagogy/open education. We will propose that open educational practice has a pivotal role to play in increasing participation not only through wider access to current degree structures, but by creating new forms of access to additional opportunities for formal and informal knowledge creation and sharing between universities and the communities in which they are located. Digital technologies are vital in allowing for the expansion of porous boundaries between universities and their various communities, and in creating greater permeability of opportunity and knowledge creation and sharing for all.

Widening Participation: Pedagogy of the Disadvantaged?

The Higher Education Policy Institute (HEPI) report "Where next for widening participation and fair access?" (2017, Number 93) poses the right questions and offers responses that are both pragmatic and critical of the present neoliberal policies for UK higher education. In his foreword, Professor Les Ebdon puts the situation thus:

> There are still stark gaps between different groups of people at every stage of the student lifecycle, in terms of whether they apply to higher education and where they apply to; whether they are accepted; the likelihood of having to leave their course early; the level of degree that they get; and whether they go on to a rewarding job or postgraduate study. (p. 3)

Overall, the report is more structural than critical and adopts a 'widening access to the current system' approach, albeit with ideas for improvement in the mechanisms providing access. The focus in the HEPI report is on features of the current admissions system that obstruct wider participation. Sociocultural inequalities are positioned as the fundamental barrier, which can be met by positive actions including (i) pre-entry programmes, (ii) modified admissions policies, and (iii) student support practices. Section 13 of the report offers some pedagogical ideas under the heading of 'innovations in learning and teaching'. Also, it is encouraging that a whole student lifecycle approach is promoted. This aligns with notions of systematic whole course development and ambitions to systematic epistemological and personal development (Anderson and Johnson 2016). However, the focus is more on taking account of the social circumstances of potential entrants, devising relevant modifications to admissions systems, and relying on the goodwill of academic and other staff to devote time and energy to helping disadvantaged students who gain admission make a success of study.

The case study of King's College London's 'full student lifecycle' approach to widening participation is an interesting example. From a critical perspective, this appears to be a mechanism for 'fine tuning' the existing system, the better to engage previously excluded populations, rather than a radical departure from the status quo. A more fundamental critique of the higher education system would tackle social and class inequalities as issues of political economy, and the associated cultural assumptions of university education, embedded in the system. Indeed, some of the other showcased strategies—Bristol Scholar, retention schemes, learning analytics to spot struggling students, and so on—seem to assume that the status quo is satisfactory and simply needs some tweaking to open it up to 'disadvantaged' people and help them 'survive' a degree programme, with relatively little pedagogical development of the curriculum required. In addition, improving retention can be seen in terms of managing institutional priorities for completion rates as well as helping students to survive a degree programme.

The approach taken in the report seems to assume a *deficit model* of the student experience as the basis for pedagogical intervention, rather than attempting a more farsighted account of a different kind of curriculum. It is a pragmatic approach in line with the policy constraints on more fundamental change, which have characterised the period of massification of university entrance in the UK. Inevitably this sets limits on educational and organisational development in universities, particularly in respect of approaches based on critical pedagogy and open education. That said, it is a timely account of an important aspect of contemporary university practice, which is often a low strategic priority for universities more engaged with the neoliberal agenda of marketisation and consumerism. The lack of Social Capital at the heart of our current system of socially 'narrower' participation is a useful construct in that it leads to reframing of the participation debate to foreground categories of excluded or 'oppressed' people. This is a perspective critical pedagogy can address which we explore in Chap. 9.

In this context the potential for digital approaches seems to be very managerial and functional in terms of providing access to information and marketing opportunities for both institutions and individuals. It is a very narrow view of the potential of developing more approaches based on participation through open educational approaches. Digital technologies allow the potential for far greater access to the outputs of universities than the traditional ivory tower model which was predicated on a level of privilege to be able to access knowledge as well as geographically imposed barriers of participation. Digital technologies allow for far more equitable access and are a key way in which it is possible to create more porosity and permeability of access and participation to and across universities and a range of communities.

Digital Access and Participation: Open Education as Conduit of Participation

We see the potential for developing digital inclusion policies to creatively reach out to a pool of potential participants for higher education; however the challenge of how to successfully engage them with higher education remains unsolved. The HEPI (2017) report sets out a number of barriers in terms of social disadvantage. A truly digitally enabled university could overcome these barriers, but it would need a more radical account of notions of the 'common good' and civic responsibilities beyond current neoliberal economic instrumentalism.

We propose that Open Education is a potential vehicle for extended participation, both in conventional 'access to courses' mode and more radical engagements with learning.

Over the past two decades, national policies and agendas directed at improving digital access and participation in an increasingly networked society as described in Chap. 2, coupled with the work of third sector groups in the areas of digital inclusion and empowerment, are beginning to address the gaps around access to and participation to digitally enabled services, from shopping to welfare benefits to education and a myriad of other services and communities in between.

As our work on the digital university concept started, we were cognisant that at a policy level, in the UK, both the Westminster and the

Scottish Governments were recognising and encouraging digital participation across all sectors of society and emphasising the notion of the digital citizen, for example, increasing use of web-based consultation exercises and increasing moves towards the notion of Open Government. Within this context the possibilities of the digital for increasing access to services, amplifying the voices and agendas of particular groups, and participating in local and national democratic process were beginning to be acknowledged and realised. These initiatives create a significant pool of new kinds of potential participants in higher education, who can be conceptualised through notions of 'digital literacy', 'digital skills', or 'digital capability' (see Chap. 6).

In parallel, within the community and higher education sectors, the development of open education practices—and the emergence of 'open' as an ethos—has created opportunities for more flexible participation in informal online and online-supported learning where access to these opportunities are more equitable with respect to the educational experiences and prior knowledge that learners bring with them. It is within this context that we use the notion of open education, and open educational practice in particular, to provide an alternative to the neoliberal developments within educational and technology use in education as discussed in earlier chapters. However, we do acknowledge that open in and of itself is not a panacea or unproblematic alternative solution.

The open education movement has been gaining traction internationally over the past two decades; however open education is not comprehensively included in the mainstream of educational practice. The dominant neoliberal pressures on universities tend to presume that the only viable models for extending digital participation are based on and provided by externally provided, often proprietary, closed services. The following section offers a wider perspective.

A Brief History of Open Education

The history of open education can be traced throughout the history of education. Weller (2014) traces the foundations of open education to the heart of notions of public education.

Openness has a long history in higher education. Its foundations lie in one of altruism and the belief that education is a public good. It has undergone many interpretations and adaptations, moving from a model which had open entry to study as its primary focus, to one that emphasises openly available content and resources. This change in the definition of openness in education has largely been a result of the digital and network revolution. Changes in other sectors, most notably the open source model of software production, and values associated with the Internet of free access and open approaches have influenced (and been influenced by) practitioners in higher education.

The Cape Town Open Education Declaration in 2007 was the first internationally supported and recognised statement of the benefits of open educational resources (OER) and practice. This was followed by UNESCO's Paris OER Declaration in 2012, which called for the open licencing of publicly funded educational materials. This in turn has formed the basis of a number of national-level declarations including the Open Scotland Declaration in 2013. The key output of the 2017 World Congress on OER was the Ljubljana OER Action Plan which provides specific drivers to meet UNESCO's 2030 Sustainability Goal around education and lifelong learning. These initiatives combine to offer a framework of international relations that could provide the foundations an alternative to the existing neoliberal order.

In 2001 MIT launched its OpenCourseWare initiative. This took the (education) world by storm. A major, international university giving away its content for free was unheard of. Many did think that this would truly cause the sky to fall in. However, as MIT knew access to content alone couldn't replace the MIT on campus experience of supported intellectual development. This project provided a way for the university to meet its mission around extending access to knowledge and provide a way to support the development of new open, digital resources.

Researching the history of open education exemplifies the ethos of extending knowledge through open sharing. The Open Education Handbook is a community-driven approach to creating a collectively authored, openly accessible, shareable, updatable resource providing a comprehensive overview of the development of the open education movement.

The Open Education consortium defines open education as:

> Open education encompasses resources, tools and practices that employ a framework of open sharing to improve educational access and effectiveness worldwide.

Movements such as community colleges, open universities, ragged schools, and more have a long tradition of supporting the opening of access to education from the privileged few to a more inclusive, if not quite yet universal, cross section of society. Whilst we in the Global North may take universal access to education as a given, access to education is still not a given in many parts of the world despite the fact that right of all citizens to education is part of the 1948 Universal Declaration of Human Rights.

This right is continually championed by UNESCO. One of the goals of their 2030 Agenda for Sustainable Development is to

> ensure inclusive and equitable quality education and promote lifelong learning opportunities for all.

The Beginning Was Not MOOCs

Despite the inherent logicality that access to education and all publicly funded educational resources should be made openly available as per the MIT model, open education has been widely and wrongly conflated and confused by the rise of the MOOC movement from the early 2010s. The origins of MOOCs can be traced to Canada (Yuan and Powell 2015) through the CCK12 course (Connectivism and Connected Knowledge 2012), a truly open course with collaboration at its heart; they caught mainstream attention after a number of angel investors provided vast start-up funding for 'massive open educational courses' instigated by academics from the American Ivy League, Stanford and Berkeley, to mostly notably Coursera and Udacity. The latter being a prime example of education conceived as a private investor opportunity operating under the guise of widening global participation.

These primarily university, undergraduate-level courses would be open to anyone, with no need for formal qualifications and no fees, and were widely hailed as bringing about a tsunami of change and radical transformation to higher education (Barber et al. 2013). In a 2013 article in *The Economist*, Andrew Ng (founder of Udacity) was quoted as stating that in 50 years there will only be ten universities left in the world. Five years later, the reality of these claims has been somewhat different. Research has illustrated initial participation in these MOOCs was mainly from those who already had a university-level degree which negated the promises of transforming global participation and access to higher education. Analysis of completion rates also showed significant variation with up to 50% drop out rates (Jordan 2015).

Far from obliterating universities, MOOCs have widely been subsumed into wider university practice, as part of marketing for paid for courses or as in Udacity's case developing into paid for, condensed, 'nanodegrees'.

Not all universities were able to jump on the 'MOOC bandwagon'. Whilst the end products maybe are free and open—in terms of no access fee—and open to all who have the means to connect to the World Wide Web, the cost of developing a MOOC is not insignificant. According to a 2015 Times Higher Education article, it was estimated at approximately £30,000 per course, which requires significant strategic commitment to find the funds for such an initiative. It appears that MOOCs are now becoming a more normal part of taster courses with paid for accreditation and other activities such as student inductions. The open element which caused so much initial hype has been subsumed into mainstream neoliberal practice.

Currently the majority of MOOC platforms have some form of charging structure for accreditation, often billed as micro credentialing. The reality of the open elements in MOOCs was always debatable. With a few notable exceptions such as the University of Edinburgh and the Open University UK, who both continue to use a range of platforms and access models, there was little if any actual openly licenced content/resources created and shared. Access was generally predicated on registration with little opportunity to truly openly access courses. This framing is consistent with our discussion of participation above. Despite this legacy, the rise of the MOOC movement did introduce the concept of open education to a wider audience.

Open Education Now

In 2017–2018 at the time of writing, macro level interest in open education is patchy. It is easy to conflate open with free; however there is always a cost to producing open resources, services, and platforms. Macro level funding, notably from large philanthropic foundations such as the William and Flora Hewlett Foundation, has been instrumental in driving forward developments in open education. UNESCO and other international agencies such as the Commonwealth of Learning have also provided support for the development of policy and formal recognition. The Ljubljana OER Action Plan (UNESCO 2017) was signed by representatives of 20 Ministers of the following countries—Bangladesh, Barbados, Bulgaria, Czech Republic, Costa Rica, Croatia, Kiribati, Lao People's Democratic Republic, Lithuania, Malta, Mauritius, Mauritania, Mozambique, Palestine, Romania, Serbia, Slovakia, Slovenia, South Africa, and the United Arab Emirates. There are notable absences in that list, including the UK.

This is despite the notable contribution to the Open Education movement from many individuals and organisations in the UK such as the Open University, the HEFCE-funded OER programmes, and the OER Research Hub. There does appear to be a lack of macro level government support for open education at both policy and funding levels. At the meso level, there is patchy support with a growing number of institutions adopting OER policies to support their staff in openly licencing materials.

It is perhaps at the micro level that open education and open educational practice are gaining more traction. Cronin (2017) uses the macro, meso, and micro levels to address some of the key questions that individuals need to address as follows:

- Macro—will I share openly?
- Meso—who will I share with?
- Micro—who will I share as?

She also introduces a fourth level—the Nano in terms of the basic question 'will I share this'?

As social media platforms have become more available at low or no (upfront) cost, many academics are now connecting and collaborating in extended international networks. It is easier to share practice, resources, and curriculum than ever before. These channels are generally outwith the provided university infrastructure and so provide a way for academics and students to circumvent institutionally closed systems. This digitally enabled sharing is allowing for more permeability of resources, research, curricula, and sharing of practice. There is still not widespread recognition of the potential value of this type of leakiness (UHI, 2017) so it is still not mainstream practice. The altruism of open education has still to be fully embraced as part of the strategic vision for the majority of universities.

Research into open educational practice is increasingly making connections to critical pedagogy theory. For example, the work of Paulo Freire is gaining new momentum within open educational research and practice (Farrow 2017; Zobel 2015).

This is largely down to a refocus and the extension of notions of praxis in terms of the relationship between open educational resources and practice, individual practitioners, learners, institutions, and wider society. Being an open practitioner forces one to re-negotiate traditional notions of ownership, distribution, and control of educational resources. The Open Pedagogy website is an example of the emerging cross-disciplinary research theme around learning and teaching practice which opens education facilities. The site explicitly presents open pedagogy as a site of praxis:

> a place where theories about learning, teaching, technology, and social justice enter into a conversation with each other and inform the development of educational practices and structures.

As we discuss in Chap. 7, universities are digitally rich spaces that have the potential to be utilised as digital, open hubs for not only extending university-level learning and teaching, but for greater community engagement for knowledge sharing and creation. For universities to disrupt and innovate education and challenge traditional market forces, open education represents an effective strategy. However, in these economically uncertain times for the UK sector, open education does seem to fall off the agenda in terms of support against the 'student as consumer' narrative. The role of the student to be contributing to the knowledge commons is often neglected in this consumer-driven narrative. Paying to be 'filled' with knowledge is more important than contributing to extending of the knowledge commons.

Many of the underlying principles of 'the university' are implicitly entwined with notions of the commons, that is, the common good. We contend that extending and enhancing understanding of the commons alongside greater institutional support for the development of open education resources and practices is vital to building critical momentum around widening digital participation to universities.

The Commons, Open Education, and Open Educational Practice

Whilst the neoliberal debate has been gaining momentum in the Global North as described in earlier chapters, the Open movement does provide an alternative vision through the notion of the (educational) commons. The notion of the commons is not new or indeed specifically unique to education. *A commons is an alternative system whereby a resource is controlled in perpetuity by a community for the shared and equal benefit of its members* (Monbiot 2017). The idea of the commons does have particular resonance with education, as fundamentally education is about participation and the sharing and extension of knowledge.

The CARE OER Stewardship Framework—contribute, attribute, release, empower—was released in spring 2018 as one model to sustain and develop open educational resources. Whilst it is still too early to comment on the success, it has already engendered a level of interest and critique around open education and the commons.

Using open education as a strategic (re)focus on the commons and civic engagement is an obvious way for developing strategy around digital participation.

The Open Conundrum

Despite the apparently altruistic nature of open education, the open sharing of practice and perhaps more importantly resources is challenging for many senior managers in universities as it disrupts traditional notions of access and control. As described earlier in this chapter, there are notable exceptions and exemplars of universities embracing aspects of the open movement. However, it appears that the kind of potential, and we would argue, positive disruption that open could bring to universities, is being subverted by the dominance at the macro level of neoliberal political and economic policies.

One area where open is having impact is in terms of research and open access. In the UK, the recommendations of the Finch Report (2012) in terms of supporting open access to research and data in a balanced way have been adopted by the UK Government and in turn the UK funding councils. The two main routes to open access publishing, Green and Gold whilst allowing for open access to research, do allow for a charging, embargo periods and what could be seen to be supporting the adage that open does not equal free. Indeed, publishers still have a viable economic model through both these routes. The irony of writing about open education and not being able to afford to publish an open version of this book is an irony the authors are all only too aware of.

On the other hand, there is growing evidence that (often collaboratively authored) open textbooks are not only having an impact on decreasing costs for students but are also changing educators' attitudes towards the benefits of creating and using open educational resources (Pitt 2015).

When a more critically informed perspective is taken, it is clear that open education in its widest sense can play a significant role in extended digital participation and the extension of knowledge creation and sharing in new ways that underline the civic role and responsibilities that all university mission statements espouse. Open practices and systems could provide transformative ways of supporting digital inclusion, participation, and access to education.

Digital Participation and Inclusion: The Wider View

Of course digital participation is not limited to the educational sphere. The expansion of digital services and technologies across all elements of twenty-first-century society is allowing for a widening of support and debate around participation and inclusion at many levels.

The Scottish Government (2011) defined digital participation as

> people's ability to gain access to digital technology, and understand how to use it creatively

During the first two decades of the twenty-first century, there continues to be substantial investment in infrastructure developments such as superfast broadband and 3/4/5 G mobile data connectivity. In the UK much of this infrastructure development is driven, subsidised, and, in the case of mobile technologies, licenced through central Government. Globally large digital service providers, sometimes referred to as the FANGs (Facebook, Amazon, Netflix, and Google), are increasingly becoming the digital gatekeepers of access to services and more importantly access to our digital data participation patterns that can be mined for commercial and increasingly political gain.

To increase digital participation and inclusion, there needs to be equitable access to the infrastructure that allows citizens to easily and affordably get online to allow them to take full advantage of the increasing number of essential state, commercial, and social services that are increasingly only available via digital gateways.

We propose that universities in the twenty-first century are uniquely placed in terms of developing and supporting digital participation and inclusion. They are relatively technologically rich spaces, situated within a defined community, for example, a city or a commonly understood geographical area.

Macro, Meso, and Micro Participation

In a UNESCO briefing paper on Learning Analytics, Buckingham-Shum (2011) highlights the convergence of macro, meso, and micro levels in terms of data and, in particular, learning analytics adoption in the education sector. He argues that this convergence of the top-down and bottom-up drivers provides a 'mutual enrichment' between the layers (Fig. 5.1).

Using this notion of mutual enrichment, and macro as in region/state/national/international level, meso as institution-wide level, and micro as individual user level, also provides a useful starting frame of reference to

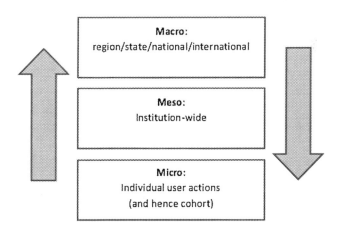

Fig. 5.1 Macro, meso, and micro participation. (Adapted from Buckingham-Shum 2011)

discuss digital participation within our context of participation in the context of the digital university.

As discussed earlier in the chapter, at the macro levels, there are strong drivers for enabling digital participation at Government level. In the UK, this works at the UK Government level and is then more contextualised at the devolved, for example, Scottish Government level. The day-to-day reality for micro level participation of students and staff working in any university is driven by their particular meso level priorities and culture. These in turn are driven by macro level priorities such as funding and Government targets. For example, in Scotland in 2017, the attainment gap and widening participation are key macro level drivers.

At the time of writing, the uncertainty over overseas student visas due to Brexit is bringing yet another level of macro level uncertainty to more general student participation in university-level education.

Digital technologies and fully online delivery is potentially one route to circumventing some of these macro level challenges. However, it brings with it additional complexities in terms of infrastructure resourcing and levels staff and student digital capabilities at both the macro and meso levels.

At the same time, increased access to information, educational content, and personal/professional networks through digital technologies, services, and networks offers an increasing range of new possibilities for participation at the individual, micro level. These include the opportunities offered through more open approaches as outlined in earlier sections of this chapter.

Students and staff are also fully embracing the opportunity to bring your own devices (BYOD) for learning. They are bringing multiple devices and their own networks and connectivity. Whilst access to stable Wi-Fi is still a key priority for students in both the HE and FE sectors, this change in use of personal technology challenges traditional university IT provision and access to services. The provision, and thereby control of access to devices, is no longer solely provided by the university. Micro level participation is no longer predicated on macro and meso level structures. University control and regulation around access to infrastructure has to evolve to embrace these changes.

Whilst the cachet of a degree awarded through the traditional university system, that is, three to four years of undergraduate study, is still prevalent, the traditional university meso level is under unprecedented attack from the macro government level and also, in terms of digital technology, from the growing influence of technology investors/companies who purport the 'education is broken' meme and are constantly trying to find new ways of 'fixing' education through new, so-called disruptive technologies (Watters 2016).

As we have argued in the first section of this book, the first quartile of the twenty-first century has produced a neoliberal renaissance where the macro business/market-led trend for innovation/disruption in education has aligned perfectly with increased pressures around university funding, student fees from government, and the growing notion of university-level education as being a market-driven sector and consumer led.

Who ultimately pays for education has already caused divides with the macro level of Government. For example, in the UK, the Scottish Government did not follow the UK Government decision to introduce undergraduate fees in England.

The tension between education as a market-driven business and that of an (quasi) independent, critically engaged space for the growth of knowledge across all disciplines has never been greater. A combination of open educational practice and critical pedagogy could provide a means to challenge and rebalance discourse in this area and allow for greater levels of relevant and engaged participation.

Conclusion: Digital Oppression Versus Digital Transformation?

In this neoliberal environment, we argue 'the digital' is being used, in a Frierian sense, as a tool of oppression. University management need to find ways to problematise the current social and economic climate HE is operating in.

If universities are really in a transition stage in the digital age, the sector needs to articulate and explore if it is actually in a state of retreat or transition. Building on Freire, we need to ask: are universities 'in' or 'of' a digital transition dictated by external forces? To be truly 'in' transition and to allow for enhanced participation, shouldn't universities embrace a more radical stance, that is

> predominantly critical, loving, humble, and communicative. (Freire 1974, p. 9)

We firmly believe that there is a significant role for open education resources, open practice, and pedagogy to offer alternative, participatory approaches inclusion and the widening participation agenda.

As our own thinking has progressed, we now see the digital university Matrix as a symbol in which to explore the potentiality of digital transformation from a number of perspectives, but in particular through open education and critical pedagogy. This will be explored further in Chap. 9.

References

About the Open Education Consortium. (n.d.). Retrieved from http://www.oeconsortium.org/about-oec/

Buckingham-Shum, S. (2011). Learning Analytics – UNESCO IITE. https://iite.unesco.org/publications/3214711/. Accessed 3 Sept 2017.

Cronin, C. (2017). Openness and Praxis: Exploring the Use of Open Educational Practices in Higher Education. *The International Review of Research in Open and Distributed Learning, 18*(5). https://doi.org/10.19173/irrodl.v18i5.3096.

Farrow, R. (2017). Open Education and Critical Pedagogy. *Learning, Media and Technology, 42,* 130–146.

Freire, P. (1974). *Education for Critical Consciousness.* London: Bloomsbury Academic.

HEPI. (2017). *Where Next for Widening Participation and Fair Access? New Insights from Leading Thinkers.* HEPI. http://www.hepi.ac.uk/2017/08/14/next-widening-participation-fair-access/. Accessed 1 June 2018.

Jordan, K. (2015). Massive Open Online Course Completion Rates Revisited: Assessment, Length and Attrition. *International Review of Research in Open and Distributed Learning, 16*(3), 341–358.

MIT OpenCourseWare. (n.d.). Milestones|MIT OpenCourseWare|Free Online Course Materials. Retrieved from https://ocw.mit.edu/about/milestones/
Open Education Handbook/History of Open Education. (n.d.). Retrieved from https://en.wikibooks.org/wiki/Open_Education_Handbook/History_of_open_education
Pitt, R. (2015). Mainstreaming Open Textbooks: Educator Perspectives on the Impact of OpenStax College Open Textbooks. *The International Review of Research in Open and Distributed Learning, 16*(4). https://doi.org/10.19173/irrodl.v16i4.2381.
UNESCO. Ljubljana OER Action Plan 2017 Adopted to Support Quality Open Educational Resources. https://en.unesco.org/news/ljubljana-oer-action-plan-2017-adopted-support-quality-open-educational-resources. Accessed 18 June 2018.
Watters, A. (2016). The Curse of the Monsters of Education Technology. Retrieved from http://monsters3.hackeducation.com/
Weller, M. (2014). *The Battle for Open: How Openness Won and Why It Doesn't Feel Like Victory*. London: Ubiquity Press.

6

Information Literacy, Digital Capability, and Individual Agency

Introduction: At the Intersection of Economy, Information, and Education

Thus far we have challenged the baleful influence of neoliberalisation on higher education and proposed a combination of open education and critical pedagogy as a means to restore the university to its rightful position as a public good in a democratic society. Our educational aim is for learners to develop a holistic awareness of themselves in relation to the powerful, but challengeable, socio-economic conditions shaping their lives. This aim is in addition to students attaining the knowledge and skills of their disciplinary studies at university. This transformative project should not be dismissed as mere idealism, at odds with the common sense desire for education to support the economic aspirations of individuals and society. Rather we are developing a critical logic, which balances the economic with the personal, social, and moral aims of education (Giroux 2000). To that end we argue that universities need to replenish a narrow and impoverished 'training for the neoliberal labour market' vision of pedagogy with a dynamic critical pedagogy and replace corporate management styles with a revitalised collegiality capable of bringing about the necessary strategic changes involved.

In the preceding chapters, we described our thinking in part through the lens of our Matrix (Chap. 3), which offers a tool for analysing university organisation. We also offered thoughts on the future of curriculum, wider participation, and open learning environments, in a context of digitally rich spaces, texts, practices, and learning patterns. In this chapter we begin with a focus on the Information Literacy quadrant of the Matrix and introduce notions of agency and personhood to the debate on the nature of digital capability in higher education. We will also draw some brief conclusions on the nature of critical pedagogy.

Information is a central concept in twenty-first-century political economy as (i) an economic resource, (ii) a powerful factor in political decision-making, and (iii) a key cultural resource for learning, employment, citizenship, and everyday life in general (Mason 2015; Anderson and Johnston 2016; Buckland 2017). These prominent features of information are highlighted by the rise of the Internet, search engines, mobile technology, social media, and other characteristics entailed in the idea of a 'Fourth Industrial Revolution' (Peters and Bulut 2011; Boutang 2012; Schawab 2016). Also the Internet is inherently porous and provides a core information space and digital apparatus, which cuts across borders and which people can use to access knowledge, learn, communicate, try to make money, and engage in political discourse. Thus the Internet experience is open and not restricted to formal academic usage and is relevant to our concerns with wider access, participation, and open education. Consequently, any conceptualisation of the digital university, in these dynamic socio-economic and technological circumstances, needs to have a means of conceptualising the informational components of digital capability and suggesting approaches to enhancing student experience in course designs and pedagogical practices.

From our critical perspective, learning influenced by such circumstances needs to include a critical understanding of how the information industry works and relates to the socio-political domain, as well as developing specific expertise in digital and other information sources, channels, and texts. We suggest that Information Literacy provides a sound disciplinary basis to develop such critical learning and design-relevant pedagogy to develop student expertise. The starting point is to acknowledge that Information Literacy is a substantial subject area in its own right, and the following indicative review of literature is intended as a basic guide to an evolving discipline. That said, our view is that the notion of Information Literacy remains unfamiliar in strategic discussion of universities, certainly by comparison to notions of learning environment and curriculum/course design, and we believe this imbalance needs to be redressed in our consideration of what it means to be a digital university. We suggest that educational developers, academics, technologists, and strategic leaders should all make themselves more familiar with this field in order to balance and complement their understanding of digital technologies, TEL, and related areas such as digital and media literacies.

Information Literacy and Related Literacies: Enhancing Learning in a Digital University

Information Literacy can be described concisely as:

> ... the adoption of appropriate information behavior to obtain, through whatever channel or medium, information well fitted to information needs, leading to wise and ethical use of information in society. (Johnston and Webber 2003)

This description posits the research field of information behaviour (Wilson 2010) as the frame for personal and collaborative information activity whilst also highlighting the importance of Information Literacy to society, the workplace, and the economy. The description encompasses (i) a narrow conception in terms of the techniques individuals use to access sources, formulate searches, and select relevant information, irrespective of whether the information is in digital or other forms; and (ii) the holistic aspect of the description referring to "wise and ethical use of information in society", which expresses Information Literacy's potential as a force for progressive change. We suggest that both senses of the term need to be on strategic agendas for curriculum change and reflected in practice at course and classroom level in universities.

By contrast Information Literacy in universities has typically been associated with libraries and classroom settings, often positioned as a 'study skill' in the early stages of degree studies, with an emphasis on basic skills development in relation to knowledge of sources, searching skills, and evaluation of found materials. The main educational benefits being associated with forms of assessed coursework, such as essay writing, combined with the more general aim of helping students extend and refresh their subject knowledge. In this narrow view, Information Literacy occupies a subordinate place in relation to the main academic tasks, and its pedagogy has typically been circumscribed to brief 'one slot shot' classroom interventions, backed up by reliance on digital resources made available online as part of a local VLE. Typically, any systematic strategy to align the development of Information Literacy to epistemological development, and a more critical consciousness, is missing from university degree courses (Anderson and Johnston 2016). This limited state of development is insufficient and unsustainable in a twenty-first-century world where information is a key socio-economic and political resource, readily available via the Internet, albeit controlled and shaped by global tech monopolies combining interests in media, publishing, online services, searching, social media platforms, business enterprise, finance, and political influence.

The term Information Literacy is generally credited to Paul Zurkowski (1974), and his paper locates it in an economic frame. Given his role as president of an information industry association, he was understandably keen to market his member's wares, so his call for widespread development of Information Literacy makes good sense. However, he was equally aware of the relevance of his ideas to free speech, democracy, and education and discusses the implications in some detail. Spitzer et al. (1998) provide a useful overview of the early years of development, charting the systematic harnessing of Zurkowski's ideas to the democratic process, education, and librarianship in particular. Webber and Johnston (2000) set out generative perspectives for the twenty-first century. They proposed Information Literacy as a soft applied discipline for the emerging information era (2005) and elaborated the idea of an information literate university (2006). Their revisited and updated perspectives (2017) highlight the positioning of Information Literacy as a discipline for an information culture, emphasise the importance of interdisciplinary to its development, and propose a connection to human development and social change by adopting a lifecourse framing of Information Literacy.

Lloyd and Williamson (2008) and Lloyd (2010) emphasised the contextual nature of Information Literacy, an approach which chimed well with phenomenographic and other qualitative studies and also widened the horizon beyond education to encompass other settings and communities of practice. Anderson and Johnston combined Information Literacy with social epistemology and insights from psychology to create a broader horizon for the twenty-first century, uniting pedagogic strategies for improving learning in universities with a clear alignment to the social value of information and knowledge as democratic resources. A key reference is the 10th anniversary issue of the Journal of Information Literacy (2017), which draws together reflective papers from major international scholars. A relevant emerging strand is a focus on the notion of critical Information Literacy (Elmborg (2012), Baer (2013), Smith (2013), Downey (2016), Nicholson and Seale (2017)). This strand draws down on radical educational scholars such as Freire and argues for opposition to capitalist managerialism in library and information work.

Higher education has been a key sector for developing Information Literacy. Bruce (1997) published a seminal work based on phenomenographic research, which neatly conjoined Information Literacy with an established approach to pedagogic research in higher education—an approach developed by Lupton (2003), Edwards (2006), and Boon et al. (2007) and extended in a comparative study by Limberg et al. (2012). The phenomenographic strand has grown steadily over several decades and has provided the basis for a number of doctoral studies in Europe, the UK, Australia, the USA, and parts of Asia, thereby locating Information Literacy firmly in pedagogical scholarship around the world.

Whilst the 'one-shot-slot' approach to teaching remains in evidence as the default approach to pedagogy in universities, much work has been done to escape the limitations of this form. The following give a flavour of the richness and variety of contributions: Johnston and Webber (2003) reviewed the status of Information Literacy in higher education and gave a case study of their credit-bearing module; Lupton (2004) illuminated student concepts and practice of information and learning; Hepworth and Walton (2009) and Kuhlthau et al. (2015) provided in-depth accounts of Information Literacy in relation to inquiry-based learning; Webber and Johnston (2013) detailed the connections with the theory and practice of lifelong learning; Anderson and Johnston (2016) applied insights from cognitive psychology and the theory of transformative learning to elaborate a model of Information Literacy linked to student epistemological development at university. Consequently, a rich source of strategic and practical guidance is available to lecturers and developers to support their efforts in curriculum enhancement and course redesign.

Several recent national developments are worthy of note. The American College and Research Libraries Association (ACRL)-revised Framework for Information Literacy (2015 – Check Ref.) is a major revision of their earlier standards and is based on Meyer and Land's (2003) pedagogical theory of Threshold Concepts as opposed to ACRL's earlier skills-based model. This is a major departure from previous thinking and practice and is having significant impact within disciplines and at course level in universities in the USA (Godbey et al. 2017). In the UK, Secker and Coonan's (2013) work on a new curriculum framework for Information Literacy is a major attempt to provide a structure to re-design courses and integrate Information Literacy in the curriculum.

UNESCO has made a number of international contributions in the form of proclamations and statements from expert panels (2003, 2005, 2006) and reports on the future of the Internet (2016). UNESCO's approach emphasises human rights, particularly freedom of speech, and lifelong learning. Horton (2007) provides a useful basic account of aspects of Information Literacy aimed at busy senior leaders and managers, which will be of interest to university leaders. However, Horton's pragmatic and simplified approach must be balanced by a reading of the research and scholarly literature. A significant development from UNESCO has been the convergence of its work on Information Literacy and Media Education, to form a new strand of Media and Information Literacy (2016). This new strand offers a potentially productive focus for the kind of critical analysis and challenge we wish to direct at the intersections of economy, education, information, and media. There is also scope to engage with established academic centres such as the Glasgow Media Group.

We suggest that an understanding of Media and Information Literacy is a promising entry point for learners to develop critical consciousness of society's contradictions and inequalities. For example, in situations where much information is provided by open public media (both mass and social), it is essential to develop an understanding of how meaning is constructed within a given media and communicated for particular purposes. This project entails traditional academic values of validity and accuracy of information, but perhaps more importantly raises questions of motive and intention. Thus it would not be sufficient to be able to expose 'fake news' by seeking out the correct information, important as that is, it would also be necessary to analyse why and how such information entities had been constructed, particularly in relation to the overarching socio-political themes and contexts involved.

In summary, the trajectory of Information Literacy over the decades has been from the practical and professional to the reflective and academic. The focus is now very much on people in a networked world and their information behaviour in a variety of settings, by contrast to earlier concentration on functional activity in libraries and basic educational applications. Also there is now no shortage of sources and examples to draw on for strategic guidance approaches to practical improvements. Information Literacy as described above is not a simple assemblage of digital and information skills, which can be 'picked up' within a course of study, albeit with some modest interventions by librarians and others. Rather Information Literacy is more usefully conceived as situated epistemological practice within a given context, which can be understood using a variety of theoretical approaches and research methods, and developed by more sophisticated pedagogical strategies.

A full academic development of Information Literacy in the curriculum would in the first instance involve networks of disciplinary teachers working with librarians, technology experts, and educational developers on course redesigns. The aim would be to ensure students had the requisite capability to find, manage, and critique information in varied texts, including digital texts, whilst achieving progressively more sophisticated epistemological and situational awareness. In this framing Information Literacy can be seen as a major strategic aspect of the digital university, albeit an aspect in need of serious attention. It can also be discussed productively in the context of other complementary strands of interest in university learning and teaching, which use literacy as a descriptor.

Related Literacies: Media, Digital, and Academic

Several important strands of scholarship and practice share an association with notions of literacy (Lankshear and Knobel 2011; Coleman and Lea 2015). They enhance our understanding of learner engagement with disciplinary content and academic practices in the university. However there has been limited overlap between these scholarly communities, and attention tends to be located in different practice zones including librarians, academic skills tutors, technical support staff, lecturers, and students. This is unfortunate as they all contribute to our understanding of university education in the digital age and offer insights into areas of the student experience including engagement with digital and other information sources, understanding the nature of TEL, and engaging with digital study practices. A synthesis would help but may not be possible without research-based academic development work around the concepts and their location in pedagogical practice across the disciplines.

Koltay (2011) reviews relationships between the media and literacy in relation to the Internet and digital technologies, by analysing relationships between media literacy, Information Literacy, and digital literacy. He presents these as the most developed concepts used in understanding communication media in the digital age. From our perspective, Koltay approaches the digital university from the 'outside', in that he is focused on the global media-sphere within which universities are immersed. He notes a growth of academic interest in literacy as a consequence of this new digital media-sphere, committed to understanding how people engage with digital media. The approaches taken assume an evolution of literacy from verbal, visual, and print modes to converge on the digital. In addition, he notes the interdisciplinary nature of scholarly attention including literacy, culture studies, race and gender studies, literary theory, psychology, library and information studies, linguistics, and media studies.

All of these theoretical and methodological approaches seek understanding of how people engage with digital affordances and the nature of their epistemological and cultural relations.

To summarise, his analysis of the three 'literacies' would be beyond the scope of this chapter. However certain common features can be identified:

* Linear process models including access to sources, searching, evaluation of content, creation, and communication of new content
* Differentiation between technologies, content, and literacy
* Multiple modes, forms, conditions, and contexts for engagement with media, digital technologies, and information
* Concerns over ownership, regulation, rights, and democratic oversight
* Focus on understanding how individuals and groups make sense of the various new media

From our perspective several conclusions can be drawn from Koltay's review. Firstly, the three literacies vary in their emphasis on the primacy of their three key words—media, digital, and information. Secondly, the nature of this emerging field is porous, and that porosity seems to be a property of the Internet, the media-sphere, and the academic fields implicated in understanding the territory. These are key aspects of the potential debate on the nature and composition of 'literacy' areas. Let us develop the perspective via two important contributions to the discussion of the digital university: Goodfellow and Lea (2013); and Gourlay and Oliver (2018). These edited collections of essays offer a rich source of topics, which combined with insights from Information Literacy could form agendas for research-based educational and organisational development.

Goodfellow and Lea (2013) provide useful perspectives with the main focus on learning, scholarship, and technology—arguably a staff/institution provider emphasis. Unlike Koltay they do not acknowledge Information Literacy. However, they identify a number of conceptual reference points, which should be part of any educational development strategy. Firstly, on Literacy key concepts include authorship, practice(s), hybrid texts, and openness. Secondly, on the Digital, concepts include tradition versus the new, sociocultural practices, sociotechnical systems, assemblages, textual modes, economic utility, digital text-making, innovation and uncertainty, future visioning, and digital age. Thirdly, on the University, concepts include value and trust; power and control; permeable boundaries; engagement; digital natives; ICTs, learning management systems, blended learning, and learning analytics; revenue and efficiency versus pedagogy; and OERs. The three major constructs—literacy, the digital, and the nature of the university—offer foci for strategic agenda setting, whilst the topics clustered around the three offer thought-lines to be explored and innovated.

Gourlay and Oliver (2018) focus on the literacy of academic learning and identify important features of the digital university. The emphasis is on the nature and practice of student engagement with the digital university. By contrast to Goodfellow and Lea, they acknowledge and discuss Information Literacy (P48/50) but have a restricted perspective emphasising the library contribution. In particular, they discuss SCONUL's 7 Pillars of Information Literacy model (2011), which they critique as being overly linear in its depiction of complex systems and patterns of Information Literacy. We would tend to agree with their assessment of that model, although it is a useful focal point for initial discussion of Information Literacy by staff and students unfamiliar with the concept. However, they do not reference arguably more significant contributions such the ACRL Framework or Secker and Coonan, which became available in the mid-2000s.

Both collections offer useful insights into the nature of digital capacity and pedagogical development, and contribute options for both pedagogical and organisational development in universities. However, it may be at present that the literacies position is too narrowly specialised, a scholarly bubble within which experts elaborate their fields and, justifiably, lament that not enough attention has been paid to their insights by university management or colleagues at the meso/micro levels of pedagogical practice. That said, if these perspectives were extended and combined in the form of a major effort of educational development, and aligned with insights from Information Literacy, we might begin to get somewhere in terms of a shift in awareness, strategic thinking, and practical change. The question of disciplinary traditions, differences, and sensibilities would need to be part of such a programme and could usefully explore insights from, for example, Trowler et al. (2014).

Critical Perspectives on the Nature of Digital Capability: Institutional Agendas for Learning and Student Skills

The discussion of Information Literacy and related literacies provides guidance for strategic thinking about digital capability and ideas for curriculum reform. Firstly, by offering a rich field of ideas to counter narrow thinking about digital capability. Secondly, by expanding the idea of the digital to include a fuller account of the informational dimension of the Internet and digital technologies. This expansion can be enhanced by the inclusion of emerging ideas from Media and Information Literacy. Thirdly, by offering a foothold in practice around the efforts of librarians, lecturers, educational developers, technologists, academic literacy people, and their practice communities. In short a proto 'workforce' is available to engage with the development of the digital university. However, at present staff expertise appears concentrated at micro and meso levels, is somewhat scattered between academic and service units, and is often deployed in time-limited projects. We suggest a combined academic and organisational development approach involving a whole university span of action focused on whole course renovation is needed to reverse the trend of uncoordinated effort displayed in current arrangements.

In advocating this approach, our sense of digital capability is holistic and goes beyond the boundaries of student technological competence, existing subject curricula, and the current responsibilities of librarians, archivists, student counsellors, and others. To take a practical example, being 'search engine savvy' is arguably a basic digital capacity for all students and citizens. So the support and improvement of search engine expertise offers an initial, concrete focus for advancing digital capability in universities and more widely. How this objective can be related to effective pedagogical practice, and how it is valued in the student learning experience, are questions for educational developers as they seek to influence institutional agendas and support pedagogical change.

As a basic approach though, process models of searching drawn from Information Literacy (source, search, select processes) offer a practical means to conceptualise that aspect of search engine expertise and shape interventions at course level. However, such a narrowly described conception of Internet engagement will not necessarily help students to understand the deeper organisational structures of digital resources or the personal dynamics of the information behaviour involved, or the nuances of academic 'literacy' and culture in different disciplines. In contemplating the nature and fostering of such expertise, there is also a need to address the wider social implications of understanding how search engines function as key components of the digital information economy and how global tech businesses like Google operate. Meeting this requirement means going beyond particular curricula and professional silos and engaging critically with the characteristics of how digital business is conducted in a neoliberal political economy.

A possible intermediate framework is provided by the Jisc Digital Capability programme offering heuristic models to describe a number of interrelated areas of digital capability, and provides resources to support staff development and mount practical interventions in learning and teaching. For example, it would be possible to use the Jisc materials in combination with models from Information Literacy and Digital Literacy to analyse existing disciplinary courses and redesign them to make better pedagogical use of the array of technological affordances available. Part of the Jisc Guide to Developing Organizational Digital Capabilities case study from Glasgow Caledonian University (2017) focuses on flexible course design and how the Jisc tools are being used by staff to benchmark their curriculum design and also to gain an insight into their own digital capabilities. This approach is also providing additional information for the academic development team for the design and development of staff support resources and to inform wider strategic decision-making around technology investment.

For example, an academic staff survey highlighted that there was inconsistency across the university in relation to staff technology provision. Many staff did not have microphones or headsets and so were unable to provide audio feedback to students or effectively utilise web conferencing software in their teaching. This led to a significant investment by the university to provide all academic staff with new laptops, 2 x monitors, and headsets with built-in microphones. This was part of a wider initiative around assessment and feedback which included a programme of staff development around effective use of a number of institutional assessment and feedback systems, working towards providing all assessment and feedback online.

To summarise, digital capability is not simply a technical matter to be managed by training in effective searching, or other specific aspects of digital systems, but entails wider educational and social concerns. Knowing more about how it comes about that certain links 'come up' before others in an online search adds to a student's ability to evaluate found information, but should also relate to the student's consciousness of the potential for large-scale tech utilities to have disproportionate influence in digital society and political economy by their capacity to 'manage' information in certain ways. Both issues provide focal points for university curriculum development and pedagogical practice. At present our experience is that the former is perhaps more common as an aspect of intervention by librarians, lecturers, and support staff at the micro level of the classroom, whilst the latter is unlikely to be addressed outside courses with a particular disciplinary focus on the issues in relation to academic specialisms such as media studies, information science, sociology, and politics. We suggest that this is not a sustainable situation and requires systematic revision at all levels of university decision-making and pedagogical activity to achieve the full scale of transformation needed.

Agency and Personhood

Our aim in this section is to explore how the preceding perspectives might be reflected in the lives and personal development of students and the implications for organisational strategy and pedagogy. We will do this by offering descriptions of agency and personhood and relating them to aspects of the digital experience at university. This is important because without a sense of personal agency, and the scope for self-managed development, discussion of 'the Internet' or 'digital capability' can be quite systems-driven and separate from the everyday reality of students. To begin with, we view agency as a social, as well as an individual, phenomenon. From a critical perspective, agency can be characterised as self-awareness, resistance to oppressive conditions, commitment to a better self and society, and cultural engagement. We view personhood as a holistic construct allied to agency, which incorporates the totality of experience and meaning and should be considered in the frame of a person's lifecourse. Exploring agency and personhood therefore takes us well beyond simplistic notions of digital natives, Prensky (2001), and beyond White and Le Cornu's (2011) critique of Prensky's crude personification of the relations between the personal and the digital.

Developing agency and personhood is therefore a part of the university experience and demands a personal commitment from individuals to identify the forces influencing their lives and create the ability to challenge negative forces. Consequently, agency is understood to an extent in terms of democratic engagement, as students explore the political discourse of their times as it effects them and as they wish to steer its future direction. This exploration is as much about reflection on experiences of value, belief, and meaning, including the possibility of change in deeply held perspectives, as it is about the subject content of disciplinary education. This is very different from a notion of agency based in purely economic aspirations, as tends to be the assumption of the neoliberal 'value for money' transactional model of student engagement with university. Personhood in our sense of the term is at the core of a critical idea of what a university is for. Pedagogy therefore needs to embrace these holistic understandings of learning and render it visible in course designs and pedagogical practice.

At present the balance of design activity in university courses is impoverished in these respects and seems to assume (i) a restricted idea of agency as a function of long-standing disciplinary traditions of learning and teaching and (ii) the narrower models of education for employability, which have grown in strength over the last four decades. Consequently, students are guided through the main features of their discipline, as in the past, but within a state-driven culture, which defines benefit not so much as academic excellence in its own right, but as a pathway to enhanced graduate income. Under these conditions, little attention is paid to more holistic and critical development of students as persons and active citizens in a democracy, although specifics like improved searching, or simply becoming 'digital savvy' (Chatterton & Rebbeck 2015), are quite feasible under such conditions, provided systematic effort and resource are applied.

How might this situation be improved upon? Let us begin by posing the question—how do students form the opinions and beliefs that define their sense of self and agency in society? Obviously taking part in a degree course should provide opportunities to reflect on the beliefs that give meaning to their lives, traditionally that is what a university is for. More specifically in terms of online digital contexts, do they have a theory of how media, including the Internet and social media, work as potential influences on their personal identity and behaviour as well as provide information and communication capacity? For example, do they understand how algorithmic choice, embedded in software codes, can channel the choice of online content 'found' by users searching for information to the advantage of content providers?

We know that searching for information is a fundamental digital capability and plays a role in shaping subject knowledge and understanding. More so if aligned to a conscious epistemological growth from basic dualism to complex evaluative relativism (Anderson and Johnston 2016). So, we suggest that insights and strategies from Information Literacy and the related literacies could extend and enhance the fundamental digital experience of searching for subject information to encompass critical analysis not only of acquired information, but also of the digital media-sphere itself and how it is framed by the present monopolistic and manipulative practices of its owners. The Stanford Civic Online Reasoning project (2016), which bases its epistemological development strategy on enhancing student capacity to evaluate information on the Internet, is a substantial example of educational development work to engage students in critiquing the links between media, information, democracy, and critical thinking.

The enhanced digital capability demonstrated in the Stanford project is a useful pointer towards forms of learning experience, which can be developed within disciplines and across the curriculum. In practice it would be possible to treat individual searching as a micro level of activity, and a whole class of searchers involved in a project takes the activity to a meso level. Suitably designed and supported such initiatives could constitute not only an enhancement of the learner's capacity to evaluate new information and incorporate it in understanding of disciplinary topics, but also a potential challenge to the person's accepted system of beliefs and values. There is also a macro level where all the searching in a university is not just a call on local infrastructure, but more importantly a channel into the global Internet sphere and a challenge to develop digital understanding. At this level it would be strategically valuable to review the terms of institutional mission statements and consider amending them to include variants on the account of agency, personhood, intellectual development, and digital acuity outlined here as part of the move to become a digital university.

Critical Pedagogy in a Digital Age: What Is the Internet for?

On one reading of the contemporary digital learning map, the agenda might appear to be set by Google—apparently supplanting core features of the learning experience such as communications, libraries, email, and topic searches. Also Google Scholar opens up academic research to wider audiences, and Google Docs provides a platform for co-authoring of texts, thereby offering enhanced opportunities for learning within and outwith university communities. Search engines open the door to a web of information, media, people, and the opportunity to construct new resources. These affordances raise issues of purposive searching, skilled performance, evaluation of findings, and their contribution to assessable formats, all of which need to be reflected in course design and pedagogical practice. There is also the question of the wider social significance of the Internet's influence on public opinion and political decisions and, crucially, who owns the net and what digital rights do citizens have.

Whilst the Cambridge Analytica saga of 2018 and the current moral panics over 'fake news', 'filter bubbles' (Pariser 2011), and 'echo chambers' (Sunstein 2007) may fade with time or be replaced with new digital attention grabbers, the insights they provide into the often opaque relationships between information, economy, education, and democracy should be retained and critiqued. Investigating how these dimensions 'fit' within a neoliberal political economy is surely as important to developing digital capability as any specific programme to inculcate efficient searching practice within a given disciplinary course of study. In short, there is ample scope for curriculum development and change in pedagogical practice around generative topics such as fake news arising from complex conceptions of digital capability. Such development would be in addition to the current approach of TEL, and could be built on particular course re-design projects.

In order to meet our agenda of developing digital capacity and learner efficacy, we advocate the extension of critical pedagogy from the classroom to encompass the Internet and digital media. To that end we subscribe to Giroux's (2000) view that critical pedagogy:

> ... asserts that students can engage their own learning from a position of agency and in so doing can actively participate in narrating their identities through a culture of questioning that opens up a space of translation between the private and the public while changing the forms of self and social recognition.

Giroux relates notions of learner self-definition to notions of using knowledge to critique and challenge their world, which echoes the arguments we have been making. Also, the disciplinary field of Information Literacy, in concert with practice drawn from related literacies, offers a powerful strategic agenda for curriculum development aligned with pragmatic interventions in course design and pedagogy. Media and Information Literacy is included as a potential further area for a curriculum development, which embraces the Internet but is not controlled by it.

Conclusions

In this chapter we have argued the need for universities to take information and related literacies much more seriously than has been the case. To this end we encourage academic developers and others to adopt a wider perspective on digital capability to include Information and related literacies and to develop large-scale change initiatives. Further ideas on how this effort might be focused are developed in subsequent chapters of this book.

References

Anderson, A., & Johnston, B. (2016). *From Information Literacy to Social Epistemology: Insights from Psychology*. Kidlington: Chandos Publishing.

Association of College and Research Libraries. (2015). *Framework for Information Literacy for Higher Education*. http.ala.org/acrl/standards/ilframework. Last Accessed 3 Feb 2017.

Baer, A. (2013). Critical Information Literacy in the College Classroom: Exploring Scholarly Knowledge Production Through the Digital Humanities. In L. Gregory & S. Higgins (Eds.), *Information Literacy and Social Justice: Radical Professional Praxis* (pp. 99–119). Los Angeles: Library Juice Press.

Boon, S., Johnston, B., & Webber, S. (2007). A Phenomenographic Study of English Faculty's Conceptions of Information Literacy. *Journal of Documentation, 63*(2), 204–228.

Boutang, Y. M. (2012). *Cognitive Capitalism*. Cambridge: Polity.

Bruce, C. (1997). *The Seven Faces of Information Literacy*. Adelaide: AUSLIB Press.

Buckland, M. (2017). *Information and Society*. Cambridge, MA/London: The MIT Press.

Chatterton, P., & Rebbeck, G. (2015). *Technology for Employability*. Jisc.

Downey, A. (2016). *Critical Information Literacy: Foundations, Inspiration and Ideas*. Sacramento: Library Juice.

Edwards, S. (2006). *Panning for Gold: Information Literacy and the Net Lenses Model*. Adelaide: Auslib Press.

Elmborg, J. (2012). Critical Information Literacy: Definitions and Challenges. In C. W. Wilkinson & C. Bruch (Eds.), *Transforming Information Literacy Programs: Intersecting Frontiers of Self, Library Culture, and Campus Community* (pp. 75–95). Chicago: Association of College & Research Libraries.

Giroux, H. A. (2000). Public Pedagogy and the Responsibility of Intellectuals: Youth, Littleton, and the Loss of Innocence. *JAC, 20*(1), 9–42.

Glasgow Media Group. (n.d.). Retrieved from http://www.glasgowmediagroup.org/

Godbey, S., Wainscott, S. B., & Goodman, X. (2017). *Disciplinary Applications of Information Literacy Threshold Concepts*. Chicago: Association of College and Research Libraries, A Division of the American Library Association.
Hepworth, M., & Walton, G. (2009). *Teaching Information Literacy for Inquiry Based Learning*. Oxford: Chandos Publishing.
Horton, F. W. (2007). *Understanding Information Literacy: A Primer*. UNESCO Information for All Programme. Edited by the Information Society Division, Communications and Information Sector. Paris: UNESCO.
Jisc. (2017). *Glasgow Caledonian University: A Focus on Flexible Curriculum Design*. http://repository.jisc.ac.uk/6638/1/DigicapGlasgowCaledonianUniversity.pdf. Last Accessed 2 Mar 2018.
Johnston, B., & Webber, S. (2003). Information Literacy in Higher Education: A Review and Case Study. *Studies in Higher Education, 28*(3), 335–352.
Kuhlthau, C., Maniotes, L., & Caspari, A. (2015). *Guided Inquiry: Learning in the 21st Century*. Abington: Libraries Unlimited/Marston Books.
Limberg, L., Sundin, S., & Talja, S. (2012). Three Theoretical Perspectives on Information Literacy. *HUMAN IT, 11*(2), 93–130.
Lloyd, A. (2010). Framing Information Literacy as Information Practice: Site Ontology and Practice Theory. *Journal of Documentation, 66*(2), 245–258.
Lloyd, A., & Williamson, K. (2008). Towards an Understanding of Information Literacy in Context: Implications for Research. *Journal of Librarianship and Information Science, 40*(1), 3–12.
Lupton, M. (2004). *The Learning Connection: Information Literacy and the Student Experience*. Adelaide: Auslib Press.
Mason, P. (2015). *PostCapitalism: A Guide to Our Future*. London: Alan Lane.
Meyer, J. H. F., & Land, R. (2003). Threshold Concepts and Troublesome Knowledge: Linkages to Ways of Thinking and Practising. In C. Rust (Ed.), *Improving Student Learning – Theory and Practice Ten Years On* (pp. 412–424). Oxford: Oxford Centre for Staff and Learning Development (OCSLD).
Nicholson, K. P., & Seale, M. (Eds.). (2017). *The Politics of Theory and the Practice of Critical Librarianship*. Sacramento: Library Juice Press.
Pariser, E. (2011). *The Filter Bubble: How the New Personalized Web Is Changing What We Read and How We Think*. New York: Penguin Books.
Peters, M. A., & Bulut, E. (Eds.). (2011). *Cognitive Capitalism, Education and Digital Labour*. New York: Peter Lang.
Prensky, M. (2001). Digital Natives, Digital Immigrants, Part 1. *On the Horizon, 9*, 1–6.

Schwab, K. (2016). *The Fourth Industrial Revolution and How to Respond.* https://www.weforum.org/agenda/2016/01/the-fourth-industrial-revolution-what-it-means-and-how-to-respond/. Last Accessed 16 Nov 2018.

Secker, J., & Coonan, E. (2013). In J. Secker & E. Coonan (Eds.), *Rethinking Information Literacy: A Practical Framework for Supporting Learning.* London: Facet Publishing.

Smith, L. (2013). Towards a Model of Critical Information Literacy Instruction for the Development of Political Agency. *Journal of Information Literacy, 7*(2), 15–32. http://dx.doi.org/10.11645/7.2.1809.

Sunstein, C. R. (2007). *Republic.com 2.0.* Princeton: Princeton University Press.

Trowler, P., Saunders, M., & Bamber, V. (Eds.). (2014). *Tribes and Territories in the 21st Century: Rethinking the Significance of Disciplines in Higher Education.* London: Routledge.

UNESCO. (2003). *The Prague Declaration – "Towards an Information Literate Society".* Retrieved from http://portal.unesco.org/ci/en/ev.php-URL_ID=19636&URL_DO=DO_PRINTPAGE&URL_SE CTION=201.html

UNESCO. (2005). *The Alexandria Proclamation on Information Literacy and Lifelong Learning.* Retrieved from http://www.ifla.org/III/wsis/BeaconInfSoc.html

UNESCO. (2006). *High-Level Colloquium on Information Literacy and Lifelong Learning.* Retrieved from http://www.ifla.org/III/wsis/High-Level-Colloquium.pdf

UNESCO. (2016). *Riga Recommendations on Media and Information Literacy in a Shifting Media and Information Landscape.* Retrieved from http://www.unesco.org/new/fileadmin/MULTIMEDIA/HQ/CI/CI/pdf/Events/riga_recommendations_on_media_and_information_literacy.pdf

Webber, S., & Johnston, B. (2000). Conceptions of Information Literacy: New Perspectives and Implications. *Journal of Information Science, 26*(6), 381–397. https://doi.org/10.1177/016555150002600602.

Webber, S., & Johnston, B. (2006). Working Towards the Information Literate University. In G. Walton & A. Pope (Eds.), *Information Literacy: Recognising the Need. Staffordshire University, Stoke-on-Trent: 17 May 2006* (pp. 47–58). Oxford: Chandos.

Webber, S., & Johnston, B. (2013). Transforming Information Literacy for Higher Education in the 21st Century: A Lifelong Learning Approach. In M. Hepworth & G. Walton (Eds.), *Developing People's Information Capabilities: Fostering Information Literacy in Educational, Workplace and Community Contexts.* Bingley: Emerald.

Webber, S., & Johnston, B. (2017). Information Literacy: Conceptions, Context and the Formation of a Discipline. *Journal of Information Literacy, 11*(1). https://doi.org/10.11645/11.1.2205.

White, D. S., & le Cornu, A. (2011, September 2011). Visitors and Residents: A New Typology for Online Engagement. *First Monday, 16*(9-5), P1–10.

Wilson, T. (2010). Fifty Years of Information Behaviour Research. *Bulletin of the Association for Information Science and Technology, 36*(3), 27–34. https://doi.org/10.1002/bult.2010.1720360308.

Zurkowski, P. (1974). *The Information Services Environment: Relationships and Priorities*. Washington, DC: National Commission on Libraries and Information Science.

7

Digitally Enriched Learning Spaces

In this chapter we will define and explore in detail three key components of a typical university institutional learning environment—physical and digital, pedagogical and social, enquiry and scholarship—with a particular focus on how we design and construct learning spaces. We adopt as a starting point the view that "A learning space should be able to motivate learners and promote learning as an activity, support collaborative as well as formal practice, provide a personalised and inclusive environment, and be flexible in the face of changing needs" (Jisc 2006, p. 3). It is within such spaces that learners experience agency and develop both discipline-specific knowledge and critical awareness of society's wider digital environment. Navigating a digitally enriched learning space is, therefore, a fusion of technological acuity and epistemological growth leading to an enriched sense of self and society.

We take the stance that any successful formal learning environment in HE is one where there is an appropriate balance between the physical and the digital, and that even within wholly online courses and contexts, the student and educator will have a physical location which will enable (or not) effective participation with the digital environment. Undoubtedly the ubiquity of mobile technologies and smart devices is allowing for greater flexibility of physical location; but they also create extra demands in the physical campus. There is also an increasing concern for where student-generated digital resources and artefacts are located within the institutional and wider learning environment, and how long they 'live'. Critically, as blended learning becomes the norm for campus-based HE, we need to move beyond the technological to critically question the social and pedagogical development—and sustainability—of our formal learning environments. This would necessarily include blended learning as a form of digital enrichment embedded in both the academic development process and strategic statements of the university, as we noted in Chap. 2 in relation to the Monash University example of an institutional learning strategy.

In offering a critical exploration of digitally enriched learning spaces, we draw upon the work of theorists and researchers including Vermunt (2007) and Vermunt and Donche (2017) who identified a number of patterns, referred to as teaching-learning environments which influence effective student learning. These include preparing students for lifelong, self-regulated, cooperative, and work-based learning, fostering high-quality student learning, and within which the complexity of the problems dealt with increases gradually and systematically.

We also address the growing discourse that has emerged around effective research practice in the digital age, including digital scholarship. A key reference point here is the work of Weller (2011), which conceptualises the digital scholar, including the increasing role of networks and connections, the disconnect and tensions between traditional and new forms of self-publication platforms, and open scholarship. However, we seek to extend the notion of digital scholarship, and of being digital scholars, to students and the work they do within and through their institutional learning.

What Is a 'Learning Space'?

Before considering what a digitally enriched learning space might comprise, within the context of the digital university, we should first seek to answer the question 'What is a learning space?'. From a binary perspective that considers the physical and technological architecture of the university environment, we might define a 'learning space' as a physical or virtual space purposefully designed to support learning, and within which a range of learning and teaching activities are intended to occur. Within this binary perspective, lecture theatres, classrooms and laboratories, and the campus-based library are obvious examples of physical spaces designed for learning within the university, while the Virtual Learning Environment and synchronous virtual classroom are obvious digital spaces designed for learning.

However, this distinction is too simplistic. It does not account for the university campus as an environment within which there are multiple spaces and locations, both formal and informal, where individual and collaborative learning activities, both formal and informal, can occur. It also excludes the physical locations outwith the university where students engage in formal learning activity, such as within the field, the community, or in the context of professional working environments. Similarly, by extension, a simple binary distinction between physical and digital spaces designed for learning within the university also excludes those digital spaces and environments that sit beyond the Virtual Learning Environment and other institutionally owned or endorsed technologies and platforms, but which many learners and academics are selecting to use to support key aspects of the learning experience.

In practice, the formal learning activity of our students is distributed across formal physical spaces designed for learning within the university, physical spaces outwith the university within which formal learning-related activity is expected to occur, and across institutionally owned and learner-selected digital spaces. Physical and digital spaces designed for learning by the university, and those which learners and academics self-select to situate their learning and collaboration within, also intersect with one another. This might lead us to consider the concept of 'learning space', in the context of the university and student learning, in a more holistic way that is congruent with the ethos of the original Conceptual Matrix for the digital university (MacNeill and Johnston 2012). That is, a conception of 'learning space' in which it is recognised that the student engages with a number of physical and digital locations and places, concurrently and contiguously as required, both for specific individual and collaborative learning tasks and across their programme of studies, and one in which we recognise that a 'learning space' can be created and defined through a spatial-temporal convergence of physical and digital spaces, learners, and learning activities.

We can take an even richer, more critical view of learning spaces, drawing upon the work of scholars including Maggi Savin-Baden (2008) who explores the distinction between created and unexpected learning spaces, dialogue as a learning space, and the interplay between learning spaces, academic identity, and the reinforcement, reproduction, and also the disruption of established academic and pedagogical practices. We can furthermore look towards what 'third place' or 'third space' thinking offers in defining the characteristics of third places in the wider community which are neither work nor home, and within which difference is embraced, social and economic status irrelevant, and which support conversation, civic and democratic engagement, and a sense of belonging (Oldenburg 1989). The implication of third space thinking and practice for education is one we will return to in the next chapter.

The understanding of the digital university which we seek to offer is one that is predicated upon more democratic participation within higher education and a further extension of higher education as a public good. Here the development and provision of learning spaces that are dialogic, participative, and inclusive, which disrupt established practices where needs be, and which wherever possible support civic engagement and action through the activities and outcomes of learning, is a vital requirement. The enabling and supporting role that the digital can play in instantiating or helping to create learning spaces of these kinds is one that transcends considerations about the specific technologies that are required, and is instead concerned with the range of ways in which digital tools, and digitally enabled approaches, enrich the opportunities for learner engagement, participation, and the expression of learning in ways which value individual and collective cognition and contributions. Achieving such a vision of the digital university will require organisational change, and associated academic development of the curriculum, to build on existing practice and explore different notions of pedagogy.

The University Learning Environment

Within the original Conceptual Matrix Fig. 3.3., p. 42 (MacNeill and Johnston 2012), the learning Environment dimension quadrant identified four key components or dimensions that comprise the learning environment at an institutional level: the physical and digital; pedagogical and social; research and inquiry; and staff and resources. The first three in particular have important implications in relation to how we position our thinking about learning spaces, and the place of the digital in providing, supporting, or enriching our learning spaces and supporting and enriching the learning that we intend is enabled within them.

Physical and Digital

The physical and digital aspects of the learning environment comprise in part, as indicated above, the physical and digital locations and spaces that have been purposefully designed to support learning, as well as the physical and digital spaces that learners self-select to situate their learning within (and which could include the social spaces of the university campus, and the personal digital spaces and networks which they have created or participate in).

When considering the physical learning environment of the university, we need to ask where and how the digital is currently or potentially to be located or embedded within that environment, and for what pedagogic purpose? Beyond digital connectivity on campus, and within our designed physical spaces for learning, there are further considerations around the means of connectivity, creativity, and communication and their 'ownership' with respect to learning and teaching. Do individual learners have equity of access to the means of connectivity, creativity, and communication in relation to the digital technologies that are either made available to them or which they may bring in to the physical learning environment? Furthermore, do they have agency in the use of those technologies to actively support and contribute to the collective learning experience in an inclusive, democratic way?

The malleability of our designed physical spaces for learning is also a limiting or enabling factor in supporting either a narrower or richer range of learning activities. The extent to which physical spaces for learning can be designed or rearranged to support interaction, participation, and collaboration is a fundamental concern both architecturally and pedagogically, with important implications for either reproducing pedagogical practices that have increasingly less relevance for an increasingly diverse student body (Savin-Baden 2008) or being able to develop more active, creative, and participative forms of engagement.

In pragmatic terms, within our physical learning spaces, this may be realised through having easily reconfigurable furniture and working surfaces, expanded writing spaces including writing walls, the availability of multiple power sockets, and the "decentring of the teaching podium as the sole focus of the direction of attention" (Pates and Sumner 2016, p. 161).

When considering the designed digital learning environment of the university, we need to scrutinise the ease and equity of access both on and off-campus. This includes parity of access to resources (e.g. library collections, software applications) and wider student support services (e.g. study skills advice, IT services, careers, counselling) for learners who are part-time, work-based, and studying predominantly or fully online. Where learners who are studying part-time and/or predominantly or fully online are concerned, equity or at the very least an equivalence of access to tutors, and meaningful opportunities to engage with peers, becomes a key concern with important pedagogical, wellbeing, and support implications.

Pedagogical and Social

We have begun to explore above important pedagogical considerations in relation to the university learning environment, and the physical and digital spaces for learning that exist therein. Before proceeding further, it would be judicious to expand upon the nature and kind of learning we believe our learning environments and spaces should be supporting.

In the broadest sense, we identify the need to support learning in which learners are engaged critically in exploring and connecting concepts and ideas, applying fundamental knowledge and ideas in the context of real and realistic tasks, in which coursework and assessment activities comprise authentic learning activities in their own right, and within which feedback is the basis of ongoing dialogue and reflection. Aligned with the fundamental belief that higher education learning ideally (but not ultimately) has to be about personal development, we identify in the above with established ideas around the desire to design learning environments, spaces, and activities that support deep learning (Entwistle 1997). From a constructivist theories perspective, deep learning is enabled through an increased emphasis on learner choice and negotiation in what is to be learned and produced, exposure to multiple perspectives and views, and socially situated learning (Jonassen and Land 2000).

Vermunt's (2007) and Vermunt and Donche's (2017) work also resonates strongly within the above context. In his exploration of how to design teaching-learning environments to support effective student learning, Vermunt (2007) discusses the importance of opportunities for self-regulated, cooperative, and work-based learning, to structure learning activities in order for the complexity of the problems being dealt with to increase gradually and systematically, and through these engagements to prepare students to support their own lifelong learning. In subsequently identifying four qualitatively different patterns to the way students learn (reproduction-orientated learning, meaning-directed learning, application-directed learning, and undirected learning), Vermunt and Donche (ibid.) underline the importance of learner conceptions and understandings of task and objective in relation to the expectations for their engagement and the nature of the resulting learning. An important implication here is the need for transparency in how we are expecting students to engage within their learning spaces, and in the context of specific learning activities, and to what end. Particularly so if we are seeking them to engage individually and collaboratively in ways that disrupt their expectations or previous experiences of what learning involves, including how much agency or control they have for and within their individual and collaborative learning activities. This would naturally extend to the need for transparency in how digital tools and learning spaces are to be harnessed within the context of specific learning tasks and activities.

However, the implications of how the digital is harnessed in the kind of learning we describe, or becomes an enabler for it, extend beyond supporting designed learning tasks in designed learning spaces. In Chap. 6, we discussed how today's learner is living within an increasingly networked, global, and digital society, within which there are challenges related to being able to contend with rapidly developing bodies of knowledge, proliferation of information and data, and being able to harness digital tools and spaces to communicate and collaborate and to curate, create, and share knowledge. On this latter point, we further contend that the need for the kind of realistic or authentic learning that we discuss above must extend to the digital tools and spaces we are asking our students to engage with, and how we are asking our students to engage within them. The critical question being: are we supporting our students to use digital technologies to communicate, create, and collaborate in ways that reflect how they will be required to engage digitally to communicate, create, and collaborate beyond the university, in professional and life-wide contexts? If the answer to that is no, then we are arguably failing to help our students in developing or further developing the digital skills and capabilities they will require not only for their chosen field of vocation or practice, but also for participation in wider society including for social and civic engagement, accessing services, and engaging in democratic processes.

In considering the social dimension to the institutional learning environment, and the learning that occurs within and through it, we must also consider where the digital can play a part in the distribution of learning across learning spaces, for example, in connecting a distributed group of learners in real time, or in extending or bending the opportunities for learning, dialogue, and collaboration beyond and around the periods of time where learners are able to come together in a physical or digital learning space or across a combination thereof.

There are also important implications in the above for how digital or digitally enriched learning spaces can enable cross-cohort and cross-disciplinary learning and allow learners to connect to peers within wider learning, scholarly, and professional communities. We will explore these broader possibilities in more detail in considering the concept of the Digitally Distributed Curriculum in the following chapter, but will return to the issue of learning that is distributed across learning spaces, and within distributed groups of students, further below.

Enquiry and Scholarship

The third dimension or component of the university learning environment that we wish to consider here was presented as research and enquiry in the original Conceptual Matrix, although we place the focus here on enquiry and scholarship. As this suggests, our focus here is not on the research and investigative activity that is prioritised as strategically important for the research profile of the university at institutional or disciplinary level. Instead it is on the role and importance of research, enquiry, and scholarship in relation to our learning spaces and the learning they support through digital engagement and digitally enabled pedagogical practices.

We also want to move beyond a detailed consideration of research-informed and research-based learning and teaching. Our own position here is that to remain both relevant and current, learning and teaching in higher education, and the content of the curriculum, must always be research-informed and draw upon, and engage learners in exploring, scrutinising, and applying, both the established and the emerging research within their fields of study.

Beyond this, we would argue that learners should be engaged in research and enquiry-based activities at each stage of their studies. Firstly, as a key enabler of active engagement, deep learning, and the development of rich transferable knowledge. Secondly, to scaffold and support the development of the student as a researcher as they transition to more advanced levels and undertake final year dissertations or capstone projects, and to support those who then make the further transition into postgraduate study and research. We would argue that a commitment to the development of learners critical consciousness, and what Freire (1974) discussed in terms of their ability to question the nature of their situation and the human condition through 'reading the world', is essential to these engagements, as it is to the range of pedagogic approaches we outline above and below.

Expanding upon the pedagogic and social dimension already considered, there are a number of ways in which the digital can support or enable engagement with research and enquiry in the context of learning and teaching. Many of the possibilities are little more than common sense, for example, having students begin to harness social media in their learning to follow leading experts in their field, to participate (perhaps initially as an observer) in relevant online Twitter chats or open webinars, or to create collections of digital resources (e.g. online journal papers, videos, other materials) that can support their studies. We contend here, simply, that common sense applications such as these should be more widely distributed across the learning and teaching practices of the university as an important first step.

We can also consider how the digital can support students in engaging in more formal and structured research and enquiry-based activities, for example, through actively engaging in and asking questions of relevant online disciplinary and scholarly fora and communities or creating their own online spaces within which to write about, reflect on, and communicate their progress with particular projects or activities to their peers and tutors, or more widely.

Activities of the above kind sit clearly within the domain of what we now commonly refer to as 'digital scholarship'. The work of Martin Weller (2011) is central to understanding developments in this area and what digital scholarship has come to mean and offer in relation to the increasing role of online scholarly networks, open publishing, and the emergence and acceptance of more reflective and less-structured forms of writing in the sourcing, sharing, and shaping of academic work and other forms of scholarly knowledge.

While the discussion and debate around digital scholarship has tended to focus in the main work of academics, practitioners, and subject experts as digital scholars, we are particularly interested in what the positioning of students as digital scholars can mean within the context of the digital university. An extension of digital scholarship to the work our students do within their learning, and an embedding of digital scholarly activities within it, has obvious implications for the development of digital skills and capabilities. When aligned to more substantial individual and collaborative projects, the potential of student digital scholarship is then extended to producing digital artefacts that can benefit the learning of current and future cohorts, or which can potentially have a wider relevance for other groups and communities that sit beyond the formal learning spaces of the university.

There is some evidence to suggest that students are more engaged and motivated in their learning when they are working towards producing outputs and resources that will sit in open online domains, for example Wikipedia, but there are more progressive possibilities here. The possibilities lie for the first part in how the research and enquiry-based activities of our students, particularly for more substantial projects that have a focus on real-world problems or needs, might directly contribute to addressing those needs through being disseminated by established open digital bodies of public or scholarly knowledge. The possibilities lie for the second part in a structured re-alignment of the curriculum, and the work undertaken through the curriculum, to Freire's (1970) notion of educational praxis as "reflection and action directed as the structures to be transformed" (p. 126) and Giroux's (2000) argument, in relation to public pedagogy, that "academic work matters in its relationship to broader public practices and policies" (p. 34). Our point of departure from Giroux is that within the digital university as we envisage it, this academic work can equally be work that is undertaken by our students, through their own digitally supported research, enquiry, and scholarship.

In describing the kind of learning we believe our learning spaces should be supporting, we identified with the belief that higher education learning ideally (but not ultimately) has to be about personal development. We see in the thinking of Freire and Giroux that higher education should ultimately be about societal development, and at the micro level of learning and teaching practice, we should therefore be seeking ways in which both personal and societal understanding and development can be nurtured and supported. This might take the form of community-focused student projects aimed at sharing the benefits of university education with local communities, which we come to explore in Chap. 8.

Defining Features of Digitally Enriched Learning Spaces

The digital is not a necessary requirement for supporting the kind of learning we espouse and explore in this text, or for realising the ethos and values of higher education that seeks to be more democratic and to challenge and change that within society that needs to be challenged and changed. However digital tools, spaces, and practices can be an important enabler both of learner engagement and participation and can extend and amplify the activities of learning within, across, and beyond our formally designed learning spaces and at a macro level beyond the university itself. In coming to consider the concept of the Digitally Distributed Curriculum, the possibilities at the macro level in particular come into fuller focus. First, however, we want to clarify where our considerations in the current chapter leave us with respect to what we see as the defining features of digitally enriched learning spaces, from a pedagogical and functional (rather than technological) perspective.

Teaching as Activity Design

While we do not challenge the need for more traditional, tutor-led activities in the context of higher education learning and teaching, nor contend that activities of this kind (including conventional lectures and seminars) can never be creative or engaging, we do see an over-reliance on such methods and approaches as being increasingly incompatible with more fully realising an active, dialogic, and reflective engagement across diverse student cohorts, and for harnessing digital tools, spaces, and approaches in ways that meaningfully enable this.

We also do not challenge the necessity for good (i.e. current, relevant, at an appropriate level) course content. However, we would contend that the proliferation of subject material now available digitally (from electronic journals and library collections, Open Education Resource collections, or which can be repurposed from previous iterations of a course) means that there is less of a necessity for the tutor to be the author of course content in the form of explanatory subject material. We would further argue that the tutor being the main creator of course content is a position that is counter to the powerful learning opportunities that we now understand can be enabled when learners themselves are engaged in the sourcing, curating, and creating of learning resources, materials, and artefacts, supported through appropriate digital tools and practices that are themselves reflective of how knowledge is increasingly being created, curated, and shared in the 'media-sphere' beyond the university, which is both professional and sociocultural by nature.

Beyond reflecting how knowledge is created and shared in real-world contexts, a further part of the rationale for engaging students in formal higher education contexts in the sourcing, curation and particularly the creation of the resources that will support their individual and collaborative learning is to shift some of the intellectual challenge that is traditionally the teachers, and through which the teacher consolidates and extends their own understanding through creating resources for their students, on to the learners so that they may be more deeply engaged in their own learning (Gros and Lopez 2016).

Given the proliferation of educational content that is now available digitally, and what we know about the increased engagement and motivation to learn and the deeper learning that can be supported when students are engaged in co-creating aspects of their learning experience (Gros and Lopez, ibid.; Cook-Sather et al. 2014), we suggest that the main role of the tutor as creator of higher education experiences for their students lies primarily in activity design. That is, the design of activities that engage students with their discipline, with each other, and with the wider world in ways that are authentic, creative, meaningful, and, wherever possible, impactful on the wider world (something else we will explore in the next chapter).

We share the view of Goodyear and Dimitriadis (2013) that "the nature of the students' activity is what affects whether or not they succeed in learning, and what they actually learn" (p. 5), and that on this basis 'activity-centred design' (tutor-led where needs be, but ideally through co-production with or between students) should occupy a central position in learning and teaching that seeks to support engagement in rich and complex learning and the development of rich and complex knowledge that has academic and real-world relevance.

Democratic Engagement in Designed Learning Spaces

The engagement of learners in the design and co-design of the individual and collective learning activities that will be undertaken within and across their formal learning spaces is one important dimension to ensuring democratic engagement in higher education learning that is both personally and socially relevant. In this context, the digital may serve either as an enabler in what is designed, the medium for what is designed, or may support engagement in the learning activity itself if the student cohort is temporarily or geographically dispersed.

However, democratic engagement in designed learning spaces, as a defining feature of digitally enriched learning spaces as we envisage them here, extends beyond the co-design of learning activities. It also needs to encompass the technologies that are there support collaboration within both physical and digital learning spaces, and which in themselves (either individually or collectively) need to support democratic engagement in learning.

In pragmatic terms, this would include considerations such as the visibility and number of displays or screens for projection and classroom interaction that are in a physical learning space, and the adequate availability of workstations or other required technologies for the number of individuals or small groups that are to be working in the space. It would also include access to assistive technologies, such as hearing loops, to allow equal or equitable opportunities to engage, and flexibility in the potential layout of the physical learning space so that wheelchair users are not restricted to being on the periphery of the space.

In both physical and digital designed learning spaces, democratic engagement in learning can be supported through the use of technologies that allow learners to express their views and positions equally, safely, and when necessary anonymously. This could include the use of handheld voting technologies or mobile apps that allow students to give an indication of where they stand in relation to potentially contentious or divisive issues without revealing their identity, and the use of asynchronous discussion boards to extend classroom discussion and enable those who are less confident or forthcoming in classroom debate to consider, articulate, and communicate their views. Discussion boards may serve a similar purpose in online learning contexts to allow everyone in the group time to reflect on and communicate their views, while anonymous forums may also support the exploration of topics and issues within which individuals may not necessarily want to be identified.

Opportunities for dialogue and debate, within which common and divergent views and perspectives can be shared and explored, are critical for democratic learning in designed learning spaces. The benefits of students engaging in dialogue within which they are exposed to multiple perspectives, understandings, and solutions, and through which they collectively challenge and co-construct meaning, are well established and can include contextually and culturally richer knowledge, an understanding of opposing views, depth of understanding, and interdisciplinary knowledge (Goodyear and Zenios 2007). As we also observe in the following chapter, the use of digital space to engage in such dialogue brings with it the possibility of extending collaborative discourse across different groups of learners, in different locations, and further enriching the exchanges that are possible as a result.

Democratic engagement and social change are intertwined in the world beyond the university, and to this end the kinds of authentic activities we allude to earlier should, wherever possible, involve collaborative projects that have a wider social value beyond he designed learning space(s) of the university. We explore this further in the next chapter, when we return to the notions of praxis and public pedagogy in relation to the curriculum.

Asynchronicity and Participation

The use of asynchronous technologies, including but not limited to discussion boards, wikis, blogs, and shared social bookmarking tools, allows opportunities for cohorts of learners to collaborate across multiple sites of learning, and outwith the times when they are able to come together in real time within either the physical or digital learning space.

We have highlighted above what that can mean in relation to extending the opportunities to engage in discussion and debate, including for those who are less forthcoming in face-to-face discussion or who would benefit from further time to articulate and share their views. As indicated in our opening chapter, there is an established evidence base in this area that underlines particular benefits for learners who are studying in a second language, who are less confident in face-to-face situations, or who are simply more reflective, to harness discussion boards in realising more democratic, egalitarian opportunities to contribute to discussion and debate. There is also evidence suggesting that for topics which are not contentious, or require a quick resolution of divergent views, the increased time to reflect on and articulate personal view, and to reflect on the views of others, can often lead to deeper thought and understanding that is possible in a very time-limited real-time debate.

These possibilities also extend to the use of blogs to support reflective and scholarly writing, usually on the part of the individual, and to the use of wikis for collaborative writing or for the co-production of learning artefacts. As for the kinds of learning activities that might particularly benefit from what asynchronous technologies can offer, and how this might be realised in ways that support democratic forms of engagement in learning, approaches could include having students take turns in pairs or small groups to summarise a classroom or real-time online discussion and post that summary with two or three follow-up questions for the rest of the cohort to engage with during an agreed timeframe, or alternatively having two or three students take turns each week to research and define key concepts in a collaborative class glossary (e.g. in a wiki) to complement issues that are being explored in the following lecture or seminar or the upcoming coursework or collaborative project.

Beyond these relatively simple examples, more sophisticated forms of engagement and learning can be enabled through activities that shift the locus of control and responsibility further towards the students themselves, for example, through student-designed and student-led online seminars, or collaborative learning approaches that require students to investigate a particular topic, issue, or problem and produce a digital case study of their findings.

This latter example, and the example of the collaborative glossary, also points towards the possibilities for participative, co-productive approaches to digitally supported learning to generate learning and knowledge artefacts that can be repurposed for subsequent cohorts, and supports sustainable pedagogic approaches in which activities can be repurposed and the tutor is not always required to produce, update, or reproduce online learning content.

The kinds of approaches, which harness digital tools and spaces for activities that support co-production and co-creation of learning and learning artefacts, have been the focus of various design frameworks for digitally enabled learning in recent years, including the 3E Framework developed by one of the co-authors of this text (Smyth 2013; Smyth et al. 2016).

Making Thinking Visible

The transparency of thinking, and enabling the transparency of thinking, is another defining feature of a digitally rich learning space, and of digitally enabled learning that is participative, meaningful, and democratic. However, we propose that there is more to this than the simple fact that the use of digital tools and spaces for learning generates visible communications (written and visual) that are often either semi-permanent or remain visible over time.

This in itself is important, for example, in making visible the split of opinion gauged through classroom voting or in sustaining shared reflective dialogue and debate through online discussion. Yet it also extends, crucially, to ensuring the visibility of engagement and contribution to collaborative work and parity and fairness with respect to this. We have a specific perspective on this, and it is not concerned with gauging, assessing, and attributing grades based on individual contributions to collaborative work (although we recognise this is an area within which there is much debate and where various guidance is available). Instead our concern is with the transparency of collaborative working in relation to the collaborative process versus the collaborative product. We think there are simple ways to support a parity of engagement in digitally supported collaborative work, for example, through asking each project group to post a bullet point summary of progress that week to a shared online space visible only to the group and their tutor, but requiring group members to rotate in taking turns to post that summary. While this is a very simple intervention, we think approaches like this can also help role model democratic and ethical use of digital communication media, as a counter to the misuse of social media to marginalise, uncritically challenge the views of, or abuse other people.

Similarly, we think tools like wikis to support the collaborative authoring of outputs are valuable as they record the history and various revisions that a group report, for example, has gone through. This can usefully reflect the input that each individual has had to the overall intellectual endeavour, even if the editing and refinement of the final output does not reflect the entirety of their contribution over the duration of the project. In this respect, we think the extent to which various digital tools make collaborative thinking visible is much more valuable in ensuring fairness in participation than accounting for how and where an individual is represented in the finished piece of work (they may have contributed substantially to the thinking and ideas, even if other peers contributed more to the final text presented).

Bringing the Outside In

In relation to bringing the outside in, we are essentially proposing that digitally enriched learning spaces, either physical or online, present increased opportunities to connect learners with others in their professional field who they would otherwise have limited potential to interact with, and for learners to bring in what they have learned from their engagement in other online communities and spaces that are beyond the university.

In relation to the former, this may take the simple form of guest speakers coming into the physical or virtual classroom via virtual classroom or webinar technologies, to offer a guest lecture or question and answer session. Or it may include joint online discussions (real-time or asynchronous) with groups of learners from similar cohorts at another institution.

In relation to the latter, then this might include 'flipped classroom' kinds of approaches in which learners engage in exploring various resources, potentially including resources they locate for themselves, to then share or communicate what they have learned ahead of reconvening with their cohort either in the classroom or online. It could also include activities in which learners engage in relevant online networking activities in their discipline area, for example, following key experts or researchers on social media or joining online professional networks and bringing what they have found out back into the formal learning space(s).

Virtuality and virtual reality technologies can also characterise 'bringing the outside' into digitally enriched learning spaces. For example, through using a combination of technologies to facilitate a virtual field trip to a specific location or place that would be difficult or impossible to access in person or through using virtual reality and augmented reality to enable an immersive, interactive experience that closely replicates the genuine one. Here we note the developments in virtual reality technologies that mean that this is not necessarily the isolated individual experience it once was, for example, through the emergence of virtual reality domes which allow collaborative VR learning experiences.

Situating the Digital Outside

Recognising that digitally enriched spaces for formal learning are not just designed physical or digital spaces within the university, but can also be those outside spaces within which formal learning is situated and expected to occur, we propose that a defining feature of some digitally enriched learning spaces will come through the situating of the digital outside. Here augmented reality, VR, QR codes, and approaches including geocaching can all have an important role in placing a digital layer or interface over external locations and landscapes to facilitate 'in the field learning'. Equally, the use of mobile technologies can play an important role in allowing learners to capture and document what they have found in the field, or to evidence the learning they have undertaken in the field or a professional environment.

Porous Learning and 'Leaky Knowledge'

Digitally enriched learning spaces, and certainly those that support democratic engagement in learning, the co-production and sharing of digital knowledge artefacts, and a bringing of the outside in are characterised by a porosity in terms of boundaries, and where various spaces for learning intersect and overlay, and by a leakiness with respect to the knowledge that is brought into, and shared beyond, the formal curriculum and the university itself. We further develop this point in the following chapter, in which we identify porosity as one of four enabling dimensions in our conceptualisation of the Digitally Distributed Curriculum.

Permanence and Portability

Our identification of the features that define digitally enriched learning spaces reflects our own perspective on the kinds of learning we should be seeking to engage our learners in and the ways in which digital tools, spaces, and approaches can enable those forms of engagement. We recognise that there are important implications of the kinds of approaches we describe, including in relation to the permanence and portability of, for example, digital artefacts created by students and the materials and resources students and their tutors curate and co-create. This is with respect both to IPR and also how students can retain ownership of the digital work they have created and co-created, and retain this beyond their time within the university. We suspect the solution to the latter extends beyond ePortfolios and is perhaps enabled most effectively through a 'Domain of One's Own' form of solution. This would position the student as their own digitally enabled/curated/represented learning space and provide a further dimension to how the notion of 'learning space' can be conceptualised.

Conclusion

In this chapter we have offered our perspective on the broad nature of learning spaces, their relationship to the university learning environment, and what we view as the defining characteristics of digitally enhanced learning spaces. In doing this we have also explored the possibilities afforded by digital learning spaces as allied to pedagogical perspectives and approaches which value and enable greater autonomy and critical agency on the part of learners. In the next chapter, we will synthesise and extend our thinking in the above and related areas through considering the role of the digital in relation to the location and co-location of the university, an 'unbounding' of the curriculum, and the extension of formal and informal higher education learning opportunities. Our lens for this exploration will be the concept and nature of what we have come to define as the Digitally Distributed Curriculum.

References

Cook-Sather, A., Bovill, C., & Felten, P. (2014). *Engaging Students as Partners in Learning and Teaching: A Guide for Faculty*. San Francisco: Jossey Bass.

Entwistle, N. (1997). Contrasting Perspectives on Learning. In F. Marton, D. Hounsell, & N. Entwistle (Eds.), *The Experience of Learning: Implications for Teaching and Studying in Higher Education* (2nd ed., pp. 3–22). Edinburgh: Scottish Academic Press.

Freire, P. (1970 in 2000). *Pedagogy of the Oppressed: 30th Anniversary Edition*. New York: Continuum.

Freire, P. (1974). *Education for Critical Consciousness*. London: Bloomsbury.

Giroux, H. A. (2000). Public Pedagogy and the Responsibility of Intellectuals: Youth, Littleton, and the Loss of Innocence. *JAC, 20*(1), 9–42.

Goodyear, P., & Dimitriadis, Y. (2013). In Media Res: Reframing Design for Learning. *Research in Learning Technology, 21*, 1–13.

Goodyear, P., & Zenios, M. (2007). Discussion, Collaboration and Epistemic Fluency. *British Journal of Educational Studies, 55*(4), 351–368.

Gros, B., & Lopez, M. (2016). Students as Co-creators of Technology-Rich Learning Activities in Higher Education. *International Journal of Technology in Higher Education, 13*(28), 1–13. https://doi.org/10.1186/s41239-016-0026-x. Last Accessed 23 Feb 2018.

Jisc. (2006). *Designing Spaces for Effective Learning: A Guide to 21st Century Learning Space Design*. https://www.webarchive.org.uk/wayback/archive/20140616001949/http://www.jisc.ac.uk/media/documents/publications/learningspaces.pdf. Last Accessed 23 Feb 2017.

Jonassen, D. H., & Land, S. M. (Eds.). (2000). *Theoretical Foundations of learning environments*. Mahwah/London: Lawrence Erlbaum.

Pates, D., & Sumner, N. (2016). E-learning Spaces and the digital university. *The International Journal of Information and Learning Technology, 33*(3), 158–171.

Savin-Baden, M. (2008). *Learning Spaces: Creating Opportunities for Knowledge Creation in Academic Life*. Maidenhead: Open University Press.

Smyth, K. (2013). Sharing and Shaping Effective Institutional Practice in TEL Through the 3E Framework. In S. Greener (Ed.), *Case Studies in E-learning* (pp. 141–159). Reading: Academic Publishing International.

Smyth, K., MacNeill, S., & Hartley, P. (2016). Technologies and Academic Development. In D. Baume & C. Popovic (Eds.), *Advancing Practice in Academic Development* (pp. 121–141). New York: Routledge.

Vermunt, J. D. (2007). The Power of Teaching-Learning Environments to Influence Student Learning. *British Journal of Educational Psychology, Monograph Series II, 4*, 73–90.

Vermunt, J. D., & Donche, V. (2017). A Learning Patterns Perspective on Student Learning in Higher Education: State of the Art and Moving Forward. *Educational Psychology Review, 29*(2), 269–299.

Weller, M. (2011). *The Digital Scholar: How Technology Is Transforming Scholarly Practice*. Basingstoke: Bloomsbury Academic.

8

The Digitally Distributed Curriculum

At first glance the title of this chapter might be interpreted along the lines that curriculum is a well-known and uncontested construct, which can be readily observed in the reality of universities and how they organise the formal educational opportunities, resources, and activities that they offer through programmes of study. On that reading the key words become 'digital' and 'distributed', and this may suggest that technology is in play in the delivery of the curriculum and that the curriculum and the role of technology in relation to it can be reduced to largely practical issues of choice of methods, media, and management.

However, we are of the opposite view, and contend that the curriculum is far from being a settled construct, despite appearances and common approaches to the (mainly modular) organisation of the curriculum in universities. We endeavour to show that the concept and reality of the curriculum can be subject to more radical interpretations and implementations, which bring with them the promise of more open, democratic, and progressive education.

Despite 30 years of technological changes, the appearance of new disciplines, and mass enrolments, the popular image of a university degree 'course' has remained remarkably stable. The organisation of learning and teaching within modularised programmes, with learning predicated on engagement through lectures, tutorials, and labs, may be more technologically enhanced than at any point thus far, but it still presents a recognisable and largely unchanged model of how the curriculum is instantiated and engaged with.

In this chapter we seek to draw upon our preceding narrative, and emerging conceptions of curriculum design, to present an alternative view of the curriculum itself as a digitally distributed, co-located space which extends learning and teaching across cohorts and communities, can meet diverse needs around lifelong and work-based learning, and through which the intellectual work of learners is allowed to resonate beyond the institution.

We are concerned here with notions including that of 'third place' or 'third space' (Oldenburg 1989) in conceptualising the university as a located and co-located space; one that exists within and across physical and digital spaces that can be both inside and outside of the institution itself. The metaphor of the porous or 'leaky university' (Wall 2015) is one we will explore in thinking about open and openness, where physical and digital spaces meet or diverge both within and through the curriculum, and where learning is enabled between and across different cohorts of learners within formal and informal settings and contexts.

From a critical pedagogy perspective, we will frame much of our discussion of the Digitally Distributed Curriculum, in the context of the digital university, against a deconstruction of the curriculum in higher education (Hall and Smyth 2016) through which we can identify the various ways—including the technological, cultural, and pedagogical—that the curriculum and the activities of the curriculum are currently often 'bounded' within the university.

Conceptualising Curriculum

A consideration of what the curriculum is and could be, within the context of the digital university and extension of higher education as a public good, might usefully begin with the question "What is the nature and purpose of the 'curriculum' in Higher Education?".

Within the original Conceptual Matrix for the digital university, the curriculum was considered in relation to pedagogical practices and factors including the 'constructive alignment' of learning outcomes, learning and teaching activities, and assessments (Biggs and Tang 2011), and how the curriculum is organised and represented through learning designs and course content (MacNeill and Johnston 2012).

Our work in applying the Conceptual Matrix in various contexts, and work undertaken in parallel by one of the co-authors of this text in exploring the 'bounded' nature of the curriculum in higher education (Smyth 2015; Hall and Smyth 2016), has informed our current position with respect to what we will come to describe as 'the Digitally Distributed Curriculum' and our attempt to conceptualise what this represents in practice.

Our concern is with how the Digitally Distributed Curriculum, as a key dimension and realisation of the digital university as we envisage it, can help us to position the curriculum as a means for realising higher education and higher education pedagogical practices as a participatory, communal good. However, the extent to which this can be realised is dependent on how our universities, and academics, define and instantiate the curriculum.

In our following exploration of how the curriculum can be defined, and the ways in which we can identify the curriculum as a 'bounded' space, we draw extensively upon the previously cited work of one of the co-authors of this text (Smyth 2015; Hall and Smyth 2016), before then exploring our initial emergent thinking, and our current position, in relation to the concept and implications of what we refer to as the Digitally Distributed Curriculum.

As addressed in Hall and Smyth (2016) and Smyth (2015), the general perspective of the curriculum that has prevailed to date is one in which the curriculum comprises the range of learning opportunities that are offered to learners by their educational institution, within the context of a planned course or programme of study that is benchmarked to the established requirements or frameworks for a particular level of study, is formally assessed, and is criterion-based (e.g. Macdonald 1977; Print 1993; Gosper and Ifenthaler 2014).

However, beyond this generalisation, 'curriculum' is a heavily contested concept that can be defined and enacted in order to place different emphases on what it is, where it is located, who it is for, and, crucially, its wider societal purposes.

In a wide-ranging consideration of what curriculum means for both informal and formal education, Smith (1996, 2000) distinguished between curriculum as a body of knowledge to be transmitted; curriculum as a product, that is, as a means to achieve certain ends in or by students; curriculum as a process of interaction between teachers, students, and knowledge; and, finally, the curriculum as praxis. These conceptualisations are related in terms of: first, where and with whom the ownership and control of the curriculum rests; and second, the defined role of the curriculum within higher education, and then beyond the institution.

Freire's (1970, p. 126) definition of praxis as "reflection and action directed at the structures to be transformed", which by this point is well established as a central motif within the narrative presented in this book, addresses the need for educational practices to engage beyond formal institutional learning spaces and contexts. When applied to the curriculum, this definition of praxis suggests a positioning and re-positioning of the curriculum in relation to that within society which needs to be challenged and changed—a supposition which is extended in more recent work concerned with directly connecting the content and activities of the formal curriculum to wider societal needs (e.g. Hall and Smyth 2016; Fung 2017).

On specifically discussing the curriculum as praxis, Grundy (1987) suggests that:

> … the curriculum itself develops through the dynamic interaction of action and reflection. That is, the curriculum itself is not simply a set of plans to be implemented, but rather is constituted through an active process in which planning, acting and evaluating are all reciprocally related and integrated into the process. (Grundy 1987, p. 115)

Smith (ibid.) contends that curriculum as praxis is manifested through a focus on collective understandings, an emphasis on human emancipation, and interventions designed humanely for a 'collective good'. In illustrating how this might be realised in practice, Smith (ibid.) offers a number of examples of the curriculum as praxis, including learning and teaching interventions that seek to explore the experiences of different cultural and racial or racialised groups in society, and within which academics and learners would expect to confront the material conditions through which social attitudes are constituted. Smith also underlines the need for an explicit linking between clearly articulated beliefs about what is important for human wellbeing and actual practice, within curricula that are not only informed, but which are informed and committed to action (Smith's definition of praxis).

Hall and Smyth (ibid.) argue that the idea of curriculum as praxis is dialectically opposed to the notion of curriculum as product, a perspective which Smith (2000) observes as being heavily influenced by the development of 'scientific management', and within which the curriculum is based on values aligned with the division of labour, and detailed attention to what people are expected to know. When viewing the curriculum as praxis, we are essentially positioning the curriculum—and formal education—as a means to improve society and the human condition. There are important synergies here with the notions of 'outside curricula' and 'public pedagogy' (Schubert 2010), of porosity which we will come on to explore, and more broadly to higher education as a social or communal good.

There are key tensions and contradictions inherent in enacting a curriculum defined by praxis, which we will also come on to address. However, at this point we recognise the contested nature of 'curriculum' and contend ourselves that a curriculum committed to praxis, and within which there is increased space for critical discourse, democratic planning, and social engagement, is one that reflects "the need for critical educators to act on the belief that academic work matters in its relationship to broader public practices and policies" (Giroux 2000, p. 34). There are implications here, as we began to explore in the previous chapter, for the roles of students (not just academics) as public scholars, for the legitimisation of specific voices and issues within the context of learning and social action, and for the role of the digital in instantiating curricula that are characterised as above.

The Bounded Curriculum

Before positioning the curriculum 'as it could be' in relation to the digital university, and the extension and distribution of the university and the activities of higher education as a public good, we must first consider how the curriculum is commonly organised and implemented within our universities. As argued by Smyth (2015) and Hall and Smyth (2016), a critical consideration of the curriculum within this context reveals a number of ways—pedagogical, technological, and cultural—within which the curriculum is limited, constrained, and 'bounded'. Of the constraining factors which Hall and Smyth (ibid.) identify, a number have previously been subjected to strong challenge, for example, the limitations of modularisation and culturally narrow curricula. Other factors, including the bounding of intellectual property through assessment and the need to reframe the open education debate, are emergent and worthy of further scrutiny. What links all of the factors identified is that each either reduces or negates the potential value and impact of the curriculum, and the learning that it supports and the knowledge it produces, from contributing to democratising access to higher education, addressing societal challenges and needs, and better situating and co-locating the university within and across the communities to which it belongs and should contribute.

We consider below the range of ways in which the curriculum is commonly 'bounded' within the university, in relation to how it is designed, organised, and enacted. We draw extensively and with permission on Hall and Smyth (2016) and Smyth (2015) in describing the eight 'dimensions' below within which the curriculum can be seen as bounded, but contextualising and also extending their observations to the ideas we are exploring in relation to the concept of the 'digital university'.

The Prevalence of Curriculum as Product

The idea of what the curriculum is, or could be, remains narrowly defined within notions of what the university will offer or provide to their students by way of closed courses and course content, which we contend has particular implications relating to widening access to higher education, including participation in the wider learning opportunities that the university can provide through open education approaches and practices. This narrow view also tends to reinforce the neoliberal notion that universities exist to provide their 'customers' with neatly packaged and potentially valuable knowledge products to be traded for higher earning power in the graduate labour market. Whilst these are important common-sense assumptions about the purpose of higher education, they are by no means the only forms of value involved and should not set the limits of student development. Nor should they be the sole criteria to evaluate the worth of an educational experience.

In a considered and broad-ranging review of curriculum models and conceptions for the Quality Assurance Agency for Higher Education, undertaken to inform a national enhancement initiative around the development of the curricula in the Scottish higher education sector, Fotheringham et al. (2012) looked at issues of curriculum design, ownership, and participation, alongside wider societal implications. In their model of Factors Influencing Curriculum, it is evident that the locus of control of the curriculum is still very much with the institution, accrediting and awarding bodies, and sector policy makers, with a strong explicit and implicit focus on the curriculum as a body of knowledge to be mastered, and the curriculum as a product which is concerned with achieving certain ends within the skills and attributes of students. This reflects a key tension within higher education curricula between what is defined as desired academic knowledge and the needs of 'external stakeholders', including employers, but also professional and accrediting bodies who will have their own requirements relating to the knowledge and skills to be learned and evidenced, but also the means through which learning is to be evidenced and assessed. In some instances, this will be encapsulated in requirements for what might be categorised as traditional, abstract forms of assessment including closed book exams.

Whilst Fotheringham et al. (2012) put forward and argue for alternatives, and provide examples of university initiatives that very effectively enact the curriculum as praxis, and through which the activities of the curriculum have a wider societal purpose, the examples that they put forward (Students as Change Agents at the University of Exeter, Student as Producer at the University of Lincoln) remain amongst the prevalent examples today. While other examples of 'curriculum as praxis' have emerged more recently, for example, the Connected Curriculum work at University College London (Fung 2017), the overall picture is one of fragmented and relatively slow progress, certainly within the sector as a whole.

Modularisation

It is well-established point of critique that the modularisation of higher education curricula, by default and when not managed carefully, can result in fragmented learning experiences that tend to be limited to, and kept within the confines of, enrolled module and programme cohorts (Savin-Baden 2008; Morris 2009). The challenge here is that unless academics 'design in' interdisciplinary or cross-cohort learning experiences, the organisation of the modularised curriculum tends to simplify the complexity of the real world and can create false distance between concepts, bodies of knowledge, and disciplines that are closely related or which interlink with one another. In turn this also simplifies the range of ways in which knowledge is created, shared, challenged, and re-created outside of formal higher education. A contributing factor here can be an over-reliance on abstract forms of assessment focused on specific isolated learning activities and outcomes, as opposed to authentic forms of assessment (Kvale 2007) that better reflect the complexity of how knowledge is developed and applied in the 'real world' including assessment that is designed to support learning in complex social contexts, and to respond to social needs and contexts.

Furthermore, the modularisation of the curriculum, as part of an information-based rather than learning-based systems architecture that links the curriculum, student records system, and the Virtual Learning Environment, contributes to the bounding of the curriculum and institutional digital learning spaces as limited and limiting spaces for learning.

Institutional Digital Silos

In further exploring the last point above, we can further observe how the institutional systems and technologies through which academics organise and deliver the curriculum often place unhelpful space and distance between learners. Particularly problematic is the information architecture of institutional digital spaces like Virtual Learning Environments (VLEs) or the alternatively named Managed Learning Environments (MLEs). In these spaces, a student is typically represented by a matriculation number that is linked to module and programme codes that in turn determine which learning resources and spaces each individual is allowed to access, alongside the peers with whom they are able to work. In this respect the student records system and the VLE might be viewed as working in combination to 'design out' opportunities for students and academics to cluster around shared needs and interests. In turn this disenables and delegitimises forms of collaborative and co-operative learning and actions across disciplines or levels of a course and across formal and informal boundaries. The organisation of the curriculum and cohorts of learners, within institutional VLEs, therefore becomes both an outcome of modularisation and a factor that exacerbates the educational challenges, difficulties, and limitations of modularisation as a curriculum model.

There are also additional challenges inherent within modularisation, and the related problem of institutional digital silos, for particular groups of learners. This includes mature and part-time students who within a modularised system, and one through which they engage in at least some degree of online activity, may be "less likely to form the tightly-knit peer support groups that [they] have recounted as being invaluable for their survival in the HE system" (Morris 2009, p. 108). This observation can be extended to other marginalised groups of learners, and for whom "the fragmented nature of programmes will inhibit the opportunities for connected and creative thinking that HE can offer" (Morris 2009, p. 108).

Clustering and Social Action

The opportunity for learning and teaching approaches and activities that can create within the curriculum opportunities for cross-cohort and cross-disciplinary learning, can connect the curriculum to wider opportunities for more democratic engagement in education, and connect the university and curriculum to social action and change requires learners and the academics who support them to be able to 'cluster' around topics, projects, and concerns of shared interest. Within the context of the curriculum as praxis, and the broader context of extending the university and higher education as a public good, clustering reinforces learning, communal wellbeing, social interaction, and social action. The instantiation of the curriculum within higher education through modularisation and imposed virtual walls and silos greatly restricts the potential for clustering and in this respect is dialectically opposed to how online social networks of various kinds enable and empower people out with the university in the sharing, co-construction, and curation of knowledge, and in their engagement in democratic debate and action, in areas of mutual areas and concern.

Within the context of higher education, and in extending its purpose, there is a need to understand who could cluster around and through the curriculum, and how the curriculum might be relocated or co-located across formal and informal boundaries.

Assessment and the Bounding of Intellectual Property

The assessment practices embedded within the curriculum often limit what learners are allowed, or able, to do with their own work and knowledge, and for whom. Many forms of assessment result in the intellectual work of the learner remaining within the institution. This applies particularly to more abstract forms of assessment, including the academic essay and the written exam which would have limited relevance or value beyond being an instrument of assessment. However, it also applies to more authentic forms of assessed coursework, including design and development projects, case studies, investigative and research-based projects, and social enquiry, if that work is not shared beyond the cohort and the academics who assess it. The problem and challenge here is not simply one of allowing our learners to share their work more easily (as an e-portfolio or personal domain). Instead, the question becomes for whom are our learners producing assessed work? Moreover, are there alternative purposes for which they could be sharing the knowledge they create, to the wider benefit of particular groups, or for the wider benefit of particular needs, within the wider community? We know the answer to this is yes, and we see in relation the Connected Curriculum (Fung 2017), and the other similar examples previously mentioned, practices that link assessment, and what is produced for assessed work, to the needs of small businesses, third sector and community groups, and to wider societal needs.

A key implication here, in relation to digital educational practice, concerns how we can harness digital media and spaces in the production and dissemination of student coursework that has a value, especially a social value, beyond the physical and virtual walls of the university. To return to an earlier point, we contend here that there is a hitherto relatively underexplored potential to engage our students in digital public scholarship, able to produce and distribute digital knowledge artefacts (e.g. digital social issue reports, rich media case studies) and contribute to online public bodies of academic and disciplinary knowledge. Here we argue that the modularisation of assessment practices, an overreliance on abstract forms of assessment, and the confinement of written and other student work within online submission and text-matching systems limit the individual and collective production of knowledge or artefacts that can then be applied by students across their own or other communities.

Culturally Bounded Curricula

The curriculum is often limited in acknowledging and celebrating diverse needs, views, and practices by being too narrowly defined in cultural terms. The dominant cultural context within which the curriculum has been devised acts as a critical limit. The Why is My Curriculum

White? campaign and associated movement established in 2015 continues to explore the problems and challenges of culturally exclusive curricula, and collectively our students, and their academic supporters, may equally seek to ask why the curriculum is able bodied, or why it is straight, or more pragmatically why it is full-time, or urban, or campus-based. With respect to how we develop more culturally inclusive curricula, both De Vita and Case (2003) and Welikala (2011) stress the critical need to look beyond internationalisation and cultural inclusion as something we apply to the curriculum, and instead celebrate them as dimensions that should enrich, shape, and determine the curriculum and its activities. De Vita and Case (2003) observe how the 'flavouring' of the curriculum with global or internationalised elements is a failure to address more fundamental issues and opportunities in creating culturally inclusive and authentic forms of learning. Welikala (2011) argues that a globally and culturally sensitive 'multi-perspective curriculum' can develop rich knowledge and values of respect, alongside the broader skills needed in a complex world.

When considering what the digital can offer within this particular context, and what it can offer more broadly for a 'cultural unbounding' of the curriculum, we can look at practical issues in relation to improved access and more fluidity in terms of accessing and engaging with higher education curricula. More critically we can look towards the harnessing of digital tools and spaces to connect learners and groups of learners from different cultural and geographic backgrounds in reflective, dialogic, and socially relevant learning activities; to engage individuals with a broader range of perspectives and world views; to better meet the needs of learners with requirements related to disability, location, or who have limitations related to when they can engage; and to situate formal higher education learning within and across relevant wider social communities, cultural contexts, and professional networks.

The Distributed Curriculum as Learning and Praxis

Emerging notions of the distributed curriculum, including different conceptions of 'the community as curriculum' (Starratt 2002; Cormier

2008), offer useful ways of thinking about how the curriculum can be further reimagined and repositioned within the narrative of higher education as a public good, and within the narrative of this book concerning the concept of the digital university as a means of extending higher education as a public good. Cormier's work on the rhizomatic model of learning is particularly relevant within the context of learning within and across online or online-supported communities, but applies equally to other contexts in which the curriculum itself is negotiated collectively:

> In the rhizomatic model of learning, curriculum is not driven by predefined inputs from experts; it is constructed and negotiated in real time by the contributions of those engaged in the learning process. This community acts as the curriculum, spontaneously shaping, constructing, and reconstructing itself and the subject of its learning in the same way that the rhizome responds to changing environmental conditions. (Cormier 2008, p. 3)

This work also underscores a consideration of the importance of 'clustering' within and through the curriculum, and a challenge to understand how the curriculum can be distributed to enable a diffuse intellectuality. With further development, the notion of the community as curriculum (and of the curriculum as community) may come to provide a nuanced extension to the notion of curriculum as praxis, possibly enabling a better understanding of 'the curriculum as place' (including as a distributed and co-located space or place). Our own thinking on the Digitally Distributed Curriculum may provide part of such a response.

Reframing Open Education

In considering the curriculum as a conduit for education as a public good, and our wider consideration of the digital university itself, there is a strong need to reframe the current debate around open education, and open educational practice, so that it moves away from addressing (almost exclusively) open online education and begins to challenge universities to make greater use of their physical spaces as open spaces for learning. If education is a communal good, then universities have to be good (and certainly much better than present) at using both their physical and online spaces for wider engagement. As we have explored in earlier chapters, the instantiation of the curricula within open online spaces and contexts may have widened access to education in some respects, but it has also served to amplify access to higher education for those who already have a higher education experience. This includes distancing the university from learners in the wider community who may be digitally excluded or disenfranchised, which as we explore further below requires a challenge to our universities to make more effective use of their campuses as digitally rich spaces in their wider communities within which digital access, digitally enabled education, and digital skills development can become a possibility for those who would otherwise be disenfranchised.

Towards the Digitally Distributed Curriculum

The concerns we explore above, in our consideration and application of the 'bounded curriculum' critique of Smyth (2015) and Hall and Smyth (2016), both inform and relate directly to what we have come to conceptualise as the 'Digitally Distributed Curriculum'. The current position we have arrived at in relation to the Digitally Distributed Curriculum has, like the revised Conceptual Matrix for the digital university we will offer in the next chapter, been the outcome of an applied and developmental refinement of our thinking.

As we have documented in more detail elsewhere (Smyth et al. 2015), and in Chap. 3, the broad notion of the Digitally Distributed Curriculum first emerged as an outcome of the work undertaken in applying the original Conceptual Matrix, and associated tools, in the context of an institutional 'digital futures' consultation at a post-1992 university in the UK.

Through our work in applying the original Conceptual Matrix, and subsequent dialogues concerning the further development of our thinking about the digital university, our initial representation of the Digitally Distributed Curriculum proved a useful focal point for exploring a wider role for 'the digital' in relation to how the curriculum is organised, who is able to engage with and benefit from the activities of the curriculum, and for a 'reframing' of open education practice in the context of the digital university (MacNeill 2016; Smyth 2016).

However, as we identified at the time, our thinking about what would characterise the Digitally Distributed Curriculum, and how it would be instantiated, was very nascent and 'imperfect' when we first outlined it (Smyth 2016). Our initial thinking, captured in the representation above, was also 'bounded' within, and to a large extent defined by, issues that were being explored within a specific institutional context for a specific institutional purpose.

As our thinking on the digital university has continued to evolve, principally in relation to our increased focus on 'praxis' and in parallel with related activities concerning the nature of higher education curricula, our position in relation to the Digitally Distributed Curriculum has moved from one of a nascent 'organising concept' to a more fully conceptualised idea. We suggest the following account of our evolving thinking constitutes a new direction in ideas about curriculum, which extends beyond the typology of curriculum concepts presented above. In our view curriculum is not only a major pedagogical structure defining the substance of a university's contribution to knowledge and learning but also an expression of what a university is for in relation to its various learning communities and social responsibilities. From our perspective, we are positioning the digital university as a wide-ranging public good and constructing a critical narrative of that positioning, which encompasses digital technology but is not limited by narrow accounts of the technology.

Conceptualising the Digitally Distributed Curriculum: A Values-Based Structure for Renewal, Development, and Outreach

As indicated previously, the 'Curriculum and Course Design' dimension of the original Conceptual Matrix for the digital university considered the curriculum in relation to pedagogical practices and factors including the 'constructive alignment' of learning outcomes with learning activities and assessment (Biggs and Tang 2011), how the curriculum is organised and represented through learning designs and course content, and the broad notion of 'pedagogical innovation' (MacNeill and Johnston 2012). Our initial depiction of the Digitally Distributed Curriculum extended this, identifying a number of factors, features, and practices relating to the role of the digital within the organisation, implementation, and, to some extent, the location and co-location of the curriculum.

As we moved towards a fuller conceptualisation of the Digitally Distributed Curriculum, our focus shifted beyond the identification of a potentially relevant range of factors, features, and approaches and towards defining the Digitally Distributed Curriculum in relation to the 'values' that we feel should underpin it; the 'enabling dimensions' that are required to link those values to practice, through establishing the context and conditions for practice; and the specific approaches to practice through which the Digitally Distributed Curriculum is actually instantiated and enacted (Fig. 8.1).

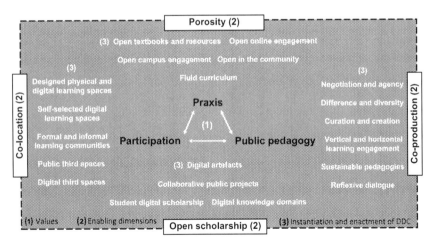

Fig. 8.1 The Digitally Distributed Curriculum

Values Underpinning the Digitally Distributed Curriculum

The values which we view as central to our conceptualisation of the Digitally Distributed Curriculum, and of this as a means to realise the digital university as we envisage it, comprise praxis, public pedagogy, and participation. Our general views relating to the first two are now well established. However in relation to the Digitally Distributed Curriculum, we are concerned primarily with praxis as a commitment to reflection and action within and through the curriculum that has a focus on social engagement and social action, criticality, and the application of knowledge and the artefacts of knowledge to meet wider needs beyond the curriculum and the university. Our perspective on public pedagogy, in relation to the Digitally Distributed Curriculum and the digital university, encompasses the aforementioned desire for academic work undertaken in the university and through the curriculum to matter in relation to broader societal and public needs, practices, and policies. However, it also recognises that our universities, our formally designed learning spaces, and the formal curricula as it is currently organised within the university are not the only locales, contexts, and spaces within which formal higher education learning, or broader learning opportunities offered by higher education institutions, should take place.

Our perspective on praxis and public pedagogy as values in turn influences our perspective on participation as a value. We view participation as encapsulating a commitment to widening, democratising, and enriching opportunities to participate in formal and informal learning; a devolvement and democratisation in ownership of the formal curriculum and the opportunities for learning therein; and the enablement of learning within and across cohorts, disciplines, and formal and informal learning communities as determined by educational purpose and need rather than how the curriculum is structured, systemised, and managed.

We depict the relationship between the values of praxis, public pedagogy, and participation as an interrelationship. We contend that they are dependent on one another in the context of the Digitally Distributed Curriculum as we envisage it and in the broader context of the digital university, and also in relation to the further extension of universities and higher education as a public good through digitally enabled practices and approaches.

Enabling Dimensions

We contend there is a comparable interrelationship between the 'enabling dimensions' of the Digitally Distributed Curriculum that we identify, and comprising co-production, porosity, co-location, and open scholarship. We view the four enabling dimensions as a translation of the underpinning values (of praxis, public pedagogy, and participation) into the context and conditions that are required, and which there must be a commitment towards establishing, in order to develop and support both the ethos and the associated pedagogic practices that we view as central to our conceptualisation of what the Digitally Distributed Curriculum is.

Co-production we view as encapsulating both a co-production *of* the curriculum, and a co-production *within* the curriculum. The engagement of students as co-designers and co-producers of the curriculum has become a well-established field of educational practice and research in recent years (e.g. Cook-Sather et al. 2014; Bovill 2013), with increased motivation to engage in the activities of the curriculum, an increased sense of ownership of learning, and the further development of collaborative and research skills emerging as key benefits for students. In the context of the Digitally Distributed Curriculum, and the extension of universities and higher education as a public good, we view the co-production of the curriculum as also requiring the participation, and partnership, of 'stakeholders' in the wider community or communities, who can either help shape the activities of the curriculum to ensure their relevance to wider societal needs or purposes, whether in local or broader contexts, or represent groups who could directly benefit from the knowledge or artefacts of knowledge that are produced through the curriculum. Regarding co-production not of but *within* the curriculum, here we are concerned with the autonomy and space for creativity our students have to shape their individual and collective learning experiences within the curriculum, in ways that reflect individual and shared interests and harness diversity to enrich collaborative learning; how students can meaningfully engage with one another within and across disciplines and levels; and what they are supported or enabled to create digitally both to evidence their own learning and for the wider benefit of others.

We view porosity, as an enabling dimension of the Digitally Distributed Curriculum, as being critically important to how we think about and position the university and curriculum in relation to opportunities for engagement within and through the university, and for enriching and reframing open educational practices. The idea of the porous or leaky university has been explored and defined in various contexts, including the geographically distributed university as a translocational and interstitial space for thinking and practice (Wall 2015) and in relation to the role of universities with respect to community engagement and lifelong learning (Preece 2017). In the context of our own work, and our conceptualisation of the digital university and Digitally Distributed Curriculum constructs, we define the 'porous university' as *a university which values open engagement in the sharing and development of knowledge, where formal boundaries are fragmented and intersect, and through which the opportunities for learning, teaching, scholarship, and research are distributed and co-located across communities within and beyond the institution.*

Co-location as an enabling dimension of the Digitally Distributed Curriculum encapsulates firstly the physical and digital spaces within and across which learning can occur, and secondly the values that we hope will help to characterise and define the nature of those spaces and who they are for. In relation to the former dimension, in the preceding chapter, we have explored the nature of our formally designed university spaces for learning (both physical and digital), self-selected spaces for learning, and where they might overlap or intersect to support formal higher education learning. This is an important aspect of co-location as we envisage it in the context of the Digitally Distributed University. However here we also extend co-location, and the notions of learning space, to those physical locations outwith the university, and in the community, where learning activities enabled or supported by the university can take place. An important concept here is that of 'third' place or space.

Oldenburg (1989) defined third place, and third places, as public places in the community that are 'not work' and 'not home' (e.g. museums, cafes, pubs, libraries, community halls), and where people can congregate for the purposes of engaging in democratic discussion and debate, community action, creative thought and expression, and for friendship and social interaction. For Oldenburg, 'third spaces' (we now revert back to the use of 'space') of this kind are typically characterised by being 'neutral ground' where difference is embraced, where social status is irrelevant, where there is a sharing of knowledge for the collective good, and where there is a bringing together of those who may otherwise not meet.

We view third space, and the use of third spaces in the community, as central to the extension of the university and higher education as a public good. In relation to the digital university and Digitally Distributed Curriculum, there is a need to identify and better harness those digitally enabled third spaces in the wider community (e.g. local libraries, community centres, and schools) where access to the university, engagement with the formal curriculum or activities therein, and engagement in informal learning opportunities offered through the university can be supported and enabled. This becomes an even greater need in areas of deprivation, and in contexts where there is disenfranchisement or a lack of opportunity to engage in learning due to distance, rurality, poor domestic connectivity, being post-school age with limited subsequent educational experience, a lack of personal access to networked technology, or lack of current opportunities for individuals to develop their digital capabilities.

In addition to the role of digitally enabled or digitally rich third spaces in the community, we envisage the co-location dimension of the Digitally Distributed Curriculum as encompassing what we might refer to as 'digital third spaces'. In common with the small body of prior work that has applied Oldenburg's (ibid.) thinking to digital spaces and places (e.g. Memarovic et al. 2014), we are interested here in digital spaces which provide a 'neutral ground', bring together individuals and groups who would otherwise not meet, and enable the sharing of knowledge for a common and collective good. In relation to 'digital third spaces' for learning, this could be seen to imply digital spaces that are either openly accessible or easily accessible to specific groups of learners and peers who would seek to come together, which are neither 'my digital institutional learning space' nor 'your digital institutional learning space', and which can easily support the amplification of issues and the sharing of knowledge and knowledge artefacts beyond the digital third space itself.

This leads into the final enabling dimension of the Digitally Distributed Curriculum that we identify, which is open scholarship. The 'open' aspect of this has two constituent elements. The first relates to the opportunity for learners, and also peers and colleagues in the wider community, to collaborate on, help shape, or contribute to scholarly public projects or scholarly projects with a clear public dimension. The second relates to the open dissemination and sharing of the scholarly work undertaken by students, individually and in collaboration with others, in various digital forms and through various digital means.

Instantiation and Enactment

Beyond values and enabling dimensions, the third component of the Digitally Distributed Curriculum we have endeavoured to capture, within each of the four enabling dimensions, concerns the range of pedagogic practices and *places of practice* that are important to the instantiation and enactment of the digitally distributed university.

We have begun to explore some of these above. We are conscious that the range of pedagogic practices and places of practice we identify will not be complete, and we do not suggest that all are essential in order to begin effectively harnessing the digital in extending the university, and higher education, as a public good. However, we would contend that the factors and practices that we identify, taken on an individual basis and especially collectively, provide a range of means for directly addressing the pedagogical, technological, and cultural ways in which the higher education curriculum is currently bounded, and through which the Digitally Distributed Curriculum can offer a response for 'unbounding' the curriculum in relation to participation within, and public good as an outcome of, higher education.

It is not our intention to define and explore in detail every aspect of the instantiation and enactment factors we identify against each of the four enabling dimensions. We have explored many of them in previous chapters, and above. However, there are further specific points to make in relation to how the Digitally Distributed Curriculum can be instantiated and enacted within each of the enabling dimensions.

In relation to the co-production dimension, we would emphasise the importance of exploring and celebrating difference and diversity (of views and culture, in experience and aspirations) as an essential characteristic of a socially inclusive, socially focused 'curriculum of praxis', and as a facet that has the potential to be even further enriched within digitally distributed educational contexts where there are additional opportunities to learn across communities and cultures. We would also underline the potential for digitally enabled learning that is horizontal in cutting across disciplines and cohorts, or vertical in allowing collaboration between learners at different stages of development within the same curriculum. In both these distinct areas (culturally enriched learning and learning across traditional curricular boundaries), we think the idea of 'digital third spaces' as we define them above becomes an important enabler and a response to the institution digital silos previously discussed.

We view 'reflexive dialogue' in which learners, their tutors, and those in the wider community explore and reflect on their views, perceptions, and lived experiences of being engaged within and through a curriculum focused on praxis, or having engaged with the knowledge artefacts produced as a result, as crucial to ensuring the integrity, continued social value, and further development of co-produced and socially oriented curricula. We also think there is an important role for reflexive dialogue of this kind in relation to the ethos and production of 'open knowledge', that is "knowledge held openly and available to all individuals", which is open to critique and discussion, and which "can enlighten the citizenry" through offering individuals "the tools and equipment that democratic societies need" (Peters et al. 2012).

On the porosity dimension, we would stress the ways in which this might be enacted through the open distribution of resources, and openness in relation to where learning opportunities can be accessed by the range of learners who may seek to engage with the university. In relation to the distribution of resources, we would contend that this is about more than access to course materials or elements thereof, including text-based and interactive resources, but a commitment wherever practicable to open access as the default, and including access to open textbooks for students of the university and other interested learners. The emerging discourse around open textbooks as a social justice, both in relation to a more affordable formal education for students and the sharing of knowledge as a public good, is one that aligns with our own narrative and conceptualisation of the digital university and the Digitally Distributed Curriculum and associated concerns of more democratic educational practices. Also aligned with these concerns is our contention that a porous university is one that enables open online engagement with learning opportunities wherever possible, and not simply in the context of open online courses (of whatever scale). Instead, we propose that there are learning and teaching opportunities within the formal university curriculum that could be further 'opened up' for wider online engagement, including guest expert webinars, streamed lectures and seminars, and live social media events.

Our perspective on porosity, in alignment with our thinking on engagement in learning opportunities in public third spaces, also advocates a 'reclaiming' or 'reframing' of open education away from the currently dominant perspective of 'open education' meaning 'open online' (MacNeill 2016; Smyth 2016), to an embracing of a richer outlook on open education that encompasses open online, open on campus, and open in the community, and the ways in which these scopes of 'open' might intersect and interplay to widen access to learning.

Finally, in relation to the porosity dimension, we would stress the need for more fluid curriculum models that more easily allow for an engagement with formal learning that is accommodating of individual constraints, opportunities, and potential patterns of engagement. This is as opposed to (mainly) modularised curriculum models than pre-determine the required patterns of engagement predicated on an x credit module or course needing to be completed in y number of weeks, determined by timetabling systems that assume the ability to engage in full-time or very narrowly defined part-time modes of campus-based attendance, and the scheduling of results boards at a few fixed points in the academic year. The need for an organised approach to the delivery of the curriculum, including assessment and ratification points, is not being challenged per se. The very fixed and rigid nature of those systems in most universities, and the broad assumptions they may make about a comparable ability and opportunity to engage across an increasingly diverse student body, is something we contend must be challenged and addressed going forward if we want to (i) fully embrace the possibilities of a higher education system that is as inclusive as possible, (ii) enable engagement in higher education from wherever the individual is located, and (iii) more fully realise the potential of open education modes of engagement.

The enabling dimension of co-location we have explored in reasonable detail. However, beyond the sites and locations for learning that we have identified, and in further clarifying what is perhaps already implied in our discussion of 'third spaces', we view the co-location dimension as also involving the co-location of learning opportunities across formal and informal learning communities. This may involve learning activities that are co-constructed and undertaken in partnership across formal and informal groups and contexts. It may also involve the location of formal learning opportunities, or the engagement of academics and students, in informal public and community learning locales and contexts. We are mindful of the work in this area of organisations such as The Ragged University, with their ethos of "Knowledge is power, but only when it is shared", and the educational opportunities they offer through harnessing 'third spaces' in the community, and harnessing third space values, to enable engagements in which academics, artisans, enthusiasts, and those with an interest in learning about a range of topics and issues can converge and converse (Dunedin 2013).

As regards the enabling dimension of open scholarship, the additional point we will offer by way of further elaboration is to underline the importance of engaging our students, within and through the activities of the curriculum, to harness the digital in producing knowledge and knowledge artefacts that can be shared, and have a relevance and resonance, beyond the university itself. We have indicated some of the forms this might take in relation to coursework (e.g. digital social issue reports, rich media case studies), and for whom it may have relevance (e.g. third sector and community groups, small businesses). Equally important, perhaps particularly for students who are further on in their studies, would be the opportunity for students to be engaged in producing scholarly outputs for dissemination online (e.g. critical essays, reflective blogs), to contribute directly to digital domains of public knowledge (e.g. Wikipedia), or to author or co-author academic papers for open journals.

These forms of open scholarship become powerful interventions and approaches in supporting, in tangible ways, the other enabling dimensions of porosity, co-production, and co-location in moving towards a realisation of the Digitally Distributed Curriculum.

Conclusion: A Critical Footnote

While we have strived to conceptualise the Digitally Distributed Curriculum as a construct that supports and advances our thinking on the digital university, and how we can rethink and reposition the curriculum in relation to digital practice and extending universities and higher education as a public good, we recognise the construct is not an unproblematic one.

As observed by Hall and Smyth (2016), "conceptualising and enacting the curriculum as praxis brings with it inherent tensions and contradictions, particularly concerning the nature and value of academic knowledge". One of these tensions lies in the nature of academic knowledge as a product of the curriculum. The development of academic knowledge positions the individual as a commodity within marketised higher education and employment sectors, while simultaneously the individual requires to develop academic knowledge, to then apply in disciplinary, vocational, and social contexts, in order to enact a curriculum of praxis and in relation to their becoming an individual who can act within and upon the world.

Our view in relation to this tension is that a continued prevalence of the curriculum as product will ultimately limit the extension of higher education as a public good, and the realisation of what the digital university as we are defining it can offer in this respect, but that the curriculum as product (i.e. as a body of academic knowledge and related skills) can and must exist in curricula (or digitally distributed curricula) that are focused on praxis.

On reflecting upon our conceptualisation of the Digitally Distributed Curriculum, we are also mindful that while we have focused on what the curriculum is, how it is instantiated, and how it could be instantiated to better harness digital practices and approaches in enabling more democratic participation in learning, our representation of the Digitally Distributed Curriculum could easily replace the word 'curriculum' with 'university' or 'higher education'. Curriculum may be our lens in the preceding discussion, but it is not the overall focus.

References

Biggs, J., & Tang, C. (2011). *Teaching for Quality Learning at University* (4th ed.). Maidenhead: McGraw-Hill/Open University Press.

Bovill, C. (2013). Students and Staff Co-creating Curricula – A New Trend or an Old Idea We Never Got Around to Implementing? In C. Rust (Ed.), *Improving Student Learning Through Research and Scholarship: 20 Years of ISL* (pp. 96–108). Oxford: The Oxford Centre for Staff and Educational Development.

Cook-Sather, A., Bovill, C., & Felten, P. (2014). *Engaging Students as Partners in Learning and Teaching: A Guide for Faculty*. San Francisco: Jossey Bass.

Cormier, D. (2008). Rhizomatic Education: Community as Curriculum. *Innovate: Journal of Online Education, 4*(5). http://nsuworks.nova.edu/innovate/vol4/iss5/2. Last Accessed 24 Feb 2018.

De Vita, G., & Case, P. (2003). Rethinking the Internationalisation Agenda in UK HE. *Journal of Further and Higher Education, 27*(4), 383–398. https://doi.org/10.1080/0309877032000128082. Last Accessed 19 June 2018.

Dunedin, A. (2013). Finding a Way to Participate. *Journal of Perspectives in Applied Academic Practice, 1*(1), 37–38. https://jpaap.napier.ac.uk/index.php/JPAAP/article/view/55/pdf. Last Accessed 19 June 2018.

Fotheringham, J., Strickland, K., & Aitchison, K. (2012). *Curriculum: Directions, Decisions and Debate*. The Quality Assurance Agency for Higher Education. http://www.enhancementthemes.ac.uk/docs/publications/curriculum-directions-decisions-and-debate.pdf?sfvrsn=8. Last Accessed 24 Feb 2018.

Freire, P. (1970, 2000). *Pedagogy of the Oppressed: 30th Anniversary Edition*. New York: Continuum.

Fung, D. (2017). *A Connected Curriculum for Higher Education*. London: UCL Press. https://doi.org/10.14324/111.9781911576358. Last Accessed 24 Feb 2018.

Giroux, H. A. (2000). Public Pedagogy and the Responsibility of Intellectuals: Youth, Littleton, and the Loss of Innocence. *JAC, 20*(1), 9–42.

Gosper, M., & Ifenthaler, D. (2014). Curriculum Design for the Twenty-First Century Curriculum. In M. Gosper & D. Ifenthaler (Eds.), *Curriculum Models for the 21st Century* (pp. 1–16). New York: Springer.

Grundy, S. (1987). *Curriculum: Product or Praxis?* London: Falmer Press.

Hall, R., & Smyth, K. (2016). Dismantling the Curriculum in Higher Education. *Open Library of Humanities, 2*(1). https://doi.org/10.16995/olh.66. Last Accessed 24 Feb 2018.

Kvale, S. (2007). Contradictions of Assessment for Learning in Institutions of Higher Learning. In D. Boud & N. Falchikov (Eds.), *Rethinking Assessment in HE: Learning for the Longer Term* (pp. 57–71). New York: Routledge.

Macdonald, J. B. (1977). Value Bases and Issues for Curriculum. In A. Molnar & J. A. Zahorick (Eds.), *Curriculum Theory* (pp. 10–21). Washington, DC: Association for Supervision and Curriculum Development.

MacNeill, S. (2016). *Reframing Open in the Context of the digital university – Part 1*. https://howsheilaseesit.blog/2016/04/14/reframing-open-in-the-context-of-the-digital-university-part-1-oer16/. Last Accessed 19 June 2018.

MacNeill, S., & Johnston, B. (2012). *A Conversation Around What It Means to Be a digital university (Parts 1 to 5)*. http://blogs.cetis.org.uk/sheilamacneill/2012/01/26/a-converstaion-around-what-it-means-to-be-a-digital-university/. Last Accessed 22 Nov 2016.

Memarovic, N., Fels, S., Anacleto, J., Calderon, R., Gobbo, F., & Caroll, J. M. (2014). Rethinking Third Places: Contemporary Design with Technology. *The Journal of Community Informatics, 10*(3). http://ci-journal.net/index.php/ciej/article/view/1048/1116. Last Accessed 03 June 2018.

Morris, A. (2009). The Stretched Academy: The Learning Experience of Mature Students from Under-Represented Groups. In L. Bell, H. Stevenson, & M. Neary (Eds.), *The Future of HE: Policy, Pedagogy and the Student Experience* (pp. 99–111). London: Continuum.

Oldenburg, R. (1989). *The Great Good Place: Cafes, Coffee Shops, Bookstores, Bars, Hair Salons, and Other Hangouts at the Heart of a Community*. New York: Marlowe and Company.

Peters, M. A., Liu, T.-C., & Ondercin, D. J. (2012). *The Pedagogy of the Open Society*. Rotterdam: Sense Publishers.

Preece, J. (2017). *University Community Engagement and Lifelong Learning: The Porous University*. Cham: Palgrave Macmillan.

Print, M. (1993). *Curriculum Development and Design*. St. Leonards: Allen and Unwin.

Savin-Baden, M. (2008). *Learning Spaces: Creating Opportunities for Knowledge Creation in Academic Life*. Maidenhead: Open University Press.

Schubert, W. M. (2010). Outside Curricula and Public Pedagogy. In J. A. Sandlin, B. D. Schultz, & J. Burdick (Eds.), *Handbook of Public Pedagogy: Education and Learning Beyond Schooling* (pp. 10–19). New York: Routledge.

Smith, M. K. (1996, 2000). Curriculum Theory and Practice. *The Encyclopaedia of Informal Education*. http://infed.org/mobi/curriculum-theory-and-practice/. Last Accessed 24 Feb 2018.

Smyth, K. (2015). *The 'Bounded' Curriculum?* https://3eeducation.org/2015/08/24/the-bounded-curriculum/. Last Accessed 24 Feb 2018.

Smyth, K. (2016). *Reframing Open in the Context of the digital university – Part 2*. https://3eeducation.org/2016/04/20/reframing-open-in-the-context-of-the-digital-university-part-2/. Last Accessed 19 June 2018.

Smyth, K., MacNeill, S., & Johnston, B. (2015). Visioning the digital university – From Institutional Strategy to Academic Practice. *Educational Developments, 16*(2), 13–17. https://www.seda.ac.uk/resources/files/publications_191_Ed%20Devs%2016.2%20v1.pdf. Last Accessed 24 Feb 2018.

Starratt, R. J. (2002). Community as Curriculum. In K. Leithwood & P. Hallinger (Eds.), *Second International Handbook of Educational Leadership and Administration* (pp. 321–348). London: Kluwer Academic.

Wall, G. (2015). Future Thinking: Imaginative Expectations for the Leaky University. *Journal of Perspectives in Applied Academic Practice, 3*(1), 6–10. https://doi.org/10.14297/jpaap.v3i1.153. Last Accessed 24 Feb 2018.

Welikala, T. (2011). Rethinking International HE Curriculum: Mapping the Research Landscape. Universitas 21. August 2011 Learning and Teaching Position Paper. http://www.universitas21.com/news/details/32/rethinking-international-higher-education-curriculum-mapping-the-research-landscape. Last Accessed 19 June 2018.

Section III

Reimagining the Digital University

9

An Extended Conceptual Matrix for the Digital University

Introduction: From Analytical Tool to Critical Representation

In this chapter, we will present a three-dimensional, extended view of the Conceptual Matrix for the digital university based on the discussion and examples of the preceding sections of the book. This enriched view of the Matrix will directly address the dynamics of institutional development and academic development, to provide a stronger base for dialogue and research relating to the concept of the digital university. In addition, the following discussion expresses how we reshaped our views of educational and organisational development at the intersections of political economy, educational policy, and university practice. The content of the extended Matrix therefore offers a contribution to the debate on what universities are for, which may offer an example of discursive construction for others to adapt.

The new Matrix aims to extend the original model by taking a more explicit critical pedagogy stance in relation to the features and potential uses compared to the original Matrix. As forecast in Chap. 4, this chapter explores this reframing of the Matrix in greater detail and uses the positioning of critical pedagogy to allow for a discussion of practice and praxis at the university/institutional level, not just the individual level as is the current norm. By taking this perspective, we hope that the Matrix can be used to stimulate discussion and debate about counter-narratives around the digital university concept that will challenge the dominant neoliberal ones we have highlighted throughout the book.

The chapter will explore how we now are positioning the extended Matrix as a critical symbol that can be used to develop discursive themes from all stakeholders involved in developing and working in a digital university. Using Freire's approaches to education as a collective, respectful dialogic process (Rugut and Osman 2013), we envisage that the Matrix and associated tools can be used to create opportunities to discuss the realities of digital engagement in modern university life compared to the myths offered to the sector of digital transformation. In this way, we anticipate that our toolset would be able to create an explicit space for critical thinking and ownership of key collectively created contextual discursive themes around different readings and contextualised adaptations of the Matrix itself. It is our hope that this would provide a more grounded, participatory approach to transformation to university developments in general, not just in terms of the digital.

In his critique of the role of pedagogy within the modern capitalist society, Giroux (2011) describes critical pedagogy as a way to create "a language of hope and critique". He highlights that education is always set within a set of contextualised political and civic power relationships, and advocates that it is only through critical pedagogy that we can begin to question our own context, develop agency, and in doing so create the necessary conditions for social transformation.

> Pedagogy is a moral and political practice that is always implicated in power relations and must be understood as cultural politics that offers both a particular version of civic life, the future, and how we might construct representations of ourselves …. (Giroux, p. 71)

The Matrix as a Symbol for/of Change

We are now positioning the extended version of the Matrix as a critical symbol. One that provides a means for a range of university stakeholders (both internal and external) to engage in contextualised discussion around organisational change that is rooted in actually practice. We propose that it should provide a way for individuals to question, construct, and increase their understanding of their own context and the wider socio-political environment of their university. In a Freirean sense, the Matrix provides an alternative way for people to contextualise their own situations and provide a range of alternative readings of institutional reality.

Ideally this would be done as part of a dialogic process, where various stakeholders could be brought together to create and develop their own generative themes based on their lived experiences of contemporary university life. In effect, we see the extended Matrix as the foundation of creating extended open, collegial spaces for knowledge exchange and organisational/individual development. Or in other words, a way to form culture circles, as derived from Freire's original work, within the context of contemporary university organisational development.

It is our hope that this would provide a critically informed socio-constructive way to create a meaningful alternative to the neoliberal discourse around the role of the digital within universities, one that was cognisant of the potential to increase participation, social justice, and the civic responsibilities of a university based on core values of praxis, participation, and public pedagogy—not one based on the neoliberal, student as customer led approach to the 'student journey'.

How the Matrix Has Been Used and Developed

The Matrix is based on our model of the dynamics of the university (Fig. 3.2, i.e. participation, Information Literacy, learning environment, and curriculum), thereby allowing us to address the major change factors we saw as critical to conceptualising the digital university. As described in Chap. 3, the

Matrix in its original form has been used in practice to develop discourse around the concept of the digital university.

The quadrants of the Matrix were specifically selected to provide a holistic view of the concept of the digital university that was accessible and relatable to everyone—staff and students—working within a university. The selected dimensions were also chosen to balance familiar and unfamiliar ways of examining university organisation and academic practices in order to open up new channels of discussion. As we have illustrated, the Matrix has indeed provided a flexible tool for engaging staff (and some students) in identifying and formulating systematic programmes for change through harnessing, or developing, digital spaces, practices, and provision.

The Matrix has been used primarily at a strategic level and has provided a means for strategic development of contextualised digital developments and strategies, for example, Edinburgh Napier's Digital Futures Programme and the developing Digital Strategy at Glasgow Caledonian University.

In summary, the Matrix has had some proven success in providing a mechanism to:

- Analyse university policy documents.
- Channel discussion in universities and amongst wider professional communities.
- Shape future division of labour in relation to developing digital practice.
- Coordinate discussion/decision/actions.

Chapter 4 illustrated how the Matrix has allowed for a form of organisational constructive alignment, for example, alignment of strategic plans such as learning and teaching strategies and institutional priorities such as institution-level missions with and across the quadrants, that has allowed for a level of holistic engagement around the concept of the digital university, which extends thinking beyond narrow technist and managerialist formulation.

Chapter 8 'The Digitally Distributed Curriculum' (Fig. 8.1) explored how an output derived from a university-wide consultation driven by the

Matrix has and could possibly be extended into practice. In this chapter, we will also explore how the extended concept of the Digitally Distributed Curriculum integrates with the enhanced version of the Matrix as part of our evolving set of tools to foster critical engagement, discourse, and action around the concept of the digital university. Our developed Digitally Distributed Curriculum now includes a set of values and enabling dimensions that can link the context and conditions for practice through which a Digitally Distributed Curriculum could be instantiated and enacted.

As stated earlier in Chap. 4, we have reflected on our own predisposition towards the concept of constructive alignment (Biggs 2003) in relation to course design and pedagogical practice. In our earlier work, we were naturally, perhaps more habitually, using the Matrix to constructively align emerging and existing strategic systems design approaches to organisational development alongside emerging academic development in terms of digital learning and teaching practice and digital scholarship/research. For example, the starting point at Glasgow Caledonian University was to map existing university policies to the Matrix to create a gap analysis of university policy in relation to the quadrants of the Matrix and overall university strategic direction. This was followed by workshops where staff and students mapped their current practice to dimensions of the Matrix.

In this way, we were in effect blending the academic practice of adopting constructive alignment as an approach to good educational design at the course level, to incorporate a notion of organisational alignment as a guide to improving organisational management and development. By combining educational and organisational factors in the Matrix in this way, we sought to unify the micro, meso, and macro levels of university activity in our exploration of ways of understanding the digital university.

This approach to our original discursive construction of the concept of the digital university was one which we increasingly realised lacked sufficient critical perspective on the current socio-political environment—the neoliberalisation of university missions and actions. In our original context, a justified critique of the Matrix could be that it was simply another tool to support the status quo by providing a useful analytic framework for co-ordinating discussion and not something that actually extended or raised the debate about what a (digital) university is and could be for.

Through our increasingly critical dialogue, we began to explore the concepts of value pluralism and critical pedagogy as key theoretical constructs upon which to base our next iteration of the Matrix. In effect, it moves the Matrix to a higher stage of analytic complexity expressing a revised sense of the nature of decision-making in universities. Based on our practice and growing awareness, we also realised that practice, praxis, and open educational practice were central to the development of our theoretical perspective.

The Revised Matrix

It is within this context that our revised Matrix becomes a symbol for stakeholders to read and adapt based on their own context (Fig. 9.1). This

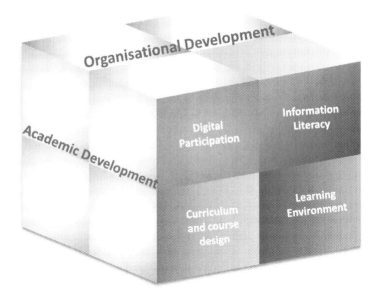

Fig. 9.1 The Revised Conceptual Matrix for the Digital University

An Extended Conceptual Matrix for the Digital University

approach would stimulate increased criticality, dialogue, and informed discussion and ownership of the various interpretations (or readings) of the Matrix. In this way, the Matrix becomes a richer discursive construct, one that can engage all stakeholders in developing their own sense of agency and criticality within commonly developed and shared understandings within their own contexts. Our aspiration is that this process will help to shine a light on the areas that universities need to focus on, not the ones that neoliberal agendas force them to focus on. Freire's insights are prescient:

> critical pedagogy forges an expanded notion of politics and agency through a language of scepticism and possibility, and a culture of openness, debate and engagement – all those elements now at risk because of the recent attacks being waged against public and higher education. (Freire, p. 159)

The three-dimensional view of the Matrix now explicitly focuses on organisational and academic development as two contrasting yet complementary areas to act as foci for broader engagement. These are the initial starting points to foster a sense of agency and criticality and in so doing begin providing a means to explore in a structured and contextualised way questions such as these raised by Selwyn.

> What have been the realities of increasing digital technology use in higher education, and how do these correspond with the long held promises and potentials of educational technology? What are the realities of digital technology for those who work with universities – i.e. academics, students, administrators and other professional staff? How are digital technologies impacting on the spaces, places and materialities of higher education – i.e. the campuses and classrooms, other learning environments and social spaces? To what extent are digital technologies simply an extension of the organizational, administration and managerial concerns of the university institution? How do these seemingly local issues correspond to wider debates regarding the future of education in the twenty first century – not least the links between education as a public good, the demands of the global knowledge economy, industry and commerce, and so on? Underlying all these specific concerns is the need to address the broader question that should *always* be asked when critiquing any are of education i.e. 'what needs to change'. (Selwyn, p. 7)

When these questions are in turn framed within a narrative of value pluralism and critical pedagogy, it is our hope that anyone engaging with the revised Matrix will be supported in a meaningful exploration and articulation of personal (and in turn institutional) agency through institutional contextualised discussions and evolving collective discourse, through the shared development of contextualised discursive themes.

> What critical pedagogy does insist upon is that education cannot be neutral. . Moreover, it is always directive in its attempt to teach students to inhabit a particular mode of agency; enable them to understand the larger world and one's role in it in a specific way …. (Freire, p. 159)

In our revised Matrix, organisational development must be cognisant of the human cost of digital transformation, not just the system/technology cost. The ongoing government obsession to transform universities into businesses with customers, KPIs, and the laws of the 'market' firmly in control needs to be balanced with empathy for the process of learning and extending knowledge and the role of education as primarily something for the public good. Not something that perpetuates grossly inflated senior management pay structures whilst at the same time creating unstable and tenuous working practices for the vast majority of staff, both academic and administrative.

Approaches to top-down organisational development initiatives must play more than lip service to bottom-up practices and needs before changes are implemented or, as all too often seems to be the case, imposed.

Similarly, in the revised Matrix, academic development is no longer seen in isolation from organisational development. It is at the heart of the development of approaches to learning, teaching, assessment, and wider research and knowledge exchange and as such cuts through organisational development.

It is our hope that the revised Matrix can act as a critical envelope. One that allows staff within and across universities to discuss and challenge the social conditions in which they find themselves products of, that is, a top-down, market-driven, neoliberal, customer-focused system, bringing to the fore issues the value of academic labour versus the value of management performance. In this way, meaningful, collectively created, and universally understood courses of actions could be developed and implemented.

This approach could well be unfamiliar and indeed uncomfortable for staff, in particular senior management. However, structuring discussion about the digital and indeed the university from a perspective that explicitly links the role and relationship between democracy and education, we believe could actually help senior management to free themselves from the oppression of neoliberal political agendas and give them the agency to embrace an informed and contextualised form of radical thinking that would bring about transformation based on the actual lived context of their universities.

Going back to the question raised in Chap. 4 by Collini (2017) in terms of what is a university for, we can now pose the question, who is a university for? Equally, looking at the Matrix from an open education practice perspective creates another dimension to discussions and explorations in relation to wider community engagement, access, participation, knowledge sharing and creation, and social justice. This in turn links to notions of the civic role of responsibilities and how they interact within the communities in which they sit.

As discussed in Chap. 3, the Matrix now becomes a symbol of potential for reforming the university to refocus from the distraction of the complex code word 'digital', particularly when used in conjunction with 'university'. The Matrix becomes a symbol that individuals can explore, modify, and build agency and praxis through shared understandings of situated practice (Fig. 9.2).

Looking at each of the quadrants in more detail, we can begin to unpack the types of critical reflections we would expect to develop in and across each of the quadrants, an organisational perspective that is rooted within principles of academic development. In turn, these are informed through the lenses of critical pedagogy and open educational practice.

Although it is possible to look at each of the quadrants on an individual basis, there is the underlying concept of a flow across the original key constructs of Information Literacy, learning environment, curriculum and course design, and digital participation.

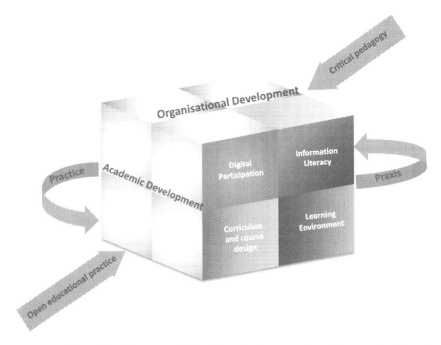

Fig. 9.2 The Revised Conceptual Matrix as the intersection of open educational practice, critical pedagogy, organisational development, and praxis

How the Matrix Could Be Used

In Chap. 2, we highlighted a number of different scholarly approaches around the concept of the digital university, namely, Collini (2012, 2017), Selwyn (2014), and McCluskey and Winter (2012). We now revisit the latter two approaches to provide an illustration of how the revised Matrix could be used to create critical generative themes through an adaptation of Freire's culture circles methodology.

A central theme from Selwyn seems to be a "…critical, pessimistic approach…", which characterises his analysis of the failings of the digital as both innovative technology and transformative ideology, and provides a platform for his thinking on what to do about the situation. His posture seems to be grounded in the identification of alternative uses of digital technologies and speculation on the prospects for engaging various communities to take action for change. The dialectic seems to be between the negative position of a digital technology for universities shaped by neo-liberal corporatism and institutional managerialism, and a potential for 'grass roots' opposition to those shaping powers. In effect, Selwyn seems to present the way forward as residing in a 'counter cultural' challenge to the dominant forces of digital development in universities.

His proposals include:

* Emphasis on the (macro) social nature of digital technology situated in particular (meso/micro) settings;
* Call to 'problematise' digital technology and subject it to critical analysis;
* Adoption of some version of 'nudge' tactics to change perceptions and behaviour;
* Re-phrasing the language used to describe technologies;
* Reconfiguration of physical space to expose the digital component;
* Collective action to produce alternative statements, for example, Bill of Rights/Manifesto;
* Individuals asserting their rights and perspectives against corporate/institutional dominance of technology;
* Widening the range of 'publics' engaging in 'problematising' technology and proposing alternatives;
* Engaging more organisations and groups in the debate, for example, trade unions, charities.

In contrast, McCluskey and Winter take different tone, where they seem to largely accept digital technology as a given. Their focus is more around getting things done rather than encouraging reflection or mounting any form of critique. There is a strong emphasis on data, measurement, analytics, tracing, and so on allied to a belief in rational, purposive action as the basis of positive change.

Some key points from McCluskey and Winter include:

* The "market smart, mission driven" mantra of business management as applied to universities;
* Need for student 'digital literacy' for employability;

- Strong support for academics in traditional roles but enhanced by digital technology;
- Differentiation between categories and kinds of universities based on mission and performance;
- Promotion of local data analytics to shape the experience of student cohorts, identify achievement of learning outcomes, and exemplify mission success;
- Promotion of large-scale external data collection for quality regulation and sector direction—TEF and LEO spring to mind;
- Advocacy for 'critical thinking' across the curriculum;
- Promotion of some level of STEM subject knowledge and methods across the curriculum;
- Proposals to distinguish academic and administrator roles in relation to technology and business processes;
- Strong support for the use of 'dashboards and data warehouses' along with 'digital report cards'.

Whilst the latter might be more palatable to senior management, the extended Matrix can be applied to both to provide, again in the Freirean sense, a codification of the university from which different stakeholders can then create their own generative themes.

For example, in terms of McCluskey and Winter's perspective on data analytics, the use of dashboards, data warehouses, and digital report cards, if explored from the information (and data) literacy quadrant could raise a set of questions around the politics of metrics. That is, who decides on what metrics should be used and for what purpose, how and where are they collected, who owns the metrics, and who has access to them. These questions start to arise in a context where staff and students can question the socio-political context in which they are occurring. These questions should be asked before entering any discussion around what type of platform(s) should be used to gather, store, and generate reports. This would go some way to address Selwyn's need to problematise technology and subject it to greater critical analysis. Using the idea of culture circles developing generative themes based on participants' own critical understanding of their context again could balance Selwyn's need for re-phrasing the language used to describe technologies with McCluskey and Winter's need to identify achievement of learning outcomes and exemplify mission success from a democratic, critical perspective.

Whilst we are aware that this approach may not prevent meso level data gathering exercises such as the UK TEF (teaching excellence framework), it may allow staff and students the space to critically examine their own approaches to data gathering, use, and storage. It may also provide a way to review legislation such as the new European GDPR (General Data Protection Regulation) from not simply a policing excercise with its inherent negative connotations. This would allow stakeholders to make their own sense of relevant, novel ways of using and understanding how data could potentially inform and enhance other areas of the Matrix such as curriculum and course design and participation.

Facilitation of the discussion could allow the introduction of some of Selwyn's reflections around, for example, individuals asserting their rights and perspectives against corporate/institutional dominance of technology. Having a critically informed discussion about data would allow a different level of critique of vendors, and their pre-selected dashboards using the data sources and algorithms they have decided are appropriate and that will bring about digital transformation. Our approach is more grounded on developing notions of value pluralism and critical consciousness as described in Chap. 1.

Developing a Critical Perspective: Value Pluralism and Critical Consciousness

The concept of value pluralism (Johnson and Smyth 2011) has become increasingly relevant to our thinking during our own critical reflections on the digital university concept and the further development of the digital university Matrix. According to Wikipedia, value pluralism is the idea that there are several values which may be equally correct and fundamental, and yet in conflict with each other. Value pluralism emphasises the need to recognise that different, often competing, views and perspectives of the same practices and phenomena co-exist within the same institutional context. This resonated with our original, and now extended holistic, ambitions for the use of the Matrix as a means of uniting people separated by the academic and professional silos, which typify contemporary university practice and management structures.

We could argue that the original Matrix did imply some elements of value pluralism. It was, at its most basic level, designed to provide a way for the collective needs and interests of learners, academics, technologists, academic leaders, and wider 'stakeholder' groups within and outside the institution to be shared, and thereby provide a basis for developing digital practice beyond the current limitations of, for example, the current UK TEF (teaching excellence framework). However, it was only as our own discussions and reflections developed that we realised the potential for a more explicit link to both institutional practice and academic development which we address in Chap. 11.

Value pluralism combined with a more critical view of our own managerial constructive alignment process led us to try and articulate a more socio-constructivist, theoretically informed perspective of university education. This led us to the work of Freire and in particular to his early work, Education for Critical Consciousness (1974).

We see many similarities between Freire's articulation of the differences between individuals engaging in the act of problematising (the extent to which one knows the sociocultural, economic historical context one is living in) and problem solving in universities where

> an expert takes some distance from reality, analyses it into component parts, devises means for resolving difficulties in the most efficient way, and then dictates a strategy or policy. (Freire 1974, p. xi)

The essential difference between problematising and problem solving lies in the contrast between persons as active agents in challenging their situation and persons operating as 'disinterested' external parties to a given situation. It is the difference between being a constituent and a consultant.

As we have outlined in Chap. 3, we now see the Matrix as not simply a tool to align current managerial problem solving, but rather one that becomes a symbol that can allow for the development of critical consciousness at macro, meso, and micro levels. That is, from the individual to the institutional to the wider socio-economic environment.

Our aim now for the Matrix is for it to allow a university to develop a critically informed sense of collective and individual agency around the digital. This would provide an enhanced means for a university to collectively understand and co-construct its own multi-layered sense of praxis in relation to digital developments and its realisation of the concept of the digital university. Our hope is that this will allow universities to develop a more powerful articulation of what they are for, whilst at the same time allowing for a richer and more critically informed discourse to develop that would provide a counter narrative to the pervasive and distorting neoliberal ones described in earlier chapters.

This process could take a variety of forms, but would differ from the familiar hierarchical structures of governance and management accompanied by time-limited team and project-based styles of collaborative problem solving. It would not rely on external consultants from large tech/IT companies. Our sense of alternative organisational form and process can be summed up as a commitment to a revitalised and more inclusive collegiality as the driving force for change in universities. We will develop the definition and potential value of such critical collegiality more fully in Chaps. 11 and 12.

We believe that this process would enable more authentic and sustainable development for universities that would counter some of the transformation myths around the role of the digital within education.

Universities in Transition: The Myth of Digital Transformation Revisited

In Chap. 4, we critiqued the notion of 'digital transformation' in universities as a characteristic of a rhetoric of radical change drawn from neoliberal political economy. Drawing on Freire's (1974) arguments around society in transition and the development of myths as sociocultural forces interacting with the dominant political economy of the time to oppress alternative points of view, we see parallels with the current challenges universities face from the 'myths' of neoliberalism and digital transformation.

> Perhaps the greatest tragedy of modern man is his domination by the force of these myths and his manipulation by organised advertising, ideological or otherwise. Gradually, without even realising the loss, he relinquishes his capacity for choice; he is expelled from the orbit of decisions. (Freire 1974, p. 5)

For the first two decades of the twenty-first century, universities (particularly in the UK and the Global North) have been in a state of social transition, analogous to Freire's description of the turbulent conditions in Brazil in the 1950s and 1960s. Freire (1974) described this as economic and cultural oppression of a whole class of society (peasants) by a ruling elite, which monopolised ownership of economic resources, dominated the political process, restricted access to education, and could use military force to maintain these relations. Freire's work in adult literacy was aimed at liberating those peasants from their oppressive conditions, not by 'teaching' them basic literacy, rather by engaging with them in praxis, with a view to releasing their capacity to demand and achieve progressive social and economic change. We draw an analogy between that time and our own in terms of a particular sociocultural formation, that is, one of digital massification as opposed to industrial massification.

We see the political and economic power structures around neoliberal digital disruptive transformation of education narratives as not an open, democratic process. In fact, the first decades of the twenty-first century are ones where the power and control of access to technology, and increasingly data, that can be utilised for educational purposes are being controlled and directed by global, digital elite companies such as Facebook, Google, and Amazon.

We contend that there is an urgent need for senior management in universities to take a radical, critical pedagogically based approach to the role of digital within the university. One that would allow them to thoroughly explore if universities can really enter a state of transition whereby they are actively addressing the needs of our current digital epoch, instead of the current state of retreat we see being driven by the political pressures and increasing market-driven approaches to the *business* of education. One which is based on the view that universities are in crisis, decline, and turmoil (Selwyn 2014), and which has constructed a climate where the 'progressive' neoliberal elite are closing down any form of criticality or radicalisation.

> Universities are even felt to have lost their counter-cultural cachet as forums for political debate, public conscious forming and general rabble-rousing. In short, universities are no longer believed (if they ever were) to play a useful role in societal, cultural economic or civic affairs.... In comparison, growing numbers of people now contend that digital technologies offer a fairer and faster means of higher education provision that is more in tune with the contemporary era. (Selwyn, p. 4)

Similar to Freire's Brazilian peasants, who were suborned by the myth that their circumstances represented the natural order of things to be accepted without challenge, universities are now victims of the myth and hype around the transformative power of the digital age that suppresses any contradictory, counter-narratives. We believe that this is not in the longer-term interests of the universities, their students, and the wider society.

Gourlay and Oliver (2018) highlight the way in which the digital has almost been unquestionably accepted as a bringing about a transformation within education with:

> ...the implication that it is inherently different from analogue technologies and related practices which consist predominately of print literacy practices, verbal encounters and other forms of embodied activity. This viewpoint reflects a wider perception in society that there is something fundamentally distinct about digital technologies in comparison with what came before, and that they will lead to wholesale root-and-branch change, sweeping away and entirely supplanting pre-existing analogue technologies, practices and subjectivities. (p. 15)

Thus, the radical and disputed characteristics of the neoliberal project of *sociocultural transition* from one form of political economy to another are applied to characterise the notion of *digital transformation* in universities. Consequently, the trajectory of the digital in universities is presented in similar categorical terms to the radical overhaul of society as a whole. In reality, any root-and-branch transformation arising from the digital has certainly not been immediate.

There has and continues to be a more blended transition from analogue to digital practice across learning, teaching, assessment, and research. However, far from supplanting analogue practice, many digital learning technologies simply replicate current practice and then sell it back to the sector under the promise of transformation and increased digital efficiency—an admirable example of neoliberal market relations in action perhaps. In any case, Selwyn (ibid.) highlights that the relationship between digital technology and universities is messy, often superficial, and not (to date) transformational, and that the combination of technological and the social is always complex and not as straightforward as either the 'booster' or 'doomster' advocates for/against digital transformation he describes.

As we have highlighted earlier in the chapter, Selwyn (ibid.) raises a number of critical questions around the issues and realities of universities in the digital age and crucially in line with our thinking asks:

> …how is it possible – if at all – to reconcile the idea of the 'university' for the digital age in a way that retains the core essence of higher education as a public good? (p. 7)

In effect Selwyn shifts the focus from the adoption of digital technology to questions of purpose and value. Within this context, is it not time for the senior leadership at universities to see radicalization in Freire's (1974) terms as something that is not a threat, but something that is

> …predominantly critical, loving, humble and communicative. (Freire 1974)

and so embrace it as a positive force for human and organisational development and a way to articulate a counter narrative to the neoliberal 'education is broken' one?

Participation in the Digital Age: Inclusion, Data, Control, and Critique

As described in Chap. 5, the digital does provide new and extended opportunities for participation. Digital participation has been a key construct for the development of the Matrix. Developing student understanding, capacity, and agency in relation to these characteristics of the digital age needs to be incorporated into the university curriculum and made the focus of an agenda for wider participation beyond the traditional student population.

Again it is our hope that through the development of increased criticality, the Matrix could be used to explore more fully the multiple contexts and circumstances surrounding inclusion and widening participation.

Digital divides are very much in existence. There is the obvious financial aspect of being able to afford to pay for device and connection to the Internet. More disturbingly, there is increasing evidence of digital redlining, which Gillard (2016) describes as

> …technology policies, practices, pedagogies and investment decisions that reinforce class and race boundaries.

In other words, decisions around access to and participation with digital technologies that deliberately exclude certain parts of society. This is particularly worrying in an educational context, if the digital platforms used in education only serve to perpetuate existing bias and segregation. Technological implementations are very rarely neutral.

There is a further complication in terms of developing public understanding of the importance of digital capabilities particularly around access and understanding of the implications of sharing personal data with an ever increasing number of digital providers.

During the writing of this book, the Cambridge Analytica scandal exposed by *The Guardian* and *Channel 4 News* in 2018 brought to light some of the ethically unchallenged consequences of Facebook users unwittingly allowing their data and access to the data of those connected to them to be mined for political exploitation. Participating in seemingly harmless quizzes allowed the newsfeeds of individuals to be manipulated and populated with stories based on algorithmically determined preferences.

These data-driven feeds are often referred to as filter bubbles (Pariser 2011) or echo chambers (Flaxman et al. 2016). In these algorithmically created spaces, targeted news can perpetuate particular (sometimes extreme) viewpoints without any of the edited counter-balances expected with the traditional media. The biases in mainstream media can be perceived to be more widely acknowledged and understood. There is a growing counterargument against the 'liberal elite' who feel threatened by these extreme, unedited, and often un-instantiated views. The rhetoric from the Trump election campaign and subsequently around 'fake news' exemplified these tensions, as this rhetoric was used explicitly to disrupt trust in established media outlets and, as some believe, disrupt the democratic election process.

The normalisation of dismissing expert opinion and facts and the emergence of alternative facts, from the most powerful office of state in the global north has profound implications for the future of education. Arguably we are witnessing the intensification of the anti-democratic strain of neoliberal political economy and the feeding of this strain via digital channels.

As we have stated, the neoliberal agenda around education is one that looks to a systematised solution to the problem of the broken education system. Data under the guise of personalised learning and learning analytics is increasingly being hailed as the new solution to ensure the successful student (consumer) journey. The narrative is that progress can be tracked, and personalised solutions can be delivered through intelligent digital learning systems.

The emerging field of learning analytics is making conscious efforts in terms of the ethical implications of use of data in education. For example, the EU-funded LACE Project produced the DELICATE ethical checklist for analytics.

Drachsler and Greller (2016) provided an excellent overview of the development of modern ethics and how these guiding principles should be included in any learning analytics work.

However, there are still many challenging issues that need to be addressed across the education sector around student consent, transparency, and cultural understanding (Slade and Prinsloo 2013). Jisc (2018) highlights the need for more serious engagement with the role, both positive and negative, of analytics in terms of student wellbeing.

Universities could be very fertile grounds for the development and use of some of the personality-type quizzes as used by Cambridge Analytica in conjunction with the data from learning and teaching systems such as VLEs. The behavioural aspects of education and of potential student profiling have been described as neuroliberalism (Whitehead 2018). This could be problematic if not critically challenged. The neoliberal trend for personalisation of learning is often in reality little more than a repacking of homogeneous content commonly coupled with quizzes, with a veneer of personalisation through changes in user interface options, rather than a truly personalised experience that supports and encourages the development of the learner constructing their own learning. One that doesn't leave content and assessment choice to the system but offers learners freedom to construct, or at least co-construct, these features of course design.

There is a real danger that participation could be limited due to algorithmically based decisions that do not allow for failure or more importantly allow for access to potential routes to success for those in underprivileged sectors of society. Data are not neutral, neither are algorithms, or the AI developed from them. They are infused with the biases of those who construct and own them.

Again we believe that the Matrix and associate tools could provide a more informed process for universities to use and explore the potential of digital participation from a humanist, critical pedagogy perspective.

Universities as Value Systems: A Humanist Perspective

Whilst this type of critical language may not currently appeal to some in senior leadership roles, it is interesting to note that the 1998 University Magna Charta Universitatum was signed by 388 University Rectors from across Europe and offers a clear statement of purpose and value to focus on strategic thinking. This short (two-page) statement of purpose and values for (European) universities heading into the twenty-first century stated within its principles that:

> To meet the needs of the world around it, its research and teaching must be morally and intellectually independent of all political authority and economic power.

> A university is the trustee of the European humanist tradition; its constant care is to attain universal knowledge; to fulfil its vocation it transcends geographical and political frontiers, and affirms the vital need for different cultures to know and influence each other.

These principles offer reference points with which to confront neoliberalism's impoverished vision of value of a university education as graduate earnings and its' rationale of education as a service provided to consumers. The charter provides another route to answer the question we return to throughout the book that of what, and who, are universities for?

In an opinion piece for *The Guardian* newspaper in 2018, Collini used the Magna Charta to explicitly critique the neoliberal developments in UK universities, in terms of academic freedom, tenure, and increasing managerialism. It does appear that the traditional European, humanist values of universities are being overtaken in the UK by increasing neoliberal, political interventions and directives around fees, accountability, and refocus on students as consumers.

It is our hope that the Matrix and associated tools would help to provide more criticality and a refocus on the fundamental principles enshrined in the Magna Charta. Indeed, it could be possible to explore the Matrix using either of the two principles highlighted above or indeed all of them.

However, there is still a contradiction surrounding the Magna Charta in terms of sustaining a liberal elite of universities and the need for wider democratic engagement and access and participation to and with higher education.

Conclusion

In this chapter, we have elucidated the development of our original digital university Matrix within a critical pedagogy framework drawing on open educational practice and the development of praxis. Drawing on actual use of the Matrix, we have outlined a proposed methodology that extends the original dialogic uses of the Matrix to one that can be used as a basis to develop codification of generative themes to provide novel, critical, democratic approaches to organisational development. It is our hope that through this type of critical engagement and acknowledgment of value pluralism, university development in a digital age can refocus on the humanist values of education and public pedagogy and not be solely driven by neoliberal, consumer values.

References

Biggs, J. B. (2003). *Teaching for Quality Learning at University* (2nd ed.). Buckingham: Open University Press/Society for Research into Higher Education.

Channel 4 News. (2018). *Exposed: Undercover Secrets of Trump's Data Firm.* https://www.channel4.com/news/exposed-undercover-secrets-of-donald-trump-data-firm-cambridge-analytica. Last Accessed 18 May 2018.

Collini, S. (2012). *What Are Universities For?* London: Penguin.

Collini, S. (2017). *Speaking of Universities For?* London: Verso.

Drachsler, H., & Greller, W. (2016). *Privacy and Analytics – It's a DELICATE Issue.* A Checklist to Establish Trusted Learning Analytics. 6th Learning Analytics and Knowledge Conference 2016, April 25–29, 89–98. Edinburgh. https://doi.org/10.1145/2883851.2883893.

Flaxman, S., Goel, S., & Rao, J. M. (2016). Filter Bubbles, Echo Chambers, and Online News Consumption. *Public Opinion Quarterly, 80*(S1), 298–320.

Freire, P. (1974). *Education for Critical Consciousness*. London: Bloomsbury Academic.

Gilliard, C. (2016). *Teaching in Higher Ed*. http://teachinginhighered.com/podcast/digital-redlining-privacy/. Last Accessed 2 Apr 2018.

Gourlay, L., & Oliver, M. (2018). *Student Engagement in the Digital University: Sociomaterial Assemblages*. New York: Routledge/Taylor & Francis Group.

Jisc. (2018). *Learning Analytics Help or Hindrance in the Quest for Better Student Well Being*. https://www.jisc.ac.uk/news/learning-analytics-help-or-hindrance-in-the-quest-for-better-student-mental-wellbeing. Last Accessed 24 June 2018.

Johnson, M., & Smyth, K. (2011). Diversity, Value and Technology: Exposing Value Pluralism in Institutional Strategy. *Special Issue of Campus-Wide Information Systems on Learning Technology and Institutional Strategy, 28*(4), 211–220.

McCluskey, F. B., & Winter, M. L. (2012). *The Idea of the Digital University: Ancient Traditions, Disruptive Technologies and the Battle for the Soul of Higher Education, Policy Studies Organisation*. Washington, DC: Westphalia Press.

Pariser, E. (2011). *The Filter Bubble: What the Internet Is Hiding from You*. London: Penguin.

Rugut, E. J., & Osman, A. A. (2013). Reflection on Paulo Freire and Classroom Relevance. *American Journal of Social Science, 2*(2), 23–28.

Selwyn, N. (2014). *Digital Technology and the Contemporary University: Degrees of Digitization*. London/New York: Routledge.

Slade, S., & Prinsloo, P. (2013). Learning Analytics. *American Behavioral Scientist, 57*(10), 1510–1529.

Whitehead, M. (2018). *Neuroliberalism: Behavioural Government in the Twenty First Century*. Abingdon: Routledge, Taylor & Francis Group.

10

Institutional Practice and Praxis

In the preceding chapter, we presented our extended Conceptual Matrix for the Digital University as a 'critical symbol' that can provide a means for internal and external university 'stakeholders' to engage in contextualised discussion that is rooted in practice, as part of a dialogic process that can support institutional and pedagogic change for enacting the digital university as we have conceptualised it and extending higher education as a public good.

Our main concerns in this chapter lie with the means through which we can translate dialogue and a shared commitment to a more creative, effective, and democratic harnessing of the digital into enabling institutional strategies, policies, and practices. This includes extending accepted notions of distributed academic leadership, reconciling value pluralism through establishing common language and values, implementing permissive rather than prescriptive institutional strategy, and institutional praxis with respect to social justice and socially just collaborative working between universities and their wider communities. We will position the latter issue in relation to social epistemology, and human knowledge as collective achievement for collective good, before concluding by considering the future developments that we hope will advance the position we have been advocating.

The issues we turn our attention to in this chapter do not represent a full or complete picture with respect to the institutional practices, or their manifestation in praxis, that are necessary for harnessing digital approaches, technologies, and practices in the ways that we advocate in this book. The collective experience of digital practice in the higher education sector is not, we feel, at a mature enough stage for us to fully understand the range of institutional issues and implications of moving towards the more 'holistic' vision of the digital university that we are proposing. However, we do feel the issues we highlight below, in combination with Chaps. 9 and 11, underline many of the key considerations and enabling factors.

Distributed Academic Leadership

The idea and practice of distributed leadership, in which "leadership is conceived of as a process dispersed across the organization (within systems, activities, practices and relationships) rather than residing within the traits, actions and or capabilities of leaders in formal positions" (Bolden et al. 2009), has gained increasing traction within higher education in recent years (Bolden et al., ibid.; Jones et al. 2012; Rambe and Dzansi 2016).

Proponents of distributed leadership within universities point towards the need for more democratic models of leadership and decision-making in order to counter the reduction in autonomy for academic staff as a consequence of increasingly bureaucratic, managerialist, and metrics-driven university structures; reflect and harness the values of collegiality, collaboration, and academic freedom that are deeply encultured within the academic communities of our universities; support the creative and innovate thinking and practice in education, scholarship, and research that need to happen within universities; and recognise and further enable the joint working between academic and professional service colleagues that is critical to the day-to-day functioning of universities and the range of support to be provided to learners (Bolden et al. 2009; Jones et al.

2012). Whilst there is a tension between the rhetoric and reality of distributed leadership within our universities, including the extent to which distributed leadership is enacted collectively and democratically as opposed to becoming a mechanism for appeasement within still overly bureaucratic and managerialist university structures and processes, we recognise the 'ideal' as one that is consistent with and a pre-requisite for a reimagining of the university in relation to the digital, an extension of higher education as a public good, and the forms of co-production, co-location, and openness of knowledge and learning opportunities we have explored thus far.

The ideal of distributed academic leadership, a term we use broadly in reference to academic-related practices undertaken within and through the university, is critically important to reconciling the disconnect between the creative and more democratic uses of digital technologies and spaces for knowledge construction and sharing that are taking place beyond the university with our more constrained, delivery-focused practices within the university. We also view distributed academic leadership as central to the critical and reflexive dialogue we need to have with the wider communities within which our universities sit and are part of, so as to ensure the relevance of the curriculum (and the knowledge created through the learning and teaching activities of the curriculum and university) to wider societal needs.

To these ends, we take a broader view of who should be engaged in distributed leadership than is often discussed in relation to universities and their development. Many advocates of distributed leadership propose an approach that "embraces all institutional employees, engaged both in direct academic roles of teaching and learning and research or in indirect roles of designing new environments for learning and teaching, supporting students, and providing the specialist and professional activities that underpin contemporary universities" (Jones et al. 2012, p. 68), a position within which students and stakeholders from within the wider community are conspicuously absent. Here, we contend that the disconnect and broader concerns identified above can only be reconciled with the active participation and empowerment of our students and community stakeholders in decision-making dialogue, if our concern is with the nature and continued role and relevance of higher education.

We see in the above a potential relationship between more equal and inclusive approaches to distributed leadership in our universities, and the Freirean concept of culture circles we explored in the previous chapter. However, consistent with our explorations of educational strategy and practice at the macro, meso, and micro levels, we also think it useful to consider the levels at which distributed leadership could be taking place in order to advance the development of the digital university as we have been envisaging it. Here, we would argue that distributed leadership should not simply be at the institutional level, as is often presupposed, but should also be evident within specific learning and teaching contexts (supporting what we referred to in Chap. 8 as co-creation within the curriculum) and at course or programme level (supporting the co-creation of the curriculum). Mirroring the meta-narrative of this book, we also identify a need for more democratic dialogue, leadership, inter-agency engagement, and reflexive action in developing more inclusive, progressive, and democratic approaches to digital practice in the higher education sector.

The potential challenges and difficulties of distributed leadership become more nuanced in relation to the harnessing of technology within universities. Rambe and Dzansi (2016) attribute this to institutional leadership and technology adoption being regarded as different domains of expertise and responsibility in universities, which in turn generates an associated hierarchical polarity which constrains a wider recognition of all those who should be engaged in digital developments in the university, and can lead to divergent discourses and values relating to what is most important in relation to, for example, institutional priorities and strategies, learning and teaching development, and the needs of the learners themselves.

Reconciling Value Pluralism

Recognising that different and often competing values and perspectives will exist in relation to the nature, purpose, and practices of the university, and the role of the digital within it has been central to our concern with 'value pluralism' that we first introduced in Chap. 1. In their exploration of value pluralism with respect to institutional strategy and educational technology, Johnson and Smyth (2011) drew upon the work of Isaiah Berlin in recognising that different values in relation to the same phenomena "may be fundamentally and defensibly correct in different contexts" (p. 212) and from the perspectives, needs, and interests of individual actors in the same social situation. Through a series of workshops undertaken in 2010, Johnson and Smyth (ibid.) facilitated a connected programme of interventions designed to "'make visible' the needs and values of different stakeholders in relation to institutional strategy and approaches to technology", in order to identify points of conflict, establish common positions, and create a greater shared sense of realism in relation to the development of institutional approaches to technology-enhanced education.

One of Johnson and Smyth's main contentions is that exposing value pluralism within the harnessing of the digital in higher education institutions is a necessary challenge, and brings with it the opportunity to negotiate and shape future directions that are likely to be more developmental and progressive in nature, rather than re-replicating established practices or uncritically introducing new approaches to digitally enabled or supported education.

It is a view we share, as reflected in the development and application of the original Matrix for the digital university, and the expanded Matrix and Digitally Distributed Curriculum constructs that we have described in the previous two chapters and now put forward as tools to guide collective critical reflection, dialogue, decision-making, and action. To a large extent, the Matrixes and Digitally Distributed Curriculum constructs are themselves an outcome of our own work in exploring and attempting to reconcile different organisational, theoretical, and pedagogical factors, through practical application, peer dialogue, and our own reflection.

They also represent an attempt to arrive at a 'common language' for thinking about and enacting the digital university, and associated practices, as we have conceptualised them within this book. We view the establishment of shared models and constructs of the kind we propose, and of mutually understood common ideals and language, as a desired outcome of dialogue which is focused on surfacing, confronting, and moving beyond 'value pluralism'. Of the other practical ways through which this might be achieved within the university, we would also argue the need for non-prescriptive, values-based institutional strategies to support the development of digitally supported or enabled educational practices.

Permissive Institutional Policies and Strategies

Institutional policy and strategy in relation to learning and teaching, and the adoption of digital technologies to support learning, teaching, and broader aspects of the student experience, are recognised as both essential to the development of effective practice within our educational institutions but potentially also delimiting of what is possible (Sharpe et al. 2006; Czerniewicz and Brown 2009; Johnson and Smyth 2011).

The extent to which policy and strategy are either enabling or restrictive with respect to how creatively and effectively the digital is located and harnessed within the university will in part be dependent on whether policy and strategy are defined by a specific set of views and values, or reflect a wider range of views that converge, as discussed above, around a collectively constructed and agreed set of values. However, it is also dependent on the extent to which policies and strategies present either a narrowly defined 'orthodoxy' of what should characterise and define digitally enabled education practices, or recognise the importance of and enable practices that are rich in their diversity and appropriateness for different contexts, disciplines, approaches, and levels of engagement. For Czerniewicz and Brown (ibid.), prescriptive policies and top-down strategies are problematic in that they will often support a 'breadth of use' or adoption across the university, but will rarely support a depth of use and practice. They argue that "rather than telling academics what to do, and worse still telling them how to do it, policy principles would be more usefully manifest in an enabling structure and systems that encourage and reward exploration" (p. 114).

Institutional culture is a key factor here, both as a part of and in relation to how it is also enabled by organisational structures and relationships. The development of effective pedagogic practice, including emergent practices and approaches, is linked to institutional cultures that support experimentation, creative educational thinking, problem-solving, and critical reflection on the effectiveness and refinement of practice based on what are often referred to as 'bottom-up' and 'middle out' approaches to institutional leadership and change, characterised by increased autonomy and agency for colleagues, networking and mentoring, and academic development interventions that are applied and practice-based (Whitchurch and Gordon 2017; Czerniewicz and Brown 2009; Mayes et al. 2009).

As for the form that an enabling strategy for guiding contextually relevant pedagogic and digital education practice might take, there are several examples in the sector (e.g. Sharpe et al. 2006; Hall 2011; Strickland et al. 2011). Strickland et al. (2011) describe a "dynamic learning, teaching and assessment strategy" that comprises three levels: a short framing set of value statements relating to institutional-level educational aims and aspirations, school and departmental interpretations of those values to their own disciplines or areas of responsibility, and an open education resource bank designed to support the strategy through providing relevant case studies of good practice and links to further guidance.

Hall (2011) offers a rich critique of the purpose of institutional strategies for digital education practice, with a focus on resilience and responding to wider societal needs and crises. Within this, Hall describes a "pragmatic approach to catalysing a resilient use of educational technology" through developing "a vision and blueprint for joined-up systems of TEL" (p. 242) which distinguishes and provides guidance for effectively utilising 'core' technologies including the institutional VLE, 'arranged' technologies in the form of plug-ins and subscribed services, 'recommended' external technologies including social media applications and networking platforms for which support is available, and 'recognised' technologies that the institution is aware students and staff are using, but which remain under a 'horizon scanning' brief until the point where a critical mass of use is established.

Sharpe et al. (2006) present an approach to implementing an institutional e-learning strategy that is focused on devolved and distributed ownership and 'levers for change' within academic schools. Their aims comprised developing ownership and commitment to the strategy at departmental level, harnessing the energy of 'innovators' to drive change forward, supporting staff to "make educationally sound choices about using technology", and making senior managers "aware of the groundswell of energy good practice already occurring" (pp. 137–138). We think this latter point is particularly important and would contend that whatever ethos or aspirations for digital education practice are encapsulated in institutional policy or strategy, regardless of how new or 'innovate' they may seem to be, there will be practitioners and learners in the institution already engaging in the kinds of practices that are being espoused as a way forward. Institutional strategy and policy must bring these existing practices to the surface and provide a platform for recognising, sharing, and learning from pedagogic work and engagements that are already well-established at grassroots level.

In many of the examples explored above (Sharpe et al. 2006; Czerniewicz and Brown 2009; Strickland et al. 2011), the need to link 'permissive', devolved policies and strategies to wider supporting structures (e.g. advocates or 'champions', mentoring, case studies, and exemplars) in order to substantially advance digital education practice is made clear, This includes the importance of academic development opportunities and interventions which role model and immerse academics in the kinds of creative and effective practices that it is hoped they will then engage and support their own learners with and through.

We will come on to explore academic development, and the shape this might take in relation to our own vision of the digital university, in the next chapter. For now, we want to make an important related point about institutional policy and strategy that is intended to support the development of digital education practice. This concerns university policy and processes for curriculum development, approval, and renewal.

Within the UK context, although we are also cognisant of this applying in other regions too, many universities operate at best a three-year cycle of curriculum re-approval at programme level. In many institutions, the cycle will be five years. In addition, programme approval and re-approval processes tend very often to be about the completeness of curriculum documentation including availability of resources, with some accompanying description of the student market for new and continuing programmes, and of the delivery means and mechanisms within modularised curriculum structures. We would challenge the extent to which current processes of this kind can actually support, and enable in a responsive and timely manner, any curriculum or pedagogical developments that go substantially beyond replicating existing dominant approaches, or which go beyond marginal and slow incremental change (e.g. the updating of readings lists, minor changes to learning outcomes, and modifications to assignment briefs when programmes are reapproved).

Our key point in relation to the above is that permissive and enabling strategies relating to learning and teaching, and the development of digital education practices that are genuinely more creative, engaging, and progressive, must be supported by corresponding policies and processes for enacting curriculum and pedagogic change and reform within the university.

Institutional Praxis and Social Justice

Pedagogic change and reform of the kind we are advocating in relation to our conceptualisation of the digital university must also extend to and enable an institutional praxis in relation to meeting wider societal needs. We have discussed in previous chapters how this might be enabled in relation to the nature and range of open education practices, and a positioning of the curriculum and the work our students undertake through the curriculum in relation to creating knowledge and knowledge artefacts that have a value and resonance beyond the university for specific communities or specific groups within the wider community. Furthermore, in the preceding discussion above, we have identified the need for a range of 'stakeholders' to be engaged in dialogue and decision-making about the university, learning and teaching, the curriculum, and our harnessing of the digital.

We see these processes and dialogues as central to the role of our universities in contributing to social justice, and socially just engagements with and within our wider communities. As will have become apparent by this point in our book, we share with commentators including Harkavy (2006) the view that a critical goal for universities "should be to contribute significantly to developing and sustaining democratic schools, communities and societies" (p. 5), and that we can achieve this through a reframing of the curriculum and who it is for, challenging cognitive dissonance between academic knowledge and real-world needs, focusing on what Harkavy (ibid., p. 19) refers to as "significant, community-based, real world problems", and through inclusive and democratic distributed leadership that confronts value pluralism and moves us towards collective values and understandings.

We must also bring into focus here a commitment to equality agendas and confronting barriers to widening participation in formal higher education including cost of participation, entry requirements, and lack of flexible learning opportunities as identified by Brennan and Naidoo (2008). We must also consider, in the broader context of institutional praxis and social justice, the matter of social epistemology and of human knowledge as a collective achievement for a collective good. This has been implied in much our previous discussion, where we have focused on student work that has a wider public value and where we have discussed the importance of open knowledge and open knowledge practices. Here, we might make a further pragmatic distinction between knowledge for experts (e.g. within specific and highly specialised disciplines) and public knowledge (e.g. relating to social policy and welfare, politics, health, and accessing democratic processes and public services) that can and should benefit the wider populace (Brennan and Naidoo 2008, pp. 296–297). We believe there is an important dialogue and area for action, in extending the universities and higher education as a public good, to identify where 'public knowledge' is being created within and through academic engagements inside and beyond the university and curriculum and to harness digital spaces, and open approaches, in the distribution of that knowledge.

Aspirations for Future Developments

Where does the above, and associated earlier discussions, leave us with respect to the future development of the digital university, and related academic and pedagogic practices, as we have been envisaging them? Certainly we think there is a need, moving forward, to develop more democratic forms of university governance in relation to the wider community and to translate joint dialogue into actions for ensuring the relevance of the university, the curriculum, 'open digital', and 'open in the community' educational opportunities and engagement. This should be reflected in joint dialogue and leadership in relation to programmes of study and also be supported and enabled through policies and strategies that support critical reflection on learning and teaching and how this should be developed. It is perhaps particularly aspirational to think that a commitment to the ethos, concepts, and tools of critical pedagogy would frame policy and practice in the above areas, although we would argue for the necessity of this in order to develop and enact the ideas of the digital university and Digitally Distributed Curriculum as we have envisaged and presented them.

We are conscious of and welcome the development of alternative models of post-school adult and higher education, for example, the Ragged University and COOCs model as explored in previous chapters, and also including initiatives like the Free University Brighton. Universities, individually and collectively, need to challenge themselves to define and understand their position in relation to the aforementioned organisations and alternatives, who are achieving or striving to achieve more with respect to democratic and socially just access to further and higher education than many universities are. Which may beg the question, in relation to the institutional practice and praxis of formal higher education institutions, of where universities are to be placed within the 'joint project' of adult education?

Conclusion

We have considered above what we feel are some of the key issues, dimensions, and challenges pertaining to institutional practice and praxis in relation to the digital university, and for the extension of higher education as a public good. In combination in particular with the preceding chapter, and the one that now follows, we hope we are illuminating potential ways forward for the development of the digital university and the associated values of co-production, openness, porosity, community, and social value which we see as central to both the digital university construct and to more democratic higher education practice.

References

Bolden, R., Petrov, G., & Gosling, J. (2009). Distributed Leadership in Higher Education: Rhetoric and Reality. *Educational Management Administration andLeadership,37*(2),257–277.https://doi.org/10.1177/1741143208100301.

Brennan, J., & Naidoo, R. (2008). Higher Education and the Achievement (and/or Prevention) of Equity and Social Justice. *Higher Education, 56*(3), 287–302. https://doi.org/10.1007/s10734-008-9127-3.

Czerniewicz, L., & Brown, C. (2009). Intermediaries and Infrastructure as Agents: The Mediation of e-Learning Policy and Use by Institutional Culture. In T. Mayes, D. Morrison, H. Mellar, P. Bullen, & M. Oliver (Eds.), *Transforming Higher Education Through Technology-Enhanced Learning* (pp. 107–121). York: Higher Education Academy.

Hall, R. (2011). Towards a Resilient Strategy for Technology-Enhanced Learning. *Campus-Wide Information Systems*, Special Issue of on Learning Technology and Institutional Strategy, *28*(4), 234–249.

Harkavy, I. (2006). The Role of Universities in Advancing Citizenship and Social Justice in the 21st Century. *Education, Citizenship and Social Justice, 1*(1), 5–37. https://doi.org/10.1177/1746197906060711.

Johnson, M., & Smyth, K. (2011). Diversity, Value and Technology: Exposing Value Pluralism in Institutional Strategy. *Campus-Wide Information Systems*, Special Issue of on Learning Technology and Institutional Strategy, *28*(4), 211–220.

Jones, S., Lefoe, G., Harvey, M., & Ryland, K. (2012). Distributed Leadership: A Collaborative Framework for Academics, Executives and Professionals in Higher Education. *Journal of Higher Education Policy and Management, 34*(1), 67–78. https://doi.org/10.1080/1360080X.2012.642334.

Mayes, T., Morrison, D., Mellar, H., Bullen, P., & Oliver, M. (Eds.). (2009). *Transforming Higher Education Through Technology-Enhanced Learning*. York: Higher Education Academy.

Rambe, P., & Dzansi, D. Y. (2016). Informal Distributed Leadership in Technology Adoption. *African Journal of Science, Technology, Innovation and Development, 8*(2), 155–165. https://doi.org/10.1080/20421338.2016.1147200.

Sharpe, R., Benfield, G., & Richard, F. (2006). Implementing a University e-Learning Strategy: Levers for Change Within Academic Schools. *ALT-J, 14*(2), 135–151. https://doi.org/10.1080/09687760600668503.

Strickland, K., McLatchie, J., & Pelik, R. (2011). Reflections on the Development of a Dynamic Learning, Teaching and Assessment Strategy. *Campus-Wide Information Systems*, Special Issue of on Learning Technology and Institutional Strategy, *28*(4), 294–298.

Whitchurch, C., & Gordon, G. (2017). *Reconstructing Relationships in Higher Education: Challenging Agendas*. London: Routledge.

11

Academic Development for the Digital University

Introduction

This chapter will address the role and importance of systematic, institutionally managed academic staff development in implementing and embedding effective digital practice within the university. As an outcome of our own praxis through the writing of this book, we will discuss academic development as critical practice, one that is not just about enhancement and marginal change, but one that provides a fundamental basis for the development of enhanced criticality across and beyond a university. A key part of our proposition is that academic development needs to be recognised as a central part of wider organisational development and change.

Academic development that is explicitly informed by critical pedagogy could provide a means to develop a greater sense of agency for both individuals and institutions. It is our belief that current academic development activity is underutilised and under-recognised as a tool for strategic change that can work effectively at macro, meso, and micro levels. Building on the work of Land (2004) and Neame (2013), we propose a new orientation for the academic developer, that of a critical, open provocateur. We also highlight the need to recognise the evolving nature of the academic developer in terms of the increasing porosity between academic developers, educational developers, and learning technologists.

This would situate academic development within a macro level role both within an institution and at sector level.

What Is Academic Development: History and Current State of Play

> We suggest an overall purpose for academic development – to lead and support the improvement of student development. (Popovic and Baume 2016, Advancing Practice in Academic Development, p. 1)

This definition is one that the majority of staff engaged in academic development activities would recognise. We acknowledge that it is within the context of improvement in learning and teaching practice that academic development is probably most commonly understood and the perception of its value resides within the HE sector. So whilst we do not disagree with the intent of the above definition, we do believe that there is the potential for an extended, more holistic role for academic development within the context of the overall organisational development of a university. This view has not been universally accepted however.

For some, the very notion of academic development was quite radical in itself. The idea of teaching university staff how to teach and work with staff to improve teaching based on theories of learning could be seen as a form of radical interference in the role of academics. One that situated learning and teaching at the heart of the educational experience at university, and staff development, and not solely on the development of the academic discipline itself. In turn, academic development units have come under pressure to justify their purpose, value, and existence within universities since their inception.

Over 20 years ago, in 1997, the Dearing Report recommended the need for a level of training for university staff. This was a catalyst for academic development units within the UK sector to gain a significant level of traction and recognition within institutions.

The subsequent development of formal, Masters level courses and PG Certificates in higher education aligned to the development of a formal professional body, the Higher Education Academy (since spring 2018 known as Advance HE), and the development of its accreditation framework, the UKPSF (UK Professional Standards Framework for Teaching and Supporting Learning in Higher Education), in 2011 is evidence of the impact and continued recognition for the need for staff development in the practice of teaching and the importance of growing and sustaining research into scholarly practice and theories of learning. Evidencing engagement with the UKPSF is aligned to professional recognition as a Fellow of the Higher Education Academy, which in the UK is a professional status that is increasingly expected of academic staff working in the UK higher education institution, with Associate, Senior, and Principal Fellow recognition open to those in supporting and leadership roles with respect to learning and teaching.

The last 30 years have also seen a growth in the development and use of educational technology. This too could be seen as a radical intervention. This technological advance brought with it the emergence of a new cohort of academic development professionals from a diverse set of backgrounds—some discipline specific, others technology specific, some from academic development. They all fell into the very broad definition of Learning Technologist. This new set of professionals was hard to categorise as the range and understanding of their practice varied widely from institution to institution and from, at that stage, individual to individual. Oliver (2002) was one of the first to try and categorise the practice of these emerging professionals. At that stage, technology, not learning theory, was a common driver for learning technologists to work with academics in the collaborative development of curriculum. As the profession and individuals within it have evolved and taken on more senior roles, so too have the characteristics of the learning technologists. Member associations such as ALT in the UK (Association for Learning Technology) have emerged and have developed their own professional peer-reviewed, portfolio-based recognition schemes, that is, CMALT (Certified Member of ALT). The Staff and Educational Development Association (SEDA) has also expanded their professional recognition framework to include professional recognition awards for supporting and embedding learning technologies, achieved through portfolio or recognised courses.

The increasing merging of departments, expansion of professional positions, and the growing adoption of technology enhanced learning have led to an overlapping of practice and roles for academic/educational developers and learning technologists. Walker and MacNeill (2015) proposed that there is now an emerging new professional tribe, which they described as digital pedagogues, who share a common focus on learning enhancement and supporting innovative practice underpinned by research and scholarly activity.

Whilst these changes to the staff who constitute an academic development department within a university are positive, questions still remain around the purpose and inclusivity of academic development. From our perspective, there is an often unrecognised opportunity for academic development units to play a more significant role in the overall organisational development of a university.

Who Is Academic Development for and is it Inclusive?

Traditionally, the remit of academic development has been aligned to supporting academic teaching staff in developing their practice and understanding of teaching within a framework provided by pedagogic research. Whilst this approach has been the staple of provision, other strands have emerged. Academic identity is a growing area of research, which adds additional dimensions to the field of academic development. It is not the intention of this chapter to critique that discourse or literature; however, we do acknowledge the everyday struggle of colleagues in developing their own sense of praxis in an ever increasingly regulated sector. Fanghanel (2012) positions academic roles and practice as being constructed through individual navigation of the tensions between formal structures and the communities in which one is situated and one's personal position towards those structures. These experiences constitute the day-to-day reality of the teaching role, and insights gained from research into that experience need to be aligned with more obvious topics of learning theory and practice when designing academic development programmes.

Digital technologies have also introduced additional opportunities and complexities to the scholarly role of academics. Web 2.0 and social media brought about a radical change in publishing with the rise of a range of platforms and services that anyone could use to publish their work, thus circumventing the traditional academic publishing process and the boundaries of institutions. In his exploration of the notion, origins, relevance, and impact of the digital scholar, Weller (2011) defines a digital scholar as someone who "employs digital, networked and open approaches to demonstrate specialism in a field".

Many academic, educational technology, and discipline-specific scholars have embraced digital technologies and their affordances in working across discipline and institutional communities and boundaries. For those academics in precarious employment conditions, digital technologies provide a vital way to participate within 'the academy' whilst not being fully part of it. Social networks and digital technologies are once again playing a vital role in the permeability and porosity of personal development and sharing of practice, knowledge, and praxis.

Sutherland and Grant (2016) provide an overview of research in academic development. Their review highlights the tension within the academic development community around the very nature of research and scholarly activity related to academic development. They highlight the differences between those who advocate that it (academic development) is a distinct disciplinary community; those who argue that it is in fact a distinctive field of practice, influenced by a multitude of other disciplinary communities; and those who advocate against the need for any such confining definitions.

Whilst we welcome the fact that research and publication into scholarly practice in HE learning and teaching is undoubtedly growing, its value is still not as widely recognised as those of the 'traditional' disciplines within universities. The very nature of academic/educational development, which is at its heart about developing people and their teaching practice, is also one that is challenging to measure.

For academic developers, and academic development units, the formal structures in which they operate have required a level of institutional reporting on impact that is slightly different to the traditional disciplines or schools within an institution. The value of academic development units has not always been fully recognised or appreciated, by traditional disciplines, who may have (and is some cases, still) considered the need to learn about teaching and theories of learning as something not entirely relevant to their discipline. Therefore, the internal worth of an academic developer/development unit is closely bundled to institutional goals and targets. Measuring progress against institutional and sector expected KPIs (key perfomance indicators), for example, staff with professional accreditation, is an obvious and relatively straightforward measurement or indicator of the contribution of academic development. Whilst there has been a gradual shift from quality assurance to quality enhancement, measuring the effectiveness of academic development is a perennial issue, made even more complex with the steady increase in the use of technology enhanced learning. Gunn, Creanor, Lent, and Smyth (2014) describe the challenges of evaluating academic development as a 'wicked problem'.

Land (2004) produced a framework that captured and conceptualised orientations to academic development. Neame's (2013) subsequent extension illustrates the tendency for attaching research in the practice of the academic developer to institutional aims/practice and impact. They identify and build on a set of key orientations or characteristics of an academic developer which are expressed in terms of organisational roles (Table 11.1).

We now suggest a further addition to that list, that of expanding the role of provocateur to that of *critical, open provocateur,* thus providing an explicit link to developing practice that is based on both critical and open pedagogical perspectives, which addresses the wider socio-political context in which any development of academic practice and organisational change is situated.

It is our hope that this change of emphasis could also allow for greater inclusivity around notions of the value and importance of developing and implementing theories of learning. Academic development tends to work firmly within the academy. Given the current neoliberal context universities find themselves in as we have described throughout the book,

Table 11.1 Orientations to educational development (Neame 2013; adapted from Land 2004)

Orientation
Managerial (Development as an institutionally mandated process of transition from one state of staff competence to another)
Political—strategic (Pragmatic: using networks to achieve a balance between 'presence' across the institution and 'impact' in policy delivery)
Opportunist (Change agent, exploiting shifts, cracks, or uncertainty in the organisation)
Entrepreneurial (Emphasis on achieving innovation, employability targets, and so on. Less focussed on community building)
Researcher (Educational development mobilised as an integrated part of the academic community's disciplinary development)
Romantic (ecological humanist) (Emphasis on development of the individual)
Reflective practitioner "Emphasis is not on competence but on the process of becoming more competent" (Gibbs 1996). Development as experiential learning for developers and their colleagues
Professional competence (Combines an 'apprenticeship' notion which aligns with 'training' to serve learner needs)
Internal consultant (Support for client-specified development, not externally instigated intervention)
Modeller-broker (Good practice identified by developer, then 'promoted' within a community of practice)
Interpretive-hermeneutic (Development as dialogue; interpretation and re-interpretation by mutually respectful colleagues)
Provocateur (Emphasis on change agents, typically drawn from within an academic community itself)

we advocate that academic developers should find ways to work more inclusively across and outwith institutions. Tertiary education is not the remit of universities alone, there needs to be greater dialogue across formal and informal sectors, including the third sector. The orientation of open, critical provocateur could develop such opportunities and link up to shared themes of criticality and openness in other contexts.

Academic Development Versus Tech Consultancy

We also firmly believe that academic development should be central to any notions of digital development and not become secondary to neoliberal consultancy modes of addressing the digital. In our critique of differing approaches to the digital and universities in Chap. 2, we highlighted a paper from PWC and one from Gibbs et al. Although differing in tone, both take a very positive, business-focused approach to university organisational change and development.

In PWC's Taking Points paper, *The 2018 digital university: staying relevant in the digital age*, their view of the digital spins a narrative web for the needed personalised, connected, data-driven, and customer-driven approaches.

> Universities that are able to harness the potential of data by analysing it intelligently and using it to deliver outcomes, such as improved academic performance, employability rates or student retention, will give themselves a considerable advantage. (PWC 2018, p. 5)

They extol the very values and measures we have critiqued throughout the book. Data is about efficiency, with no mention of ethics or bias. The need for competition, not increased collegiality as we propose, is prominent:

> universities have a new breed of customers that they need to engage with, and competitors that they need to compete with, in new and different ways. (p. 6)

Although digital literacy and the need for a focus on teaching are mentioned, there is no mention of how this will be done, apart from through the development and use of new technologies. Whilst they do highlight the need for community support, it is implicit that this support is centred around the use of digital learning systems and data to:

> Encourage the advanced use of learning platforms by academics to deliver better outcomes for students and the university and to capture valuable learning data for use in analytics.

What exactly constitutes valuable learning data is not actually described.

Their digital blueprint is firmly centred on marketing and the student consumer model. However, this type of narrative is often seen by senior management as a viable basis for developing strategy.

The Entrepreneurial University paper (Gibbs et al. 2012) provides a more academic review and proposition for university development based on research and practice in entrepreneurialism. Whilst there is acknowledgement of pluralism within universities, for example, in the tensions across disciplinary lines in terms of funding and focus, and the need to have shared common goals, their focus is again firmly based in neoliberalism and in providing leadership and structure for the success of university as a business and an entrepreneurial one at that.

Producing products (including students and research outputs) that sustain the capitalist status quo in terms of universities providing value to society is key. As we have already highlighted, this view of what a university is for tips decisively in favour of the integration of academic activity in a competitive global knowledge economy and a digitally networked society. Knowledge is produced primarily for economic gain. Student learning is focused on the development of relevant skills for recruitment to the knowledge workforce with the implication that staff research, teaching, and administrative responsibilities will be subordinate to such aims.

The digital is mentioned, for example, as part of the external environment to be accepted and adopted as a process activity contributing to the overall mission. There is reference to MOOCs and Big Data, both depicted as challenging but necessary and uniformly positive. The technological dimension is closely linked to university knowledge transfer initiatives and is therefore aligned to the business function account of a university. There is apparently no room in this model for the role of developing scholarly practice around learning and teaching practice.

We hope that our counter-narrative around the development of agency and praxis would provide a more democratic, contextualised, and inclusive approach to the organisational development of the 'business' of a university. For example, aligning curriculum development around the values and dimensions underpinning our digitally distributed curriculum model (Fig. 8.1) could provide a more engaging, contextualised way to begin to address wider issues of participation, access enabled and supported by relevant digital services and infrastructure. Equally the developer role of critical, open provocateur offers a means to channel counter narratives into strategic thinking and localised practice as a way to create the kind of digital university needed to regenerate higher education's place in society as a public good.

Academic Development as Critical Practice: A Reflection

It is not our intention to detract from current practice within academic development. We fully acknowledge the positive impact that many of our colleagues have made to developing critical, reflective practice and extending the scholarship of learning and teaching. Academic developers have, and continue to make, impact on transforming learning and teaching and developing scholarly practice. However, it could be argued that this has occurred within a vacuum of developing and defining a distinct discipline through researching and understanding scholarly approaches to practice—one that has not typically included a critique of the socio-economic contexts in which developing practice is occurring.

Roxå and Mårtensson's (2017) critique of academic development resonates with our thinking. In their paper 'Agency and structure in academic development practices: are we liberating academic teachers or are we part of a machinery suppressing them?', they provide a current, critical review of the situation facing academic development and academic developers. Drawing on a range of contemporary literature and in particular the work of Manathunga (2011), they illustrate how academic development has lost some of its original focus, what we have described as radical identity, through increasingly narrow emphasis/focus on teaching and learning, and alignment to the politics and policies (at macro and meso levels) prevalent within universities and national agencies. They describe this evolution as leading the academic developer to be increasingly "entangled in the power dynamics of our institutions" (p. 96). They then go on to unpack the nature of the power within academic development and the role of academic developer, in the sense that academic developers are afforded the power "to do things to others" (p. 96). However, this notion of power is not commonly used in current academic development discourse. Their intent is to use that notion of power as a starting point for a wider, reflexive discussion, which relates to a wider political sharing of ideologies and beliefs in higher education.

Their narrative reflection of their experiences and the routine of the academic developer lifecycle—teaching on mandatory course, developing and working within new policy frameworks, managing accountability—resonated with our own. We all have felt at times that our experiences and workload are a result of "being produced by the practice rather than being in control of what happens" (p. 96) with little opportunity for critical reflection on what and why we are doing things.

Roxå and Märtensson's practice was challenged by an external social anthropological researcher (Friberg 2015) who took a critical and provocative stance to academic development. He positioned academic developers as "prime agents for a suppressing machinery anchored in globalisation and economofication with an agenda to control academic developers for the benefit of economic growth linked to a neoliberal ideology of life". He argues that the language used in the formalisation of teaching and learning actually leads to a lack of variation and leads to the loss of academic freedom. The concept of Constructive Alignment, which forms a prominent part of academic development theory and practice, is positioned as part of a wider politically driven process, in which the student is treated as a product of curriculum and assessments. These assessments of student performance in turn are used to measure teacher performance. The discourse of academic development becomes part of a machine feeding the wider neoliberal ideologies of the student as consumers service economy approach to education.

This emotional response amongst the academic development community caused by this critique led to a reflection on the perceptions of freedom, power, and control based on the concept of governmentality in (neo) liberal society. We increasingly live in a world where there is an illusion of choice that is in fact driven by technological determinism and behaviourist approaches to consumerism—the myths of the digital, which we identified in Chap. 1 and elaborated in Chap. 4.

As Roxå and Märtensson (ibid) highlight, most academic developers, including ourselves, would not subscribe to being "footsoldiers in the frontline of an enterprise wheeled by evil machinery" (p. 103). We are all guilty of getting on with the job, trying to survive within ever-changing priorities and policies, and actually trying to keep our jobs. This leads us to not making the time to question and critique the wider socio-economic context in which we find ourselves in. Surviving the seemingly never ending rounds of organisational and policy changes within universities is often all that most of us can do. To counter this, we suggest that academic developers need to recognise and embrace the necessity to simultaneously occupy two quite distinct positions. On the one hand, we have a role to play in sustaining, supporting, and enhancing 'effective' learning and teaching practice within our universities. On the other hand, as academic developers this positions as uniquely placed to critically challenge and change what is accepted or acceptable practice and to be instrumental in the development of more progressive, inclusive, and democratic practices.

In terms of organisational change (and control), policies are often used to prescribe expected behaviour. This is very common within universities. Mapping outcomes and deliverables to strategic policies, for example, student experience or learning and teaching strategies, is an increasingly common measure of accountability for academic developers and the wider academic disciplines. Policy impacts practice at micro, meso, and macro levels and is symbolic of the power dynamics with any organisation and including universities.

Policies are linked to other policies creating an intricate web of symbols and acts of power. (Roxå and Mårtensson, ibid., p. 100)

However, as academic developers 'do things' to people, we are perhaps in a more powerful position than we or our university management realise.

We see a natural progression from the strategies of critique and resistance posited by Roxå and Mårtensson to our extended notion of the academic developer as a critical, open provocateur. The critical, open provocateur role would be to develop counter narratives through scaffolded discussions informed through a critical pedagogy stance. In this way, contextualised generative themes could be developed through the use of our Matrix and associated tools as described in Chap. 9.

Academic Development as Critical Intervention

Central to the position of the academic developer as a critical, open provocateur, and indeed to the enactment of more provocative, disruptive, and progressive academic development practices, is the need for our academic development opportunities to extend beyond enhancement and instead serve as what we have termed 'critical interventions'. Our perspective here is a simple. Wherever possible the academic development opportunities we seek to engage our colleagues in (whether these be workshops, seminars, mentoring, or formal courses) must act as collegiate but critically focused interventions. Providing extended opportunities for dialogue, reflection, and action that are orientated towards an enrichment of learning and teaching and the curriculum. Thereby disrupting, challenging, and changing the educational practices of the university beyond merely sustaining, re-creating, or marginally improving existing practices.

What this could mean in practice are dialogues focused on critically exploring the relevance of external benchmarks and frameworks, and internal policies and strategies, that influence or shape what effective learning and teaching should look like, and asking whether the values and approaches they espouse are representative of established ideals and orthodoxies or of what is possible and desirable in relation to higher education practices that value negotiation, co-production, culturally rich and diverse learning experiences, democratic engagement, and wider social benefit. This would extend to challenging our academics and academic leaders to scrutinise the curricula for which they are possible and to consider the ways in which their curricula are pedagogically, culturally, or technologically bounded as explored in Chap. 8.

In relation to academic development courses for staff, and particularly PG Cert or MEd programmes, we think the challenge is more substantial. Programmes of this kind need to encompass the opportunities for critical reflection and dialogue we outline above, whilst also immersing academics and other colleagues with a responsibility for learning and teaching in the kinds of authentic, collaborative, culturally rich, democratic, and digitally enabled learning approaches that we have been advocating and which we describe more fully in Chaps. 8 and 9. This is not merely for the purposes of supporting critical reflection and the 'role modelling' of what is possible, but for ensuring that the emerging generation of academics and academic leaders within our institutions can contribute, as critical pedagogues and critical practitioners, to ensuring the future relevance of our universities and higher education both generally and in relation to societal needs, challenges, and inequities.

Academic Development as a Means for Open, Extended Collegiality

As we have discussed, academic developers are already well placed to support communities of open practice and notions of extended collegiality across institutions. This is evident through the development of a number of micro level open CPD opportunities including #BYOD4L (Bring your own device for learning)—a week-long open 'event' to share practice based on the 5 C Model (Nerantzi and Beckingham 2015)—and the weekly #LTHEchat which runs a weekly Twitter chat centred around current issues in learning and teaching. Whilst instigated primarily through the academic development community, these initiatives are gaining traction across disciplines as they provide support for the sharing of practice based on authentic, current experiences. This creation and support for open networks and communities is one of the areas highlighted for development by Gunn et al. (2014) in terms of developing impact and evaluation of academic practice. From our perspective, these examples provide strong foundations for the extension of increased criticality and notions of porosity.

However, these initiatives tend to be formed of those working at the chalk face. With a few notable exceptions, there is little engagement from senior managers in these types of open, collegiate experiences. As senior managers get more embroiled in the business of managing a university, they become more removed from actual practice. Using a critical pedagogy informed perspective around developing generative themes and culture circles as described in Chap. 9 could provide an additional means for more transparency of senior management practice and a way for them to reconnect with others and to reveal and challenge value pluralism across their university.

This in turn could help to foster extended academic communities, which were based on what we referred to in Chap. 1 as a revitalised collegiality, and would contribute to an increased reconciliation of value pluralism across an institution based on shared common language and understandings, and we would hope on the Freirean values of love and humanity. Darder (2011) explains this type of love as:

> love that could be lively, forceful, and inspiring, while at the same time, critical, challenging, and insistent.

We stand in solidarity with our peers throughout the globe who share these values, and through our own practice hope, we can develop these ideas in the near future.

We now challenge university management to utilise the experience of academic developers to be at the forefront of wider organisational developments through the facilitation of the development of institution-wide discursive themes around digital developments, based on critical pedagogy and open educational practice. Whilst this approach might look like a conventional 'working party' format, the explicit focus on critical pedagogy and an embracing, exploration, and ultimately a reconciliation of value pluralism would change the nature of the experience.

References

Darder, A. (2011). Teaching as an Act of Love: Reflections on Paulo Freire and His Contributions to Our Lives and Our Work. *Counterpoints, 418*, 179–194. JSTOR.

Fanghanel, J. (2012). *Being an Academic*. Milton Park: Routledge.

Friberg, T. (2015). *An Anthropological Study of Profession Education and Power*. Malmö: Universus Academic Press.

Gibbs, G. (1996). Supporting Educational Development Within Departments. *International Journal for Academic Development, 1*(1), 27–37.

Gibbs, A., Haskins, G., Hannon, P., & Robertson, I. (2012). *Leading the Entrepreneurial University: Meeting the Entrepreneurial Development Needs of Higher Education (2009, Updated 2012)*, NCEE. http://eureka.sbs.ox.ac.uk/4861/

Gunn, C., Creanor, L., Lent, N., & Smyth, K. (2014). Representing Academic Development. *Journal of Perspectives in Applied Academic Practice, 2*(2). https://doi.org/10.14297/jpaap.v2i2.92. Last Accessed 6 June 2018.

Higher Education Academy, UK Professional Standards Framework (UKPSF). Higher Education Academy. https://www.heacademy.ac.uk/ukpsf. Last Accessed 1 May 2018.

Land, R. (2004). *Educational Development: Discourse, Identity and Practice*. Maidenhead: Society for Research into Higher Education/Open University Press.

Manathunga, C. (2011). The Field of Educational Development: Histories and Critical Questions. *Studies in Continuing Education, 33*(3), 347–362.

Neame, C. (2013). Democracy of Intervention? Adapting Orientations to Development. *International Journal for Academic Development, 18*(4), 331–343.

Nerantzi, C., & Beckingham, S. (2015). Scaling-Up Open CPD for Teachers in Higher Education Using a Snowballing Approach. *Journal of Perspectives in Applied Academic Practice, 3*(1). https://doi.org/10.14297/jpaap.v3i1.148.

Oliver, M. (2002). What Do Learning Technologists Do? *Innovations in Education and Training International, 39*(4), 245–252.

Popovic, C., & Baume, D. (2016). Introduction: Some Issues in Academic Development. In D. Baume & C. Popovic (Eds.), *Advancing Practice in Academic Development* (pp. 1–16). London: Routledge.

PWC, The 2018 Digital University Staying Relevant in the Digital Age. (2018). PWC. https://www.pwc.co.uk/assets/pdf/the-2018-digital-university-staying-relevant-in-the-digital-age.pdf. Last Accessed 21 Nov 2017.

Röxa, T., & Märtensson, K. (2017). Agency and Structure in Academic Development Practices: Are We Liberating Academic Teachers or Are We Part of a Machinery Supressing Them? *International Journal for Academic Development, 22*(2), 95–105.

Sutherland, K., & Grant, B. (2016). Researching Academic Development. In D. Baume & C. Popovic (Eds.), *Advancing Practice in Academic Development* (pp. 188–206). London: Routledge.

Walker, D., & MacNeill, S. (2015). Learning Technologist as Digital Pedagogue. In D. Hopkins (Ed.), *The Really Useful #EdTech Book* (pp. 91–105). David Hopkins.

Weller, M. (2011). *The Digital Scholar How Technology Is Transforming Scholarly Practice*. London: Bloomsbury Open Publishing.

12

Conclusion: Advancing the Digital and Open Education Agenda

Introduction: The Digital University as Contested Space

The title of this book expresses our sense that any definition of what a digital university might become can be found at the intersection of the policy, pedagogy, and academic practice of a given time. The present policy context for change in pedagogy and practice is extremely harsh. We are faced by a globalised neoliberal political economy allied to the spread of authoritarianism, which is creating an increasingly anti-democratic political climate. This in turn threatens academic values and marginalises dissenting voices in the academy. At the time of writing, figures such as Trump, Putin, Erdogan, General Prayuth Chan-ocha, and even Aung San Suu Kyi have directed power away from the defence and extension of basic human rights to employment, welfare, education, and free speech. This shift away from democracy towards authoritarianism in pursuit of neoliberalism is supported by the ambitions of corporate enterprise and also by powerful media strategies to manipulate information, undermine expert knowledge, and manipulate public understanding of events. In such an environment, critical thinking, of the kind our universities should engender and fight for, is under unadorned threat from 'fake news', digital propaganda, abuse of data analytics, and in some cases outright censorship.

We hold to the view that education is central to democracy and the advancement of human rights, and needs to be opened up and enriched not narrowed down and impoverished. Hence our advocacy of critical open pedagogy, public pedagogy, Information Literacy, and higher education as a public good, as key forces for positive change in universities, and also our arguments for imagining and enacting a more creative and democratic harnessing of the digital within higher education.

In the following passages, we will summarise our current reading of the state of the neoliberalisation of the universities and then distil some of our main views on pedagogy, practice, and academic and organisational development. We will also set out proposals for implementing higher education's responsibility to challenge, critique, and create new knowledge and better informed citizens.

From Here to Where?

The past decade has experienced the economic shock of the financial crisis (2008–2009), allied to stagnant wages, precarious employment, low productivity, and rising social and economic inequality. The mainstream response, often referred to as 'austerity', has been to simply double down on the neoliberal scheme of political economy, which we described in Chap. 1. In the higher education sector, this has meant a growing obsession with 'value for money', translated as graduate earnings accompanied by (i) increased reliance on the market/consumer model, (ii) introduction of the OfS in the UK, (iii) reinforcement of the impoverishment of education, and (iv) a contradictory and narrow response to technology. The result has been an increasingly oppressive and managerialist regime in universities and the marginalisation of alternative concepts of what universities are and arguably should be for in the early twenty-first century.

The staff experience of this oppressive situation might be described in terms of several major aspects of university life including:

Conclusion: Advancing the Digital and Open Education Agenda

- Working conditions defined by short-term contracts, pay restraints, declining pensions, and marginalisation of unions;
- Workloads comprising long hours, unrealistic deadlines, staff reductions, narrowing down of scope for initiative, motivation and performance, and too much overthinking of practice by managers;
- Audit culture, which in the UK involves the use of REF/TEF to police activity and increase demands for performance and conformity;
- Government negativity with respect to unsubstantiated claims about poor teaching standards, associated moral panics over freedom of speech on campus, and increasingly unrealistic demands for 'value for money';
- Inequalities through extreme pay differentials and gender-biased promotions.

The student experience must also be cited in terms of fees and long-term debt, failure to obtain good jobs, pay and mortgages, the narrowness of curricula which are often abstracted from the real world, and the lack of opportunity to fail or change direction at university. This oppressive condition in universities has been 'normalised' over decades in the form of state policies, managerialist practices, and general undermining of autonomy and sense of worth to the extent that the everyday power of academics and students has been eroded to a dangerously low level.

Whilst neoliberalism remains the dominant force in society, and acting upon our universities, there are powerful critics. Mason (2015) and Srnicek and Wilson (2016) offer critical commentary and arguments for change. These commentators reject neoliberalism as a failed system of political economy, which is inefficient, reinforces inequality, and is increasingly undemocratic. Both are dismissive of traditional social democratic and socialist prescriptions for change, which they see rooted in the past and incapable of challenging the status quo. However both are at one in proposing the power of technology, particularly the Internet and digital technologies, to provide the means for a more productive and equal economy and the basis for a new form of global participative democracy. Their vision for change is based on a belief in the enriching power of technology and the absolute necessity of evolving more human and collaborative ways of working and organising society. Whilst operating at the broader socio-economic levels of analysis, there are distinct echoes of their interest in the intersections of technology, democracy, and social activity and, to an extent, learning, which mirror the themes we have pursued in this book.

Our rejection of neoliberalism has been argued throughout the book, and we have promoted Freirean ideas around critical pedagogy as they might apply to contemporary higher education and universities. Freire is cast very much as a radical humanistic thinker whom we have aligned with Europe's Charta Universitatum ideals. Allied to critical pedagogy are (i) our commitment to public pedagogy, (ii) our account of open education and how this might be reframed as an alternative approach to creating and extending higher education, and (iii) our advocacy in relation to recognising, confronting, and seeking to reconcile value pluralism, in order to realise a revitalised collegiality as an essential force for change within universities.

In summary we have discussed the contradictions in current commentaries on the digital university (Chap. 2), detailed our way of working (Chap. 3), and critiqued the mythologising of the digital university (Chap. 4). We developed our case through themes of participation and open education (Chap. 5). In Chaps. 6, 7, and 8, we developed our approaches to Information Literacy, pedagogy, curriculum, and digital learning spaces. Chapter 9 revisited our major constructs from Chap. 3, and in Chaps. 10 and 11, we set out our suggestions for change in university organisational and academic development.

The Digital University as a Liberating Social Force: The Purposes of Learning Spaces and Environments in the Information Age

Looking beyond the contours of a university's physical, digital, and social spaces, it is clear that the value of the investment in such structures is best judged by the extent to which they allow the university to operate as a public good, and not simply a provider of degrees to a higher education marketplace. The emphasis is on pedagogical practices and institutional strategies best suited to this democratic purpose, as explored respectively in Chaps. 7, 9, 10, and 11. The organisational horizon of this democratising project might be expressed in the terms of the *porous university* as we first defined them in Chap. 8, to denote the radical redrawing of familiar boundaries between universities and various communities and also the reshaping of internal disciplinary and other organisational boundaries.

Allied to these perspectives is concern with the place of student agency, personhood, and digital capability in the digital university learning space. Evidently the university is immersed in the digital media-sphere provided by the corporate giants currently being referred to as FANG and cannot remain aloof from the penetration of those organisations as service providers, but more significantly as creators of the common digital environment. Consequently, it is axiomatic that students become not only digitally skilled but information literate in the widest sense to better engage with and make critical evaluations of the nature of the digital political economy, which seeks to shape their social identities. The university can best achieve this mission by accepting a responsibility to support the epistemological development of students, not only in disciplinary terms but also in terms of their capacity for informed citizenship. We suggest that the field of Information Literacy offers powerful support for these objectives and that the emerging UNESCO programmes for Media and Information Literacy (2016) are a valuable additional support.

A consideration of the nature of university learning spaces, in relation to student engagements with those spaces, highlights the need for academic development of the curriculum in the digital university. We do not view curriculum as a simple matter of shaping the academic programme followed by students to 'produce' the requisite degree-level credentials. Rather we view curriculum as a much more open-ended or 'porous' entity, which should be available to many participants and offer a variety of socially valuable benefits. Developing curriculum from a critical and holistic perspective is a necessary process and can be understood as an epistemological and pedagogical means by which academic developers, in the widest sense of the term, can help create the digital university as a channel of public pedagogy.

In the first instance, this requires a critical review of existing accounts of curriculum and an exploration of new directions to provide a renewed concept of curriculum appropriate to the digital university as we conceive it, which can be channelled into strategic change within universities. Our conceptualisation of the digitally distributed curriculum, in Chap. 8, is our own response to this challenge. Allied to this intellectual project is the need to develop more inclusive and challenging forms of staff working together to bring about change, in partnership with students and the wider community, even if this process is at odds with current managerialist practices.

Creating the Digital University: Prospects for Practice

In Chap. 9 we summarised our thinking on how the digital university might be visualised in Fig. 9.1. This graphic encapsulates the key elements we believe are essential to address in bringing about change in universities, and to create digitally enabled universities that are defined by values including those of porosity, co-production, co-location, and open scholarship. From our perspective, this means re-designing not just infrastructures but also human relations, pedagogies, and forms of working, to make them collaborative and committed to a renewed sense that universities are democratic spaces. In basic terms, universities should be for openness and democratic citizenship. In more formal terms, universities should be practising the values inscribed in Magna Charta Universitatum (n.d.).

Taking a human-first, not digital-first, approach could provide a type of transformation to universities that corporate disruptive innovators would never dream of. That is, one that would challenge the neoliberal market-driven business model of education we have criticised throughout this book. Focussing on curriculum development, based on the values and dimensions in our digitally distributed curriculum model (Fig. 8.1) and not the student 'customer journey', could provide a more contextualised and sustainable way to begin to address wider issues of participation which could then be supported by relevant digital services and infrastructure.

Using the dialogic processes around developing culture circles we described in Chap. 9 could provide ways for a university to (re)engage with various stakeholders and communities in a sustainable way. It could also provide a way to (re)energise staff and in turn students through a renewed sense of collegiality and greater autonomy and ownership in decision-making as discussed in Chap. 10.

In summary, we hope and feel that colleagues could use the ideas and tools developed in this book to initiate and develop change in their universities. For example, our conceptual Matrix for the university as first described in Chap. 3, and then further developed in Chap. 9, offers the means to create generative themes and openings for local discussion. Equally important is our encouragement to explore critical pedagogy and rethink more familiar accounts of educational practice, as well as rethinking and extending academic development in the form of critical interventions. Our experience has been that undertaking such activities through multi-faceted teams is most likely to widen horizons and establish commitment to change. Finally it is essential to engage at the level of strategic decision-making and in the collective creation of institutional policy statements.

Agendas for Change: Research as Regeneration and Strategic Transformation

The critical educator Antonia Darder offers this valuable insight into research:

> Traditional research has emerged from an authoritarian context bent on the prediction of the environment for the purpose of controlling and dominating its evolution, with an emphasis on the hierarchical categorization and compartmentalization of human experience. (Darder 1994)

We are not like that. Throughout the book we have argued for the need for the digital university to be perceived and understood as a holistic concept, and one to be understood collectively by learners, academics, academic leaders, and others within and beyond the university who have a vested interest in both higher education and in what universities should mean and offer within our communities and wider society.

We have proposed that our model of change and development of the conceptual Matrix and Digitally Distributed Curriculum constructs offer a field of study and application for the development of the digital university as we envisage it.

Going forward, our methods of inquiry to further develop and understand how we can most effectively harness digital technologies, spaces, and approaches in extending higher education as a public good should by necessity be both qualitative and quantitative, but with a focus and emphasis on understanding experiences, needs, aspirations, belonging, engagement, and empowerment. We suggest that ethnographic and phenomenographic approaches to research and inquiry are of the kind most likely to illuminate and provide further insight into, and the basis for informed action resulting from, future investigations into the nature of 'being' within the digital university. We expect an important stage in our own work will be to undertake further structured research and inquiry in relation to key dimensions of the digital university and digitally enabled higher education practice.

To this end, while it has not been the intention of this book to advance a detailed agenda for research related to the issues and themes we have explored, we have identified some possible themes and foci for future research.

These potential research directions include the social impacts of academic knowledge distributed through the digital university; policy and practice to enable the enactment of universities as porous institutions; the impact and nature of open educational practices that are designed to intersect the 'open online' with 'open on the campus' and the 'open in the community'; learning and engagement analytics that are contextualised to our conceptualisation of the digital university; alternative forms of academic practice and critical academic development; and media and Information Literacy within the curriculum or for the digitally distributed curriculum.

We feel there is also merit in exploring and finding ways to operationalise 'alternative metrics' and criteria to challenge neoliberal dispensations of the university, and the role of the digital within it. What would they be? How would they be operationalised? What could they tell us about how to further advance higher education practices and agendas framed by critical and public pedagogy, open education, and a commitment to democratic engagement and social action?

Conclusion

There is a direct threat to democracy, openness, participation, and criticality—the key descriptors of what a university is for. This threat is posed by neoliberal notions of market efficiency leading to an impoverished vision of universities as businesses competing for student customers and harnessing technology to the resulting limited scenarios for learning and teaching. Our response has been to challenge this distorted notion of what a university is for. We have sought to counterpoise this threat with an idea of the university as a public good, which is committed to critical thinking and challenging the currently oppressive conditions. In this context, our proposal is to liberate digital space, place, and practice to extend higher education, and to democratise the opportunities to engage with or benefit from the knowledge created within universities, for the benefit of our wider communities and society.

While our main focus in this book has been with exploring and offering a more holistic imagining of the digital university than we were able to find in considerations of this concept to date, our driving concern has been with the nature and purposes of universities and higher education and a rejection of the currently dominant neoliberal position. We are therefore opting to conclude our own narrative with an excerpt from a seminal narrative we find particularly apt. In his Rectorial Address titled 'Alienation', which set out a cogent critique of 1970s neoliberalism, Jimmy Reid (1972), trade union leader of the Upper Clyde Shipbuilders occupation, had this to say:

> To the students I address this appeal. Reject these attitudes. Reject the values and false morality that underlie these attitudes. A rat race is for rats. We're not rats. We're human beings. Reject the insidious pressures in society that would blunt your critical faculties to all that is happening around

you, that would caution silence in the face of injustice lest you jeopardise your chances of promotion and self-advancement.

References

Darder, A. (1994). Institutional Research as a Tool for Cultural Democracy. *New Directions for Institutional Research, 81*, 21–34. Jossey-Bass.

Mason, P. (2015). *Postcapitalism: A Guide to Our Future.* London: Alan Lane.

Observatory Magna Charta Universitatum. (n.d.). *The Magna Charta Universitatum.* http://www.magnacharta.org/magna-charta-universitatum. Last Accessed 10 May 2018.

Reid, J. (1972). *Alienation, Rectorial Address*, University of Glasgow. https://www.gla.ac.uk/myglasgow/news/archives/2015/december/headline_435928_en.html. Last Accessed 29 June 2018.

Srnicek, N., & Williams, A. (2016). *Inventing the Future: Postcapitalism and a World Without Work.* London/New York: Verso.

UNESCO. (2016). *Riga Recommendations on Media and Information Literacy in a Shifting Media and Information Landscape.* http://www.unesco.org/new/fileadmin/MULTIMEDIA/HQ/CI/CI/pdf/Events/riga_recommendations_on_media_and_information_literacy.pdf. Last Accessed 30 June 2018.

Index

NUMBERS AND SYMBOLS
2D, 76
3D, 76
3E Framework, 75, 143
3G/4G/5G, 98

A
Academic developer, 121, 217, 218, 220, 222, 223, 226–231, 239
Academic development, 4, 10, 14–16, 40, 41, 54–56, 111, 112, 115, 116, 128, 130, 179, 183, 185–187, 192, 209, 210, 217–232, 236, 238, 239, 241, 242
   critical, 56, 242
   programmes, 221, 230
   units, 218–220, 222

Academic knowledge, 64, 155, 173, 212, 242
Academic leaders, 192, 230, 241
Academic practices, 21, 28, 31, 35, 112, 182, 183, 222, 231, 235, 242
Access, 10, 25, 64, 66, 70–74, 78, 85–94, 97, 98, 100, 106, 107, 113, 131, 132, 140, 145, 154, 157, 160, 162, 168, 170, 171, 187, 190, 194, 197, 198, 201, 213, 226
Accrediting bodies, 155
Active/activity, 13, 14, 16, 23, 33, 34, 40, 50, 54, 69, 73, 74, 93, 107, 111, 117–120, 127, 129, 130, 132, 135, 138–143, 145, 149–152, 154–158, 160, 163, 164, 166–168, 172, 183, 192, 195, 204, 205, 217, 218, 220, 221, 225, 237, 238, 241

Activity design, 69, 138–139
Administration, 11, 46, 50, 185
Adult education, 213
Adult literacy, 13, 194
Advance HE, 219, 243
　See also Higher Education Academy
Advocate(s), 14, 32, 121, 171, 180, 196, 204, 205, 210, 221, 223
Advocating, 115, 204, 211, 230
Affordances, 77, 78, 86, 113, 116, 120, 221
Agency, 6, 94, 106, 117–121, 127, 131, 133, 147, 180, 185–187, 197, 209, 217, 226, 227, 239
Agenda/agendas, 26, 49, 52, 66, 72, 86, 88–90, 92, 96, 102, 107, 113–117, 120, 121, 185, 187, 197, 198, 212, 227, 235–244
Agenda for Sustainable Development (UNESCO), 91, 92, 94, 99, 110, 239
Alienation, 234, 243
ALT, *see* Association for Learning Technology
Alternative, 4–12, 16, 20, 21, 23–26, 29, 30, 36, 37, 39, 58, 65–67, 70, 79, 90, 91, 96, 102, 142, 150, 155, 157, 159, 181, 188, 189, 193, 194, 198, 213, 236, 238, 242
　practices, 69
Altruism, 91, 95
Amazon, 98, 194
American College and Research Libraries Association (ACRL), 110, 114

Analytics, 11, 30, 31, 42, 53, 88, 99, 114, 179–180, 183, 184, 189, 190, 198, 199, 225, 236, 242
　See also Data
Anderson, A., 87, 106, 108–110, 119
Applied, 30, 33, 34, 50, 108, 110, 119, 152, 156, 159, 162, 168, 189, 190, 196, 209
Architecture/architecturally, 7–11, 129, 132, 156, 157
Artefacts, 10, 50, 53, 128, 137, 139, 142, 143, 146, 159, 165, 166, 169, 170, 172, 211
Assemblages, 111, 114
Assessment/assessed, 44, 64, 67–69, 75–77, 108, 114, 117, 133, 151, 154–156, 158–159, 164, 171, 186, 196, 199, 227
Assessment practices, 68, 158, 159
Assistive technologies, 140
Association for Learning Technology (ALT), 219
Asynchronous/asynchronicity, 76–78, 140–144
Audit culture, 237
Augmented reality (AR), 145
Aung San Suu Kyi, 235
Austerity, 8, 236
Authentic, 13, 76, 133, 134, 139, 141, 156, 158, 160, 193, 230, 231
　activities, 141
　assessment, 156
　learning, 13, 76, 133, 134
Author/authorship, 8, 15, 33, 44, 51, 97, 113, 138, 173
Autonomy, 10, 68, 78, 147, 166, 204, 209, 237, 241

B

Baer, A., 109
Bailey, M., 27
Barber, M., 11, 19, 32, 44, 93
Baume, D., 218
Beckingham, S., 73, 230
Beetham, H., 43
Behaviour, 5, 8, 25, 29, 107, 111, 116, 119, 189, 228
Benchmark/benchmarking, 116, 151, 229
Biggs, J., 55, 151, 164, 183
Birch, K., 8
Blended learning/approaches, 35, 45, 76, 77, 114, 128, 196
Bolden, R., 204
Boon, S., 109
Bottom-up, 35, 99, 186, 209
Bounded, 54, 150, 151, 154, 163, 169, 230
  bounded curriculum, 154–162
Boutang, Y.M., 106
Bovill, C., 166
Brazil, 194
Breadth of use, 208
Brennan, J., 212
Brexit, 100
Bring your own device (BYOD), 100
Bring your own device for learning, #BYODL (BYOD4L), 100, 230
Brown, C., 208–210
Bruce, C., 109
Buckingham-Shum, S., 99
Buckland, M., 106
Buckner, K., 77
Bulut, E., 106

C

Cambridge Analytica, 120, 198, 199
Campus/campus-based, 11, 44, 64, 74, 91, 128, 129, 131, 132, 160, 162, 171, 185, 237
Capacity, 7, 14, 51, 114, 115, 117, 119–121, 194, 197, 239
Cape Town Open Education Declaration, 91
Capitalism/capitalist, 33, 109, 180, 225
CARE Framework for OER Stewardship, 96
Case, P., 160
Case studies, 57, 75, 88, 109, 116, 142, 158, 159, 172, 209, 210
Certified Member of ALT (CMALT), 219
Champions, 210
Channel 4, 198
Chan-ocha, General Prayuth, 235
Chatterton, P., 119
Citizenship, 9, 50, 86, 106, 239, 240
Civic, 85, 89, 97, 98, 130, 134, 180, 181, 187, 195
  engagement, 97, 130, 134
  responsibilities, 85, 89, 98, 181, 187
  role, 85, 98, 187, 195
  society, 130, 134, 181, 195
Civic Online Reasoning project, 119
Classrooms, 76, 107, 108, 117, 121, 129, 140, 142–145, 185
Clustering, 54, 114, 157, 158, 161
CMALT, *see* Certified Member of ALT

Co-creation, 143, 206
Cognition/cognitive, 76, 110, 130, 211
Cognitive dissonance, 211–212
Cohorts, 31, 52, 53, 76, 134, 137, 138, 140–145, 150, 156–159, 165, 170, 190, 219
Coleman, L., 112
Collaborate, collaboration, collaborative learning, 8, 22, 66, 68, 72, 76, 79, 92, 95, 97, 107, 127, 129, 130, 132–134, 137, 139–145, 157, 166, 167, 169, 170, 193, 203, 204, 219, 230, 237, 240
Collaborate to Compete (report of the UK Online Learning Task Force), 72
Collective, 5, 13, 29, 56, 66, 71, 91, 130, 131, 140, 141, 152, 159–161, 166, 168, 169, 180, 186, 187, 189, 192, 193, 203–205, 207, 208, 212, 213, 241
  good, 153, 168, 203, 212
  values, 130, 212
Collegiality, 10, 12, 106, 193, 204, 224, 230–232, 238, 241
Collini, S., 10, 25–27, 30, 32–36, 42, 43, 64, 187, 188, 200
Co-located/co-location, 5, 10, 15, 70, 79, 147, 150, 154, 158, 161, 164, 166–168, 172, 173, 205, 240
Commerce, 185
Common good, 89, 96
Common language, 203, 207, 231

Commons, 50, 56, 77, 96–101, 105, 113, 117, 136, 141, 149, 155, 168, 203, 207, 219, 220, 225, 228, 231, 239
Communicate/communication, 21, 51, 66, 77, 78, 106, 111–113, 119, 120, 131, 134, 136, 141, 143–145
Communities, 10, 12, 14, 15, 29, 45, 48, 49, 52, 53, 56, 65, 79, 85–102, 109, 112, 115, 120, 129, 130, 134, 136, 137, 144, 150, 154, 159–163, 165–172, 182, 187, 203–205, 211–213, 220, 221, 223, 225, 228, 230, 231, 239–243
Community Open Online Courses (COOCs), 79, 213
Comprehension, 15, 22, 31, 32, 76, 90, 91
Comrie, A., 68, 69, 75
Conceptual Matrix for the Digital University, 42, 45–48, 54, 70, 129, 151, 162, 163, 179–201, 203, 241, 242
  Revised Conceptual Matrix for the Digital University, 70, 162
Connected Curriculum, 156, 159
Connectivism and Connected Knowledge 2012, 92
Connectivity, 98, 100, 131, 168
Construction/co-construction, 5, 40, 45–48, 158, 179, 183, 205
Constructive alignment, 42, 55, 151, 164, 182, 183, 192, 227
Constructivism/constructivist, 133

Consumer/consumerism/
  consumerist, 3, 4, 7, 8, 11, 20,
  24, 25, 27, 47, 50, 64, 88, 96,
  101, 200, 201, 225, 228, 236
Content, 22, 35, 49, 53, 67, 79, 91,
  93, 100, 112, 113, 118, 119,
  135, 138–140, 142, 143, 151,
  152, 154, 164, 171, 179, 199,
  207
Contested, 3–7, 10, 12, 20, 36, 152,
  153
  space, 235–238
Context, 5, 7, 13, 20, 21, 23, 39,
  44–45, 47–51, 54–58, 63,
  65–74, 76–78, 85, 86, 88, 90,
  100, 106, 109, 111–113, 119,
  127–129, 133, 134, 136,
  138–141, 150–156, 158–168,
  170–173, 180–187, 190, 192,
  196, 197, 203, 206–210, 212,
  218, 222, 224, 226, 228, 229,
  235, 240–243
Continuing professional
  development (CPD), 73, 230
Cook-Sather, A., 239, 266
Coonan, E., 210, 214
Cooperation/cooperative, 128, 133
Cooperative learning, 128, 133
Cormier, D., 160, 161
Course, 12, 35, 40–42, 45, 46, 50,
  65, 67, 68, 72–74, 79, 87, 89,
  92–94, 106–108, 110, 111,
  115–121, 127, 128, 138, 139,
  149, 151, 154, 157, 164, 170,
  171, 183, 187, 191, 199, 206,
  219, 220, 227, 229, 230
Coursera, 44, 92

Coursework, 73, 108, 133, 142, 158,
  159, 172
Creanor, L., 222
Creation, 5, 33, 86, 87, 96, 98, 113,
  139, 164, 187, 231, 241
Creativity, 19, 47, 55, 131, 166
Criterion-based, 151
Critical academic development, 56,
  242
Critical agency, 147
Critical analysis, 27–29, 36, 110,
  119, 189, 190
Critical consciousness, 4, 15, 16,
  23–24, 54–57, 108, 111, 135,
  191–193
  See also Freire, P., *Education for
  Critical Consciousness*
Critical development, 119
Critical dialogue, 4, 26, 184
Critical essays, 173
Critical information literacy, 109
Critical intervention, 229–230,
  241
Critical pedagogy, 4, 7, 11–15, 20,
  25, 39, 46, 55–57, 70, 86, 88,
  95, 101, 102, 105, 106,
  120–121, 150, 179, 180,
  184–188, 194, 199, 201, 213,
  217, 229–231, 238, 241
Critical practice, 217, 226–230
Critical symbol, 217, 226–230
Cronin, C., 94
Cross-cohort, 52, 134, 156, 158
Cross-disciplinary, 95, 134, 158
Culturally bounded, 159–160
Culturally enriched, 72, 76, 170
Cultural unbounding, 95, 134, 158

Culture/cultural, 8, 13, 23, 29, 63, 64, 72, 74, 76, 79, 88, 106, 113, 118, 141, 150, 153, 154, 159–160, 169, 170, 180, 189, 194, 195, 199, 230
Curation/co-curation, 139, 158, 164
Curricula, 52–54, 69, 70, 72, 74, 95, 115, 116, 153–156, 159–160, 162, 163, 165, 170, 173, 230, 237
Curriculum, 5, 14, 15, 31, 33, 35, 40–42, 45–56, 58, 67–70, 73, 75, 79, 86, 88, 95, 106, 107, 110, 111, 115–117, 119, 121, 130, 135, 137, 138, 141, 146–176, 181–183, 187, 190, 191, 197, 205–207, 210–213, 219, 226, 227, 229, 238–240, 242
Curriculum and course design, 41, 42, 45–47, 50, 163, 187, 191
Curriculum as body of knowledge, 152, 155
Curriculum as praxis, 152, 153, 155, 156, 158, 161, 173
Curriculum as process, 153, 154, 173
Curriculum as product, 153–156, 173
Curriculum design, 14, 67–69, 75, 116, 150, 155
Curriculum implementation, 149, 164
Curriculum re-approval, 210
Customer/customer focused, 4, 6, 8, 11, 32, 39, 64, 155, 186, 224, 243
Czerniewicz, L., 208–210

D
Darder, A., 4, 9, 231, 241
Dashboards, 31, 190, 191
Data, 6, 24, 30, 31, 33, 42, 66, 97–99, 134, 189–191, 194, 197–199, 224, 225, 236
See also Analytics
Data connectivity, 98
Dawson, S., 44
Dearing Report, 218
Debt, 237
Deep learning/deeper learning, 78, 133, 135, 139
Degree, 8, 11, 46, 74, 86–88, 93, 101, 108, 119, 149, 157, 238, 239
DELICATE ethical checklist for analytics, 199
Democracy/democratic, 8–10, 12, 14, 15, 39, 47, 63, 73, 78–80, 86, 94, 105, 109, 113, 119, 121, 131, 138, 142–144, 149, 153, 163, 170, 171, 174, 187, 191, 198, 203–213, 226, 228, 230, 235–240
 engagement, 118, 130, 140–141, 146, 158, 201, 230, 243
 processes, 66, 90, 108, 134, 194
Deprivation, 168
Depth of use, 208
Design Studio, The (Jisc), 75
De Vita, G., 160
Devolved, 100, 209, 210
Dewey, J., 65
Dialogic, 4, 5, 13, 42, 48, 57, 130, 138, 160, 180, 181, 202, 203, 241

Index

Dialogue, 4, 12, 13, 15, 26, 40, 45, 49, 54, 76, 130, 133, 134, 141, 143, 162, 164, 170, 179, 184, 185, 203, 205–207, 211–213, 223, 229, 230
Digital access, 86, 89–90, 162
Digital age, 6, 21, 28, 31, 32, 43, 57, 101, 112, 114, 121, 128, 195–199, 201, 224
Digital artefacts, 53, 137, 146, 164
Digital capability/capabilities, 45, 49, 58, 90, 100, 105–125, 168, 197, 239
Digital citizenship, 9, 239
Digital domains, 173
Digital education, 71, 74, 78, 159, 209–211
    digital education technologies, 65, 76, 77
Digital futures, 40, 51–53, 56, 162, 182
Digital Futures Working Group (DFWG), 40, 51, 53
Digital literacy, 7, 30, 40, 43, 49, 51, 75, 90, 112, 116, 189, 224
Digitally distributed curriculum, 51–54, 58, 70, 135, 138, 146, 147, 149–176, 182, 183, 207, 213, 226, 240, 242
Digitally enabled learning, 76, 143, 170, 230
Digitally enriched learning spaces, 58, 127–148
Digital natives, 31, 114, 118
Digital oppression, 101–102
Digital participation, 40–42, 45, 47–51, 58, 66, 72, 75–102, 197, 199, 1187

Digital practice, 7, 26, 46, 51–53, 70, 173, 174, 182, 192, 196, 204, 206, 217
Digital resources, 68, 76, 91, 108, 116, 128, 136
Digital rights, 120
Digital scholarship, 53, 128, 137, 164, 183
    students as digital scholars, 136
Digital services, 86, 89, 98, 99, 226, 240
    digitally enabled services, 89
Digital silos, 157, 170
Digital skills, 7, 64, 70, 76, 90, 134, 136, 162
Digital spaces, 47, 70, 129–132, 141, 145, 150, 157, 167, 168, 182, 212, 243
Digital tools, 35, 66, 77, 78, 80, 130, 133, 134, 138, 139, 143, 144, 146, 160
Digital transformation, 36, 44, 58, 63–84, 102, 180, 186, 191, 193–197
Digital university, 3–17, 19–59, 70, 80, 88, 100, 102, 106–115, 120, 128–130, 136, 137, 150, 151, 154, 161–163, 165, 167, 168, 171, 173, 179–204, 206, 207, 210–213, 217–233, 235–236, 238–243
    Conceptual Matrix for the digital university, 42, 45–48, 70, 129, 151, 162, 163, 179–201, 203
Dimitriadis, Y., 139
Disadvantage, 66, 79, 87–89
Discipline/disciplines/disciplinary, 42, 49, 72, 101, 105, 106,

111, 112, 115–118, 120, 121, 134–136, 141, 156, 158, 159, 173, 221, 223, 225, 239
Disconnect, 105, 128
Discourse, 15, 47, 48, 55, 70, 77, 101, 106, 118, 128, 141, 153, 171, 181–183, 186, 193, 206, 220, 227
Discursive, 5, 40, 41, 45–48, 55–58, 179, 180, 183, 185, 186, 231
Discussion, 5, 7, 13, 15, 21–23, 28, 30, 40, 41, 43, 47, 49, 50, 56, 57, 76–78, 86, 94, 107, 113–115, 118, 136, 140–144, 147, 150, 168, 170, 172, 174, 179–182, 184–187, 190–192, 203, 211, 212, 227, 229, 241
Disenfranchisement, 168
Disrupt/disruption/disruptive, 11, 32, 42, 69, 70, 96, 97, 101, 130, 133, 194, 198, 229, 240
Distributed, 51–54, 58, 70, 125, 129, 134, 136, 138, 146, 147, 149–176, 183, 203–207, 209, 212, 213, 226, 240, 242
Distributed academic leadership, 203–206
Distributed leadership, 204–206, 212
Diverse/diversity, 21, 53, 73, 76, 132, 138, 150, 159, 164, 167, 170, 172, 208, 219, 230
Division of labour, 153, 182
Domain of One's Own, 146
Donche, V., 128, 133
Downey, A., 109
Drachsler, H., 199
Draper, S., 68, 75
Dualism, 119
Dunedin, A., 172

Dyke, M., 77
Dzansi, D.Y., 204, 206

E

Ebdon, Professor Les, 87
Edinburgh Napier University, 40, 51–53, 56
Education, 3, 19, 39, 63, 85, 105, 130, 149, 180, 203, 219, 235–244
Educational developers, 12, 20, 26, 49, 55, 107, 111, 113–116, 119–221
Educational development, 12, 20, 26, 49, 55, 113, 114, 119, 219, 221
Educational experience, 64, 68, 71, 72, 90, 155, 168, 218
Education is broken, 43, 65, 101, 197
Edwards, S., 109
e-Learning Benchmarking and Pathfinder Programme (Higher Education Academy), 67, 219
e-Learning Transformation Programme (Scottish Funding Council), 68
Elmborg, J., 109
Employability, 9, 24, 25, 30, 50, 118, 123, 124, 189
Employers, 155
Empower, 13, 57, 97, 158
Enabling dimensions, 146, 164, 166–173, 183
Enabling strategies, 209, 211
Enacting/enactment, 153, 164, 169–173, 211, 229, 236, 242

Enquiry, 42, 127, 135–137, 159
Enterprise, 8, 44, 108, 228, 235
Entwistle, N., 133
Epistemology/epistemological, 16, 87, 108–111, 113, 119, 127, 203, 212, 239
e-portfolio, 22, 159
Equity/equitable/equivalence, 10, 66, 71, 72, 76, 89, 90, 92, 98, 131, 132, 140
Erdogan, 235
Essay/essay writing, 108, 113, 158, 173
Ethical, 19, 107, 144, 198, 224
Ethnographic, 242
Ethos, 5, 74, 79, 90, 91, 129, 138, 166, 170, 172, 210, 213
Evans, S.K., 77
Exemplars, 16, 51–53, 74, 97, 210
Experimentation, 208

Facebook, 98, 194, 198
Facebook, Amazon, Netflix and Google (FANG), 98
Face-to-face, 142
  learning, 76
Fake news, 11, 120, 121, 198, 236
Farrow, R., 95
Fees, 93, 200, 237
  student fees, 24, 64, 101
FE sector, 100
Finance, 44, 85, 108
Finch Report, 97
Flaxman, S., 198
Flipped classroom, 144
Formal education, 77, 149, 152, 153, 171
Formal learning, 127–129, 137, 140, 145, 171, 172
Fotheringham, J., 155
Framework for Information Literacy, 110
Framing/framework, 4, 8, 23, 28, 42, 48, 56, 57, 64, 70, 75, 85, 91, 92, 97, 109–111, 114, 116, 143, 151, 184, 191, 192, 201, 209, 219, 220, 222, 227, 229
Freedman, D., 27
Freedom of speech, 110, 237
Free University Brighton, 213
Freire, P., v–vi, 4, 5, 12–15, 57, 95, 102, 109, 135, 137, 152, 180–182, 185, 186, 188, 193–196, 238
  Education for Critical Consciousness, 12, 57, 192
Fung, D., 152, 156, 159

Gasevic, D., 44
Gender, 112, 237
Gender biased, 237
General Data Protection Regulation (GDPR), 191
Geocaching, 145
Gibbs, A., 9, 32–36, 224, 225
Gibson, J.J., 77
Gilliard, C., 197
Giroux, H.A., 4, 6, 64, 105, 121, 137, 153, 180
Glasgow Caledonian University, 40, 51, 56, 116, 182, 183
Glasgow Media Group, 110
Global elite, 71

254　Index

Globalisation, 32, 227
　globalised society, 65
Global North, 92, 96, 194, 198
Glocalization, 42
Godbey, S., 110
Goodfellow, R., 5, 47, 113, 114
Goodyear, P., 139, 141
Google, 98, 116, 120, 194
Google Scholar, 120
Gordon, G., 209
Gosper, M., 151
Gossman, P., 73
Gourlay, L., 113, 114, 195
Government, 7, 9, 10, 22, 24–27, 30, 44, 47, 66, 90, 94, 97–101, 186, 228, 237
Government (UK), 9, 24, 97, 100, 101
Government policy, 7, 24–27, 66
Grades, 143
Grant, B., 221
Grassroots, 29, 73, 79, 210
Greller, W., 199
Gros, B., 69, 139
Grundy, S., 152
Guardian, The (newspaper), 198, 200
Guest experts, 171
Gunn, C., 222, 231

H

Haggard, S., 71, 73
Hall, R., 150–154, 162, 173, 209
Harkavy, I., 211, 212
Harvey, D., 8
Hearing loops, 140
Hepworth, M., 109
HE sector, 41, 45, 52, 64, 70–74, 80, 101, 156, 180, 196, 209, 218

Hewlett Foundation, 94
Higher education, 3, 4, 7–10, 20, 39, 63, 85, 105
Higher education (as a public good), 10, 14, 15, 21, 25, 39, 47, 64, 67, 69, 70, 78, 80, 91, 130, 150, 154, 158, 161, 166, 168, 169, 173, 185, 186, 196, 203, 205, 212, 213, 226, 236, 238, 242, 243
Higher Education Academy, 67, 219
　See also Advance HE
Higher Education Funding Council for England (HEFCE), 72, 94
Higher Education Policy Institute (HEPI), 87, 89
Holistic, 5, 9, 37, 39–59, 105, 107, 115, 118, 119, 129, 182, 192, 204, 218, 239, 241, 243
Holmwood, J., 27, 43
Hope, 27, 75, 167, 180, 181, 186, 193, 197, 200, 201, 204, 210, 213, 222, 226, 231, 241
Horton, F.W., 110
Hub/hubs, 94, 96
Human development, 109
Hybrid texts, 113

I

Identity, 14, 119, 121, 130, 140, 220, 227, 239
Ifenthaler, D., 151
Impoverished, 19–39, 43, 105, 118, 200, 236, 243
Inclusive/inclusion, 10, 14, 15, 21, 47, 49, 56, 66, 79, 85, 86, 89, 92, 98–99, 102, 115, 127, 130, 131, 160, 170, 172, 193,

197–199, 206, 212, 220–224, 226, 228, 240
Individual agency, 105–122, 193
Industrial revolution, 44
Industry, 8, 44, 65, 106, 108, 185
Inequality/inequalities, 87, 88, 111, 236, 237
Informal education, 64, 90, 147, 150, 152
Informal learning, 165, 168, 172
Information culture, 108
Information era, 108
Information literacy, 42, 45, 47–51, 58, 105–122, 181, 187, 190, 236, 238, 239, 242
Infrastructure, 7, 11, 22, 35, 42, 45, 46, 48–51, 86, 95, 98, 100, 120, 226, 240
Innovation, 15, 20, 22, 42, 47, 87, 101, 114, 164, 223
Innovators, 209, 240
Inquiry, 25, 110, 131, 242
Instantiation, 158, 162, 169–173
Institution, 3, 4, 7, 9, 12, 19, 24–26, 28, 34, 36, 45, 46, 48, 50–52, 57, 64, 66–68, 70–72, 75, 85, 89, 94, 95, 113, 144, 150–152, 155, 158, 165, 167, 170, 180, 182, 185, 192, 207–210, 213, 217–219, 221–223, 227, 230, 231, 242
Institutional development, 14, 179
Institutional policy, 67, 208–211, 241
Institutional praxis, 203, 211–212
Institutional strategy, 14, 43, 203, 206–210
Intellectual development, 91, 120
Intellectual property rights (IPR), 146

Interaction/interactive, 21, 47, 49, 64, 76, 132, 140, 145, 152, 158, 168, 171
Interdisciplinary, 109, 112, 141, 156
Internet, 19–22, 47, 49, 91, 106, 108, 110, 112, 113, 115, 116, 118–121, 197, 237
Intersect/intersection, 5, 14, 85, 105–107, 110, 129, 146, 167, 171, 179, 188, 235, 238, 242
Ivory Tower, 63, 89

J

Jisc, 67–69, 75, 116, 127, 199
Johnson, M., 5, 7, 87, 191, 207, 208
Johnston, Jo, 43
Johnston, B., vii–xi, 42, 46, 48, 49, 51, 55, 56, 106–110, 119, 129, 131, 151, 164
Jonassen, D.H., 133
Jones, C., 5, 47
Jones, S., 204, 205
Jordan, K., 93
Journals, including electronic and open, 173

K

Kennedy, E., 79
Key Performance Indicators (KPIs), 186, 222
King's College London, 88
Knobel, M., 112
Knowledge, 4, 5, 10, 13, 26, 31–34, 44, 49, 52, 64–66, 73, 76, 79, 86, 87, 89–92, 96, 98, 101, 105, 106, 108, 109, 119, 127, 133–137, 139, 141, 142, 146,

152, 154–156, 158–160, 163, 165–174, 181, 185–187, 190, 200, 203, 205, 211, 212, 221, 225, 235, 236, 242, 243
Knowledge, bodies of, 52, 66, 134, 156
Knowledge commons, 96, 168
Knowledge economy, 32, 34, 65, 86, 185, 225
Koltay, T., 112, 113
Krenelka, L.M., 74
Kuhlthau, C., 110
Kvale, S., 156

L

LACE Project, 199
Land, R., 55, 110, 217, 222, 223
Land, S.M., 133
Lankshear, C., 112
Laurillard, D., 79
Lea, M. R., 112–114
Leaders, 27, 31, 36, 69, 107, 110, 192, 204, 230, 241, 243
Leaky/leakiness, 95, 146, 167
See also Porosity/porous
Learner, 12, 13, 52, 55, 56, 58, 64, 66, 69–74, 76, 78, 90, 95, 105, 111, 112, 120, 121, 127, 129–135, 138–142, 144–147, 150, 151, 153, 157–160, 162, 168–172, 192, 199, 204, 206, 210, 223, 241
Learner agency, 58
Learner choice, 133
Learning
  activities, 69, 129, 130, 132, 133, 140, 142, 156, 160, 164, 167, 172

analytics, 88, 99, 114, 198, 199
environment/environments, 42, 45–50, 55, 76, 106, 107, 127, 128, 131–135, 147, 181, 185, 187 (*see also* Virtual Learning Environment)
evidencing, 219
experience, 14, 67, 68, 71, 72, 76, 119, 120, 129, 131, 139, 145, 156, 166, 230
gains, 75, 77
outcomes, 9, 31, 55, 69, 76, 77, 130, 151, 164, 190, 191, 211
patterns, 106
spaces, 5, 14, 35, 45, 58, 127–147, 152, 156, 165, 167, 169, 238–240 (*see also* Digitally enriched learning spaces)
Le Cornu, A., 118
Lecture theatres, 129
Lent, N., 222
Levers for change, 209
Librarians, 111, 112, 115, 117
Libraries, 50, 108, 109, 111, 112, 114, 120, 129, 132, 138, 168
Lifelong learning, 50, 91, 92, 110, 133, 167
Limberg, L., 109
Literacy/literacies, 7, 13, 30, 42, 43, 45, 48–51, 58, 75, 85, 90, 105–122, 181, 187, 189, 190, 194, 195, 224, 236, 238, 239, 242
Littlejohn, A., 43
Ljubljana OER Action Plan, 91, 94
Lloyd, A., 109
Lopez, C., 69, 139
LTHEchat (#LTHEchat), 230

Luckin, R., 19
Lupton, M., 109

M

Macdonald, J.P., 151
Maclean, N., 8
MacNeill, S., vii–xi, 40, 42, 46, 48, 49, 51, 54, 56, 129, 131, 151, 163, 164, 171, 220
Macquarie University, 51
Macro, 14, 20, 28, 29, 34, 35, 48, 71–78, 86, 94, 95, 97, 99–101, 120, 138, 183, 189, 193, 206, 217, 218, 227, 228
Magna Charta Universitatum, 200, 240
Management, 6–9, 12, 14, 19, 22, 24, 27, 28, 30–34, 39, 42, 46, 49, 50, 57, 101, 106, 114, 149, 153, 183, 186, 187, 189, 190, 192–194, 225, 229, 231
Managerialism, 9, 20, 28, 29, 109, 189, 200
Marginalise/marginalisation, 23, 144, 235–237
Market/marketisation, 3, 4, 7–11, 20, 24–26, 30, 34, 50, 58, 63, 64, 66, 88, 96, 101, 105, 108, 155, 186, 189, 196, 210, 236, 243
  of higher education, 64
Mårtensson, K., 226–229
Mason, P., 8, 64, 106, 237
Massification, 88, 194
Massive Open Online Courses (MOOCs), 11, 32, 33, 44, 70, 71, 73, 79, 92–94, 225

Masters (postgraduate programmes), 219
Masters of Education (MEd), 230
Mayer, R., 77
Mayes, T., 67, 209
McKinsey, 6
McLuskey, F.B., 42
Media, 8, 14, 21, 49, 76, 95, 106–108, 110–115, 117, 119–121, 136, 144, 145, 149, 159, 171, 172, 198, 209, 221, 235, 239, 242
Media literacies, 107, 112
  Media and Information Literacy, 110–112, 115, 121, 239, 242
Media-sphere, 112, 113, 119, 139, 239
Medium, 31, 107, 140
Memarovic, N., 168
Meme, 43, 101
Mentoring, 209, 210, 229
Meso, 14, 20, 29, 35, 48, 57, 68, 71–78, 80, 86, 94, 95, 99–101, 114, 115, 120, 183, 189, 191, 193, 206, 217, 227, 228
Method, 25, 31, 32, 111, 138, 149, 190, 242
Methods of inquiry, 242
Metrics, 25, 27, 30, 64, 190, 242
Meyer, J.H.F., 55, 110
Micro, 14, 20, 29, 35, 48, 57, 68, 69, 71–78, 80, 86, 93–95, 99–101, 114, 115, 117, 120, 137, 183, 189, 193, 206, 217, 228, 230
Micro credentialing, 93
Middle out, 209

Mirowski, P., 8
MIT, 91, 92
Mobile technology, 98, 106, 127, 145
Modular, 149
Modularisation, 154, 156–159
Molesworth. M., 64
Monash University, 27, 34–36
Monbiot, 96
Moreno, R., 77
Morris, A., 156, 157
Motivation/motivated, 4, 14, 26, 127, 137, 139, 166, 237
Multimedia, 76
Multiple perspectives, 133, 141
Myth/myths/mythologizing, 36, 58, 63–80, 180, 193–197, 228

N

Naidoo, R., 212
Narrative/narratives, 4, 7, 9, 15, 39, 57, 63–65, 70, 96, 150, 152, 161, 163, 171, 186, 193, 194, 197, 198, 224–227, 229, 243
National Student Survey (NSS), 11
Neame, C., 217, 222, 223
Negotiation, 55, 56, 133, 230
Neoliberalisation, 7–12, 15, 20, 31, 37, 39, 43, 45, 105, 183, 236
Neoliberal/neoliberalism, 3–16, 20, 21, 23–27, 29, 30, 32, 33, 36, 37, 39, 47, 50, 57, 58, 64, 80, 86–91, 93, 96, 97, 101, 105, 116, 118, 121, 155, 180, 181, 185–187, 189, 193–201, 222, 224, 225, 227, 228, 235–238, 240, 242, 243
Nerantzi, C., 73, 230

Netflix, 98
Networks (digital and human), 42, 85, 86, 91
Networks/networked/networking, 32, 34, 65, 66, 73, 79, 85, 89, 95, 100, 111, 128, 131, 134, 136, 145, 158, 160, 168, 209, 221, 223, 225, 231
Ng, Andrew, 44, 93
Nicholson, K.P., 109
Nicol, D., 68, 75

O

OER Research Hub, 94
Office for Students (UK), 10
Oldenburg, R., 130, 150, 168
Oliver, M., 113, 114, 195, 219
Online learning, 44, 45, 73, 76, 141, 143
Online Learning Task Force (OLTF), 72
Online services, 85, 108
Online submission, 159
Open access publishing, 97
OpenCourseWare (MIT), 91
Open CPD, 230
Open education, 12, 54, 57, 58, 65, 70, 73, 74, 79, 86, 88–92, 94–98, 102, 105, 106, 154, 155, 161–163, 171, 172, 187, 209, 211, 235–244
Open educational resources (OER), 5, 91, 94, 95, 97, 114
Open Education Consortium, 92
Open Education Handbook, The, 91
Open education movement, 70, 86, 90, 91, 94

Open education practice, 54, 90, 163, 187, 211
Open learning, 106
Openness, 4, 5, 11, 15, 39, 45, 91, 114, 150, 170, 185, 205, 213, 224, 240, 243
Open Pedagogy (website), 95
Open public media, 111
Open Scotland Declaration, 91
Open textbooks, 70, 79, 97, 171
See also UK Open Textbook Project
Open University, UK, 74, 93, 94
Open University, US, 74
Oppression/oppressive, 4, 5, 13, 55, 57, 101, 118, 187, 194, 236, 237, 243
Organisational development, 4, 10, 14, 16, 28, 33, 35, 37, 40, 41, 54, 88, 113–115, 179, 181, 183, 186, 188, 197, 201, 217, 218, 220, 226, 231, 236
Orthodoxy, 28, 208, 229
Osman, A.A., 13, 180
Outside curricula, 153
Ownership, 7, 57, 95, 113, 131, 146, 152, 155, 165, 166, 180, 185, 194, 209, 241

P

Parchoma, G., 77
Pariser, E., 120, 198
Paris OER Declaration, 91
Parity, 131, 143
Participative, 79, 130, 132, 142, 143, 237
Part-time, 140, 157, 171

Pates, D., 132
Pay, 20, 101, 197
  differentials, 237
  structures, 186
Pedagogical practice, 9, 14, 35, 36, 106, 112, 114, 115, 117, 118, 120, 121, 130, 132, 135, 151, 163, 183, 238
Pedagogic research, 109, 220
Pedagogy/pedagogic, 4–7, 9, 11–16, 20, 23, 25, 35, 39, 46, 55–57, 69–71, 75, 79, 86–89, 95, 101, 102, 105–109, 114, 117, 118, 120–121, 130, 131, 136, 137, 141, 143, 150, 153, 165, 166, 179–181, 184–188, 197, 199, 201, 203, 208–213, 217, 220, 229–232, 235, 236, 238–241, 243
Permanence, 146
Permissive institutional policies and strategies, 208–211
Personal development, 21, 47, 87, 117, 133, 137, 221
Personhood, 16, 106, 117–120, 239
Peters, M.A., 106, 170
Pew Charitable Trust, 67
PG Certificates (postgraduate programmes), 219
Phenomenographic/phenomenography, 109, 242
Physical, 5, 29, 42, 127–132, 134, 140, 141, 144, 145, 150, 159, 162, 167, 189, 238
  learning environment, 131
  space, 29, 129, 131, 132, 162, 189

Pitt, R., 97
Places of practice, 169
Plehwe, D., 8
Policy/policies, 3, 7–9, 23–28, 30, 35, 45, 47, 50, 52, 56, 57, 63, 66, 67, 70–72, 75, 86–89, 94, 97, 137, 153, 155, 165, 179, 182, 183, 192, 197, 203, 208–213, 223, 227–229, 235, 237, 241, 242
Political economy, 3–16, 33, 64, 88, 106, 116, 117, 121, 179, 193, 194, 196, 198, 235–237, 239
Popovic, C., 218
Porosity/porous, 15, 85–102, 106, 113, 146, 150, 153, 166, 167, 170, 171, 173, 213, 218, 221, 231, 239, 240, 242
See also Leaky/leakiness
Portability, 146
Postgraduate, 72, 87, 135
Powell, S., 92
Power, 4, 8, 10, 13, 14, 16, 19, 20, 28, 29, 45, 114, 132, 155, 172, 180, 189, 194, 195, 200, 227–229, 235, 237
dynamics, 227, 228
Practice-based, 209, 230
Praxis, 5, 13, 15, 16, 26, 39–42, 54, 57, 58, 86, 95, 137, 141, 152, 153, 155, 156, 158, 160–161, 163, 165, 166, 170, 173, 180, 181, 184, 187, 188, 193, 194, 201, 203–214, 217, 220, 221, 226
Preece, J., 167
Prensky, M., 118
Price, S., 77
Price Waterhouse Cooper (PWC), 31–32, 36, 43, 224
Prinsloo, P., 199
Print, M., 151
Problem, 23, 31, 43, 128, 133, 137, 142, 157, 159, 160, 192, 193, 198, 208, 212
problem-based, 23
problem solving, 192, 193, 208
Professional accreditation, 222
Professional bodies, 219
Program in Course Redesign (Pew Charitable Trust), 67
Programme, 47, 50, 52, 67–69, 71, 72, 74, 75, 87, 88, 94, 115–117, 121, 130, 149–151, 156, 157, 182, 206, 207, 210, 211, 213, 221, 230, 239
Programme approval/programme re-approval, 210
Progressive, 10, 19, 35, 53, 74, 80, 107, 137, 149, 194, 195, 206, 207, 211, 228, 229
Projects, including individual and collaborative, 137
Proprietary, 90
Public good, 10, 14, 15, 21, 25, 39, 43, 47, 48, 64, 67, 69, 70, 78, 80, 91, 105, 130, 150, 154, 158, 161, 163, 166, 168, 169, 171, 173, 185, 186, 196, 203, 205, 212, 213, 226, 236, 238, 242, 243
Public knowledge, 33, 173, 212
Public pedagogy, 4, 5, 15, 137, 141, 153, 165, 166, 181, 201, 236, 238, 239, 243
Public practices, 137, 153
Public projects, 169
Public scholarship, 79, 159
Public services, 8, 212
Public value, 212

Publishing, 20, 86, 97, 108, 136, 221
  academic, 20, 86, 221
Putin, 235

Q

QR codes, 145
Qualitative, 109, 133, 242
Quality Assurance Agency for Higher Education (QAA), 155
Quantitative, 242

R

Race, 112, 197, 243
Racial/racialised, 153
Radical, 4, 5, 8, 9, 12, 13, 19, 20, 27, 34, 46, 88, 89, 93, 102, 109, 149, 187, 193–196, 218, 219, 221, 227, 238, 239
Ragged schools, 92
Ragged University, 172, 213
Rambe, P., 204, 206
Read/write technologies, 68
Real-time, 134, 141, 142, 144, 161
Real-world, 76, 137, 139, 156, 212, 237
Rebbeck, G., 119
Recall, 76
Rectorial address, 243
Re-engineering Assessment Practices (REAP), 68, 75
Reflection, 13, 15, 30, 36–37, 40, 45, 48, 55, 63, 76, 118, 133, 137, 152, 165, 187, 189, 191, 192, 207, 209, 213, 226–230
Reflective, 72, 109, 111, 136, 138, 139, 142, 143, 160, 173, 226
Reflective blogs, 173
Reform, 10, 115, 187, 211

Reframing, 54, 88, 161–163, 167, 171, 179, 211
Reid, Jimmy, 243
Relativism, 119
Replicating, 211
Research, 3, 20, 26, 34, 44, 49, 51, 52, 55, 76, 86, 93, 95, 97, 109–111, 120, 128, 131, 135–137, 142, 145, 166, 167, 179, 183, 186, 196, 200, 204, 205, 219–222, 225, 241–243
Research-informed, 135
Resilience, 66, 209
Revised Conceptual Matrix for the Digital University, 70, 162
Reward, 208
Rhetoric, 43, 71, 73, 80, 193, 198, 205
Rhizomatic model of learning, 161
Robbins Report, 66
Rogers, Y., 77
Role model/role modelling, 68, 144, 210, 230
Roxå, T., 55, 226–229
Rugut, E.J., 13, 180

S

Savin-Badden, M., 130, 132, 156
Schawab, K., 106
Schellens, T., 77
Scholarly knowledge, 136, 137
Scholarship, 34, 49, 79, 109, 112, 113, 127, 128, 135–137, 159, 166, 167, 169, 172, 173, 183, 204, 226, 240
  See also Digital scholarship
Schubert, W.M., 153
Science Technology Engineering and Maths (STEM), 9, 31, 190

SCONUL Seven Pillars of Information Literacy, 114
Scottish Funding Council (SFC), 68, 75
Scottish Government, 66, 90, 98, 100, 101
Seale, M., 109
Search engines, 25, 106, 115, 116, 120
Secker, J., 110, 114
Selwyn, N., 19, 22, 25, 27–30, 36, 43, 45, 185, 188–191, 195, 196
Senior management, senior managers, 4, 12, 57, 97, 186, 187, 190, 194, 210, 225, 231
Services, 4, 8, 20, 43, 51, 64, 85, 86, 89, 90, 94, 98, 100, 108, 115, 132, 134, 186, 200, 204, 209, 212, 221, 226, 228, 239, 240
Sharpe, R., 43, 208–210
Shukie, P., 79
  See also Community Open Online Courses (COOCs)
Siemens, G., 44
Silos, 116, 157, 158, 170, 192
Situate/situated, 29, 99, 111, 129, 131, 133, 145, 160, 187, 189, 218, 220, 222
Slade, S., 199
Smith, L., 109
Smith, M.K., 152, 153
Smyth, K., vii–xi, 5, 7, 51, 52, 54, 55, 73, 75, 77, 143, 150–154, 162, 163, 171, 173, 191, 207, 208, 222
Social action, 153, 158, 165, 243
Social capital, 88
Social change, 109, 141
Social context, 21, 63, 65–67, 156, 173

Social disadvantage, 89
Social epistemology, 109, 203, 212
Social good, 34
Social inclusion, 85, 86
Social justice, 70, 96, 171, 181, 187, 203, 211–212
Socially situated, 133
Social media, 49, 95, 106, 108, 119, 136, 144, 145, 171, 209, 221
Social networks/social networking, 73, 158, 221
Social spaces, 131, 185, 238
Social value, 16, 109, 141, 159, 170, 213
Societal needs, 66, 152, 159, 166, 205, 209, 211, 230
Society/societal, 3, 4, 11, 12, 20, 21, 23, 31, 32, 34, 43, 49, 64–66, 72, 86, 89, 90, 92, 95, 98, 105, 107, 111, 117–119, 127, 134, 137, 138, 152–155, 159, 165, 166, 170, 180, 194–197, 199, 205, 209, 211, 225, 226, 228, 230, 237, 242, 243
Sociocultural, 6, 48, 87, 114, 139, 192, 194, 196
Sociocultural transition, 196
Socio-economic, 6, 34, 85, 105, 106, 108, 193, 226, 228, 238
Socio-political, 13, 55, 106, 111, 181, 183, 190, 222
Spitzer, K.L., 108
Srnicek, N., 8, 237
Staff and Educational Development Association (SEDA), 48, 219
Stakeholders, 4, 155, 166, 180, 181, 184, 185, 190–192, 203, 205, 207, 211, 241

Stanford University, 119
  See also Civic Online Reasoning project
Starratt, R.J., 160
Strategic, 3, 8, 11, 14, 15, 20, 28, 32, 35, 36, 39, 49, 50, 54, 56, 57, 68, 88, 93, 95, 97, 106, 107, 111, 114–116, 120, 121, 128, 135, 182, 183, 200, 217, 226, 228, 240–243
Strategy (institutional), 14, 43, 203, 206–210
Strategy/strategies, 5, 6, 9, 14, 25, 31, 35, 36, 40, 43, 56, 66, 72, 88, 96, 97, 108, 109, 111, 113, 117, 119, 128, 182, 192, 203, 206–211, 213, 225, 228, 229, 235, 239
Streek, W., 8
Strickland, K., 209, 210
Student, 3, 4, 6–11, 13, 15, 16, 19, 22, 24, 25, 30–35, 39, 43, 46, 47, 49–51, 55, 56, 64, 68, 69, 72, 74, 76, 78, 79, 87, 88, 93, 95–97, 100, 101, 105–112, 114–121, 127, 128, 132–142, 146, 152–157, 159, 160, 164, 166, 167, 169, 171, 172, 181, 182, 185, 186, 189–191, 198–200, 205, 208–212, 218, 224, 225, 227, 228, 237, 239–241, 243
Student as consumer, 96, 228
Student as Producer, 155–156
Student-as-tutor, 69
Student journey, 64, 181
Students as Change Agents, 155
Students as digital scholars, 136
Sumner, N., 132
Sunstein, C.R., 120

Sutherland, K., 221
Swan, K., 76
Synchronous, 129
Systems, 4, 8, 13, 20, 22, 25, 29, 35, 40, 43–46, 49, 50, 54, 55, 65, 66, 75, 85, 87, 88, 95, 96, 98, 101, 114, 117, 120, 156, 157, 159, 171, 172, 183, 186, 198–201, 204, 208, 209, 225, 237
Systems design, 54, 183

Tang, C., 151, 164
Teachers, 4, 12, 55, 111, 139, 152, 226, 227
Teaching excellence framework (TEF), 10, 191, 192
Teaching-learning environments, 128, 133
Technist, 11, 12, 36, 37, 182
Technologists, 107, 115, 192, 218–220
Technology-enhanced learning (TEL), 22, 23, 68, 74, 107, 112, 121, 209, 220
Tertiary, 25, 85, 223
Text-matching, 159
Textual modes, 114
Thinking, 8–10, 15, 16, 20, 23–29, 31–33, 35, 37, 39–58, 70, 102, 106, 110, 114, 115, 119, 130, 131, 137, 143–144, 147, 150, 151, 157, 161–163, 167, 168, 171, 173, 180, 182, 187, 188, 190, 191, 196, 200, 204, 207, 208, 226, 235, 240, 243
Third place, 130, 150, 167, 168
Third sector, 89, 159, 172, 223

Third space, 130, 150, 168–172
Threshold Concepts, 55, 110
Transactional, 36, 63, 69, 118
Transformation, 4, 13, 15, 19, 31, 36, 39, 40, 44, 46, 57, 58, 63–80, 93, 102, 180, 186, 187, 191, 193–197, 240–243
Transformative, 29, 63, 78–79, 98, 105, 110, 188, 195
Transforming and Enhancing the Student Experience through Pedagogy (TESEP), 68, 69, 75
Transforming Curriculum Design and Curriculum Delivery through Technology (Jisc programme), 67, 69
Transparency, 78, 133, 143, 199, 231
Trowler, P., 115
Trump, 198, 235
Tutor, 69, 74, 112, 132, 136, 138, 139, 143, 146, 170
Tutor-as-learner/tutor-as-student, 69
Twenty-first century, 3–16, 28, 48, 63, 98, 99, 101, 106, 108, 109, 185, 194, 200, 236
Twigg, C., 67
Twitter, 136, 230

U
Udacity, 44, 92, 93
UK eUniversities (UKeU), 74
UK Online Learning Task Force, 72
  See also Collaborate to Compete (report of the UK Online Learning Task Force)
UK Open Textbook Project, 70
UK Professional Standards Framework for Teaching and Supporting Learning in Higher Education (UKPSF), 219
Unbounded, 147, 160, 169
Undergraduate, 101
UNESCO, 91, 92, 94, 99, 110, 239
  See also Agenda for Sustainable Development (UNESCO), Paris OER Declaration
United Kingdom (UK), 8–12, 22, 24, 32, 35, 36, 43, 44, 48, 50, 55, 64, 66–68, 70, 72, 74, 87–89, 93, 94, 96–99, 101, 109, 162, 194, 200, 210, 219, 236, 237
United Kingdom Government, 9, 24, 97, 99, 100
United States (US), 25, 66–68, 71, 74, 76, 109, 110
United States Department of Education, 67, 76
Universal Declaration of Human Rights, 92
Universities and Colleges Information Systems Association (UCISA), 12, 22, 23, 26, 35, 36, 74
University Centre Blackburn College, 79
University College London, 156
University of Dundee, 50–51
University of Edinburgh, 93
University of Exeter, 155
University of Greenwich, 51
University of Lincoln, 156
Upper Clyde Shipbuilders, 243

V

Valke, M., 77
Value for money, 9, 16, 24–25, 118, 236, 237
Value pluralism, 5, 7, 11, 55, 184, 186, 191–193, 201, 203, 206–208, 212, 231, 232, 238
Value/values, 4–9, 11–13, 15, 16, 20, 24–26, 28, 33, 34, 50, 55, 64, 66, 69, 78, 91, 95, 109, 111, 114, 115, 118, 120, 130, 138, 141, 147, 153–155, 158–160, 164–167, 169, 170, 172, 173, 181, 183, 184, 186, 191–193, 196, 200–201, 203, 204, 206–209, 211–213, 236–238, 240, 243
Vermunt, J.D., 55, 128, 133
Virtual classroom, 129, 144
Virtual Learning Environment, 74, 129, 156, 157
Virtual reality (VR), 145
Visual media, 76
Vocational, 173

W

Walker, D., 220
Walker, R., 22, 74
Wall, G., 150, 167
Walton, G., 110
Watters, A., 101
Web 2.0, 221
Webber, S., 107–110
Webinars, webinar technologies, 73, 136, 144, 171
Web/World Wide Web, 93, 117, 120, 224, 229

Welikala, T., 160
Wellbeing, 21, 132, 153, 158, 199
Weller, M., 65, 90, 128, 132, 221
Westminster, 89
Whitchurch, C., 209
White, D.S., 118
Whitehead, M., 199
Why is My Curriculum White?, 159–160
Widening access, 50, 52, 66, 72, 73, 79, 85–102, 155
Widening participation, 49, 64, 87–89, 100, 102, 197, 212
Wikipedia, 137, 173, 191
Williamson, K., 109
Wilson, T., 107, 237
Winter, M.L., 25, 26, 30–31, 36, 42, 188–191
Wintrup, J., 79
Work-based, 53, 109, 128, 132, 133, 150
Working conditions, 237
Workstations, 140
World Congress on OER, 91

Y

Yuan, L., 92

Z

Zenios, M., 141
Zhenghao, C., 71, 73
Zobel, G., 195
Zones, 112
  of practice, 22, 86
Zurkowski, P., 108

Printed in the United States
By Bookmasters